Competing Sovereignties

Competing Sovereignties provides a critique of the concept of sovereignty in modernity in light of claims to determine the content of law at the international, national and local levels. In an argument that is illustrated through an analysis of debates over the control of intellectual property law in India, Richard Joyce considers how economic globalisation and the claims of indigenous communities do not just challenge national sovereignty – as if national sovereignty is the only kind of sovereignty – but in fact invite us to challenge our conception of what sovereignty 'is'. Combining theoretical research and reflection with an analysis of the legal, institutional and political context in which sovereignties 'compete', the book offers a reconception of modern sovereignty – and, with it, a new appreciation of the complex issues surrounding the relationship between international organisations, nation states and local and indigenous communities.

Richard Joyce is based in the Faculty of Law at Monash University, Australia.

Competing Sovereignties

Richard Joyce

Routledge
Taylor & Francis Group
a GlassHouse Book

First published 2013
by Routledge
2 Park Square, Milton Park, Abingdon, Oxon OX14 4RN

Simultaneously published in the USA and Canada
by Routledge
711 Third Avenue, New York, NY 10017

A GlassHouse book

Routledge is an imprint of the Taylor & Francis Group, an informa business

British Library Cataloguing in Publication Data
A catalogue record for this book is available from the British Library.

Library of Congress Cataloging in Publication Data
Joyce, Richard John, 1978-
Competing sovereignties / Richard Joyce.
p. cm.
Includes bibliographical references.
ISBN 978-0-415-67814-8 (hbk)
1. Sovereignty. 2. Intellectual property. 3. International relations. I. Title.
KZ4041.J69 2012
320.15–dc23 2011052497

ISBN: 978-0-415-67814-8 (hbk)
ISBN: 978-0-203-11541-1 (ebk)

Typeset in Baskerville
by Cenveo Publisher Services

For Premala

Contents

Acknowledgements

This book began life as a PhD thesis at the School of Law, Birkbeck, University of London. My doctoral studies were generously supported by the University of Melbourne (Rae and Edith Bennett Travelling Scholarship), the Birkbeck School of Law (Ronnie Warrington Research Studentship in Law) and the UK Government (Overseas Research Student Award). Subsequently, the School of Law at the University of Reading and the Faculty of Law at Monash University have provided stimulating and supportive environments in which to complete the book and my thanks go to colleagues at both institutions.

I owe an enormous personal and intellectual debt to my two PhD supervisors, Professors Peter Fitzpatrick and Fiona Macmillan. Both provide an exemplary model of scholarship and I thank them for their attentive, rigorous and creative supervision. Peter's influence on the thesis (and by extension, this book) and my development as a scholar has been particularly marked. I am quite sure Jacques Derrida would have gained an even more acute sense of unconditional hospitality if he had been lucky enough to have Peter as a supervisor. I would also like to thank my examiners Professors Peter Drahos and Andreas Philippopoulos-Mihalopoulos for a searching viva and their helpful comments on preparing the thesis for publication.

I have been fortunate to enjoy the support of too many friends over the course of this project to thank them here and will resort to thanking them personally. Special mention must be made, though, to two of my PhD colleagues, Sundhya Pahuja, whose encouragement was instrumental to my commencing a PhD at Birkbeck, and Ben Golder, who among much else provided a model of how to complete the thing. Particular thanks also to Chris Warren, for illuminating discussions of early modern history, literature and international law.

The research on patent law and traditional knowledge in India was aided immeasurably by the opportunity to travel to New Delhi to meet with people working in those and related fields. For their time, interest and suggestions of sources, I would like to thank Pratiksha Baxi, Upendra Baxi, Sachin Chaturvedi, Nagesh Kumar, R. A. Mashelkar, Suman Sahai, Devinder Sharma, Vandana Shiva and Jaivir Singh. For providing contacts, thanks to Peter Fitzpatrick, Abdul Paliwala and Dwijen Rangnekar. Thanks also to the staff at the Institute of Social Sciences in New Delhi for providing access to its library and the University of London Central Research Fund for financial support.

The team at Routledge has been patient and supportive beyond measure and particular thanks go to Colin Perrin and Melanie Fortmann-Brown.

To my parents, Margaret and Eric, and parents-in-law, Mary and Rajan, thank you for your love and support throughout the preparation of this book and beyond.

Above all, I wish to thank my wife, Premala. Her singular capacity to hone in on any weakness in my arguments might not always work to my advantage, but it has certainly helped this book. Without her brilliance, selflessness, patience, kindness and love, this whole endeavour would not have been possible. And while supporting me on this book she has also brought into the world two of its most delightful children, Benjamin and Anna. It is with deep gratitude and love that I dedicate this book to her.

Introduction

The Crisis of Modern Sovereignty

'Everything must begin by uprooting.'[1]

Modern sovereignty is in crisis. The nation-state, presumed to be the sole site of sovereignty in modernity, appears threatened by a multitude of challenges. The intense flow of goods, information, capital, people and violence across national borders suggests a world whose various forces cannot be contained and regulated by national polities.[2] These factors prompt many to ask whether or not the sovereignty of the state is in decline.[3] However, beyond the limited question of the perceived rise and fall of state sovereignty lies the question of what, if anything, the factors which

1 Jacques Derrida, 'The Laws of Reflection: Nelson Mandela, In Admiration', trs M. Caws and I. Loenz in Jacques Derrida and Mustapha Tlili (eds), *For Nelson Mandela*, New York: Seaver Books, 1987, p. 22.

2 Barbour and Pavlich eloquently evoke the sense of crisis and its commonly perceived causes in their introduction to Charles Barbour and George Pavlich (eds), *After Sovereignty: On the Question of Political Beginnings*, Abingdon: Routledge, 2010, p. 1.

3 See, e.g., Saskia Sassen, *Losing Control? Sovereignty in an Age of Globalisation*, New York: Columbia University Press, 1996; Manuel Castells, *The Rise of the Network Society*, 2nd ed., Chichester: Wiley-Blackwell, 2010, p. xviii; David Held and Anthony McGrew, *Globalisation/Anti-Globalisation: Beyond the Great Divide*, 2nd ed., Cambridge: Polity Press, 2007, pp. 1–10; James Fulcher, 'Globalisation, the Nation-State and Global Society', *The Sociological Review* 48, 2000, 522–43.

seem to put sovereignty in crisis reveal about sovereignty itself. That question is the focus of this book. In short, its premise is that the crisis of sovereignty necessitates a critique of sovereignty.

The ubiquity of claims that sovereignty is in crisis is perhaps unsurprising when one considers the etymological connections between these two words. 'Crisis' derives from the Greek *krisis*. Its various meanings include 'turning point', which is perhaps the one most closely connected to the present usage of crisis.[4] But other meanings include 'separating', 'distinguishing', 'decision' and 'judgment'[5] all of which, we will see throughout this book, are central to the figure of the sovereign itself. Sovereignty involves the act of marking out borders and boundaries, of separating and distinguishing between inside and outside. It also involves the power to determine law, to decide and to judge. This suggests that sovereignty is not (only) in crisis, but that sovereignty is crisis. Not only is crisis intimately bound up with sovereignty itself, but the etymology suggests it is intimately connected to critique. Critique derives from the Greek *kritikē*, which means the 'act of discerning', but both *krisis* and *kritikē* derive from the verb *krinō*, 'to decide'.[6] Like crisis, critique is somehow embedded in sovereignty itself. Sovereignty lends itself to critique, it demands questioning.

This book will cede to that demand and provide a theoretical critique of the concept of sovereignty in modernity. Its chief aim is to break the seemingly exclusive link between sovereignty and the nation-state and open the field to other claims to authority to determine the content of law. I will argue that the received conception of sovereignty, exclusive to the state, fails in significant ways to allow us to adequately comprehend and respond to the relationship between rival claims to determine law at the local, national and international levels. In its place, a new conception of

4 Henry Liddell, Robert Scott and Henry Jones, *A Greek-English Lexicon*, Oxford: Clarendon Press, 1968, p. 997. Thanks to Emeline Marquis for invaluable guidance on the meaning and use of these terms in ancient Greek.

5 Ibid.

6 Ibid., p. 996.

sovereignty will be offered. This conception will build on and combine the work of Jacques Derrida on sovereignty, Jean-Luc Nancy on community, and Peter Fitzpatrick on law. I will argue that sovereignty in modernity is not grounded in the state but is in fact, to use Derrida's term, 'autopositioned'.

This kind of thinking on sovereignty takes place in light of the void announced by what we might call, using a shorthand Derrida would hesitate to adopt, the death of God.[7] It is, of course, axiomatic that modernity marks the end of our reliance on God for legal and political authority on earth. Indeed, if pre-modern sovereignty in Europe could be accounted for by the concept of the divine right of kings, the Enlightenment and its revolutions would leave us without both the divine and the king. In its place we have authority grounded in the 'nation' and its 'people'. What God used to do for sovereign authority was to provide a settled point of transcendent reference guaranteeing the authority of those who had the strength to claim it in His name. Without such transcendent reference, as has been pointedly observed, the heirs of divine authority – 'nation' and 'people' – are required to take on and effect qualities which, if not easily characterised as 'sacred', then at least put incredible strain on the secularity of modern authority.[8]

Indeed, while awareness of the death of God might be commonplace in thought on modern sovereignty, its consequences are usually overlooked or suppressed.[9] What distinguishes the

7 Jacques Derrida, 'Faith and Knowledge: The Two Sources of "Religion" at the Limits of Reason Alone', tr. Samuel Weber, in Jacques Derrida, *Acts of Religion*, ed. Gil Anidjar, New York: Routledge, 2002, p. 65.

8 See Peter Fitzpatrick, 'What are the Gods to Us Now?: Secular Theology and the Modernity of Law', *Theoretical Inquiries in Law* 8, 2007, 161–90; Carl Schmitt, *Political Theology: Four Chapters on the Concept of Sovereignty*, tr. George Schwab, Chicago: University of Chicago Press, 2005.

9 For example, Kant's acute awareness of the difficulties in grounding legal authority without God was accompanied by a stern warning against questioning the origins of an existing legal authority. See Immanuel Kant, *The Metaphysics of Morals*, ed. and tr. Mary Gregor, Cambridge: Cambridge University Press, 1996, p. 95. See also Chapter 1 below, text accompanying notes 125–9 and 142.

line of thought which takes us to Derrida's conception of 'autopositioning' is its rigorous insistence on the void which God's death announces. For Derrida, the death of God, or more precisely '[t]he "deaths of God," before Christianity, in it and beyond it, are only figures and episodes' of a fundamental absence.[10] 'Everything begins with the presence of *that* absence.'[11] The absence of a settled and settling transcendent reference to guarantee our social formations, including sovereignty, nation, people etc., means that it is left up to us to bear witness to their validity. Derrida's 'deconstruction' operates in view of this lack. It 'tries to show ... that convention, institutions and consensus are stabilisations (sometimes stabilisations of great duration, sometimes micro-stabilisations) ... of something essentially chaotic.'[12] This 'chaos and instability' is 'fundamental, founding and irreducible'.[13] Derrida's analysis and critique of sovereignty takes place against the background of this void.

What does this mean for modern sovereignty, which has taken the contours of its form from Jean Bodin's definition of the sovereign as a person recognising 'nothing, after God, that is greater than himself'?[14] Would we not find that in the absence of divine authority, the sovereign is simply an entity which recognises no authority greater than itself, with respect to that over which it claims authority? If the sovereign recognises no authority greater than itself, then it has only itself to justify its authority. It is this line of thought that takes us to Derrida's notion of sovereignty as self-authorising and self-justifying – or, in his precise term, 'autopositioned'.[15] Viewed in this way, the crisis of modern

10 Derrida, 'Faith and Knowledge', p. 65.

11 Ibid. (original emphasis).

12 Jacques Derrida, 'Remarks on Deconstruction and Pragmatism', tr. Simon Critchley, in Simon Critchley, Jacques Derrida, Ernesto Laclau and Richard Rorty, *Deconstruction and Pragmatism*, London: Routledge, 1996, p. 83.

13 Ibid., p. 84.

14 Jean Bodin, *On Sovereignty: Four Chapters from the Six Books of the Commonwealth*, ed. and tr. Julian Franklin, Cambridge: Cambridge University Press, 1992, p. 4.

15 Jacques Derrida, *Rogues: Two Essays on Reason*, trs Pascale-Anne Brault and Michael Naas, Stanford: Stanford University Press, 2005, p. 142.

sovereignty lies in its having to distinguish and separate, decide and judge, without any guarantee of its own validity.

The theoretical critique advanced in this book will be contextualised by reference to two particular challenges to the sovereignty of the nation-state. One comes from the international level. It is the challenge to national sovereignty posed by the World Trade Organisation (WTO). The second comes from the local level, from local and indigenous communities which challenge the primacy and exclusivity of the sovereignty of the state. Both challenges manifest themselves in many different settings and in a wide variety of locations. Here, the focus will be on control over intellectual property law in India, in particular patents and traditional knowledge. This may seem a very narrow and particular example to illustrate the much broader question of the grounds of law in modernity. It has been chosen for a number of reasons. The first and most important reason is that the example provides a single substantive area of law in which two key challenges to national sovereignty, economic globalisation and the rights of indigenous and local communities, meet. By addressing the challenges of economic globalisation (via the WTO) and of local and indigenous communities claiming sovereignty, the example goes beyond its narrow substantive confines. Those substantive confines, though, are also significant. Since the argument here suggests that the boundaries of rival sovereign claims are to be found in the detail of the law, the focus on a single area of law helps to illustrate this point by enabling close consideration of the law itself and not just the broader politico-legal formations at play. The second is that participants (on many sides) in the intense and vibrant debates over the control of patent law and traditional knowledge in India have frequently turned to the concept of 'sovereignty' to advance their causes. Often these uses are contradictory, and the theoretical argument pursued here assists to understand why such contradictory uses are possible (indeed, perhaps, inevitable).

I will take two common claims about sovereignty in India which present themselves in this field. The first is the claim that India's sovereignty was undermined by the requirement that it enact strict patent laws in order to meet its obligations as a

WTO member. The second is the claim made by and on behalf of local and indigenous communities that they hold 'sovereignty' over their 'traditional knowledge', thus seeking to place a certain mode of regulating knowledge and information beyond the reach of the state. I will spend some time now setting out the nature of these challenges so as to enable the reader to keep this context in mind throughout the theoretical analysis which forms the core of this book.

I International and Local Challenges to National Sovereignty: Patent Law and Traditional Knowledge in India

The context for the first claim is India's membership of the WTO. The WTO oversees the most comprehensive multilateral system of trading rules in history. Its 153 member states are required to comply with common standards in a wide range of policy areas affecting trade. Given the breadth of the areas covered and specificity of many of these standards, the WTO is commonly seen as something which marks the decline of the sovereignty of the state. Even within the United States, the state with the most negotiating power at the WTO, the possible impact of the organisation on its sovereignty was highly contentious.[16] However, the argument that the WTO undermines state sovereignty is most frequently made in respect of its developing country members. The gist of this argument is that the rules administered by the WTO reflect the wishes of powerful states and that the organisation operates as a neo-colonial tool used by those states to control the law of less powerful states. One particular example of this argument concerns the effect of India's membership of the WTO on its patent law.

As a condition of India's membership of the WTO, it was required to adopt patent laws (and other intellectual property laws) which met the minimum requirements of the Agreement on Trade-Related Aspects of Intellectual Property Rights (1994)

16 John Jackson, 'The Great 1994 Sovereignty Debate: United States Acceptance and Implementation of the Uruguay Round Results', *Columbia Journal of Transnational Law* 36, 1997, 157.

(TRIPS). As a 'developing country', India was afforded the luxury of a ten-year grace period. Having been a founding member in 1995, its deadline for full compliance was 1 January 2005. On this date, India would relinquish the exclusion from patentability of medicines, food and agricultural products; an exclusion it had enacted in 1970 in the first major revision of the patent law inherited from its colonial masters. A bill to give effect to this change was introduced in December 2003, but having been referred to a parliamentary committee, lapsed during the 2004 elections.[17] And so, through an executive ordinance, and without any scrutiny by Parliament, the requirements of TRIPS became Indian law.[18] Some measure of scrutiny would come a few months later, when amidst walk-outs by opposition members (some of whom had been members of the previous government which had introduced the bill in 2003), a refusal by the Government to refer the matter to another parliamentary committee, and some last minute concessions, Parliament passed the Patents (Amendment) Act 2005.[19]

More than ten years of anticipation of this event had sharpened opposition to it. Both within India and outside, enormous concern was expressed for the viability of India's then thriving generic pharmaceutical industry and the cheap medicines (including treatments for HIV) it produced both for local consumption and for use in other developing countries.[20] For many who

17 B. K. Keayla, 'Amended Patents Act: A Critique', *Combat Law* 4(2), 2005, India Together, at: http://www.indiatogether.org/combatlaw/vol4/issue2/patents.htm (last accessed 6 December 2011).

18 Patents (Amendment) Ordinance (No. 7 of 2004) (India). The President can only pass legislation by ordinance when Parliament is not in session and he or she is satisfied that 'circumstances exist which render it necessary ... to take immediate action': Constitution of India, art 123.

19 Ibid. The passage of the Act was necessary because Presidential ordinances expire six weeks after the reassembly of Parliament: Constitution of India, art 123.

20 Khabir Ahmad, 'India's New Patent Bill Threatens Generic Industry', *The Lancet Infectious Diseases* 5, 2005, 265; New York Times, 'India's Choice', Editorial, 18 January 2005, at: http://www.nytimes.com/2005/01/18/opinion/18tues2.html?oref=login (last accessed 6 December 2011).

opposed TRIPS, and saw it as the result of the influence of rich countries and their corporations, the requirements constituted nothing less than an 'assault on India's sovereignty.'[21] According to former Indian Supreme Court Justice Krishna Iyer, India was 'as a nation, trapped into TRIPS and stripped of its sovereign power to defend the people's right to life in good health (an inviolable basic feature).'[22] In Iyer's terms, not only does the WTO constitute 'an assault on India's sovereignty'[23] but, agreeing to TRIPS may have been an abdication by the Indian Government of its constitutional obligations, including the right of the people to 'life in good health'.[24] The hurried passage of the ordinance and the Patents (Amendment) Act 2005, together with the public concerns about it, seemed to emphasise the notion that this law responded to external concerns.[25] It provides an example of a wider concern about the fate of national sovereignty in the wake of 'globalisation'. A concern about a world in which nation-states cease to be sovereign, where policy is decided 'globally', and in that term beloved of intellectual property bureaucrats, laws are 'harmonised'. In this setting, the effectiveness of state sovereignty is called into question while at the same time it appears as the only legitimate force which can be opposed to the shifting forces of globalisation.

Claims by local and indigenous communities in India to authority over their 'traditional knowledge' present a different challenge to the sovereignty of the state. Before considering that challenge, it is worth briefly noting that the question of how one should define

21 V. R. Krishna Iyer, 'Human Health and Patent Law', *Frontline* 17(21), 2000, at: http://www.frontline.in/fl1721/17210790.htm (last accessed 6 December 2011).

22 V. R. Krishna Iyer, 'The Doha-Delhi Odyssey', *Frontline* 19(6), 2002, at: http://www.hindu.com/fline/fl1906/19060900.htm (last accessed 6 December 2011).

23 Iyer, 'Human Health'.

24 Ibid.; See Constitution of India, art 21. See also: Iyer, 'Doha-Delhi'; V. R. Krishna Iyer, O. Chinappa Reddy, D. A. Desai and Rajinder Sachar, *Peoples' Commission on GATT: On the Constitutional Implications of the Final Act Embodying the Results of the Uruguay Round of Multilateral Trade Negotiations*, New Delhi: Centre for Study of Global Trade System and Development, 1996, pp. 127–64.

25 See Keayla, 'Amended Patents Act'.

'traditional knowledge' is complex and contested. The present draft articles on the protection of traditional knowledge developed by the World Intellectual Property Organisation's Intergovernmental Committee on Intellectual Property and Genetic Resources, Traditional Knowledge and Folklore (IGC), contain two alternative definitions and related criteria. The first defines traditional knowledge as: 'know-how, skills, innovations, practices, teachings and learning, resulting from intellectual activity and developed within a traditional context' and provides that the knowledge must be 'the unique product of' or 'distinctly associated' with its traditional holders, and be 'collectively generated, shared, preserved and transmitted from generation to generation' and 'integral to the cultural identity' of those holders.[26]

The second alternative definition adds that traditional knowledge is 'dynamic and evolving' and includes 'knowledge associated with biodiversity, traditional lifestyles and natural resources.[27] While agreement on the precise definition has eluded the IGC since it was formed in 2000, the terms above reflect many of the broad definitional concepts used by participants in the debates and can be used as a way of understanding the use of the term in this book.

The claims put forward by local and indigenous communities in India intensified over the same period of time as opposition to the WTO and TRIPS. Partly in response to the impending patentability of medicines, food and agricultural products, local and indigenous communities began to challenge both the authority of the Indian state and of the WTO to determine the law applicable to local knowledge and innovation. Drawing on support from non-government organisations and examples of challenges made

26 Intergovernmental Committee on Intellectual Property and Genetic Resources, Traditional Knowledge and Folklore. World Intellectual Property Organisation, 'The Protection of Traditional Knowledge: Draft Articles', Annex to Document WIPO/GRTKF/IC/21/45, 18 January 2012, at http://www.wipo.int/tk/en/igc/ (last accessed 20 April 2012), art 1, paras 1.1–1.2 option 1.

27 Ibid., art 1, option 2.

by indigenous peoples to the authority of colonial and post-colonial states (often arising first in the context of land rights), these communities began to claim that their traditional knowledge was always and already subject to the traditional law of the community. It was not for the state, much less the WTO, they argued, to impose laws providing for private rights over the use or products of that knowledge. Instead, the state and the WTO should recognise and respect local communities' 'sovereignty' over traditional knowledge.[28] In this setting, it is the validity of state sovereignty, not its effectiveness, which is called into question.

The issue of control over Indian patent law and traditional knowledge thus presents a situation in which the concept of state sovereignty is challenged from both the international and local levels. In most of the debates of this kind, there is a sense that state sovereignty is in decline. That tends to presuppose that state sovereignty has, or once had, a clear and stable content from which a decline could be measured. The starting point remains the assumption that sovereignty is a quality which resides only in nation-states. Sovereignty itself is not put in question.

In the remainder of this introduction, I will argue that the issue of control over Indian patent law and traditional knowledge prompts a much more fundamental investigation. Indeed, I will argue that it presents a concentration of issues which prompts us to consider nothing less than the nature of modern sovereignty itself. I will firstly outline the received conception of sovereignty which is under attack in this book. I will then briefly illustrate how this conception fails to grasp the complexity of the relationship between these rival sites of authority. Specifically, I will argue that an attachment to the received conception places strict limits on the range of ways it is possible to think about rival claims to authority. It leads to stifling debates in which key participants speak past each other in increasingly strident terms while difficult,

28 See, e.g., Vandana Shiva, Afsar Jafri, Gitanjali Bedi and Radha Holla-Bhar, *The Enclosure and Recovery of the Commons: Biodiversity, Indigenous Knowledge and Intellectual Property Rights*, New Delhi: Research Foundation for Science, Technology and Ecology, 1997.

complex issues are overlooked. I will then briefly state the terms of the re-conception of sovereignty pursued throughout the book. While the book will focus on developing a new theory of sovereignty, frequent reference will be made throughout to the implications of the theory for thinking about rival claims to patent law and traditional knowledge in India. Chapters 4 and 5, in particular, will focus on these implications. But the reference to the context of the claims in India is not intended to act as proof of the validity of the theory, but rather to illustrate, in context, the lines of thought opened up by that theory.

2 The Received Conception of Sovereignty and its Limitations

In the received view, sovereignty in modernity is an exclusive feature of nation-states and all legal authority is exercised by national institutions or by a body whose authority has been delegated to it by a nation-state.[29] International law, including the international economic law administered by the WTO, would be simply the accumulation or aggregation of delegated or transferred authority and would have no 'life' of its own. Similarly, claims to legal authority by local communities and indigenous groups would be obliterated by the establishment of the state – and what we see as remnants of that authority would in fact be delegated to the group or otherwise permitted by the state. In all of this, the nation-state would be the unmoved mover – and its sovereignty prime and generative of all law. Much then, has been invested in the notion of the sovereign nation-state as the foundation of the modern legal order at both the domestic and international levels. Indeed the idea of the sovereign state forms

29 See Dan Sarooshi, *International Organisations and their Exercise of Sovereign Powers*, Oxford: Oxford University Press, 2005. Sarooshi argues that sovereignty is an 'essentially contested concept' and yet finds that all exercise of sovereign powers by international organisations originates with nation-states and is then bestowed on those organisations by agency, delegation or transfer.

the basis for the very division between the domestic and the international.

In opposition to this settled notion of sovereignty and modern legality, the WTO and local and indigenous communities in India appear as significant challenges. The WTO seeks to respond to and regulate forces which cannot be regulated by nation-states alone and which are external to them (the transnational flow of goods, services, information, capital) while at the same time facilitating those very forces. As both facilitator and regulator of these forces, the WTO appears as something more than just the simple sum of authority delegated by states and seems to be one significant marker of the end of the modern era in which states were sovereign. Local and indigenous communities in India, on the other hand, present a different kind of challenge. Their persistence bears witness to the failure of the modern sovereign state to supplant all other prior forms of political belonging relevant to the production of law. This would make us question whether the era of the modern sovereign state ever really began.

A rigid attachment to the received view leaves us with limited tools to either understand or respond to the challenges to the sovereignty of the state which the debates about Indian patent law and traditional knowledge put in sharp relief. National sovereignty might serve as a useful shorthand for those who oppose the substantive content of the law that India's membership of the WTO requires it to adopt. But at a conceptual level it is a sterile tool with which to challenge the WTO's influence. This is primarily because states are at the very least complicit in constituting the WTO's authority and this relies on the formal notion that they are sovereign. Similarly, the received view leaves us bereft of the tools necessary to understand the potency and resilience of the claims made by local communities to 'sovereignty' over traditional knowledge. On a strict application of the received view, such claims should be impossible. How, then, can we account for their persistence – and with them the claims of indigenous groups in colonial and post-colonial settings the world over? In the remainder of this section of the Introduction I will explain in a little more detail the nature of these failures.

2.1 Sovereignty and the WTO: a coincidence of the grounds of law

The controversy over patent law in India raises significant questions about the appropriate distribution of legal authority between the state and international organisations. For this reason opponents of the reforms frequently turn to the concept of sovereignty to ground their opposition. In doing so, they rely on the conventional conception of sovereignty in which the nation-state is the ultimate and exclusive source of legal authority. Against this figure of the sovereign state, the WTO appears as an illegitimate intruder.

The history of Indian patent law, from the colonial period, through the post-independence reforms, and now under TRIPS, does allow a convincing story to be told in which India's sovereignty over patent law is denied by the WTO. It is possible to show that India's patent law was initially created to suit its colonial masters.[30] It also is possible to show that following independence, a determined effort was made to fashion a patent law in India's national interest.[31] Further, it is possible to show that TRIPS was included within the WTO agreements largely on the initiative of the United States, itself acting under the influence of powerful industry lobby groups and multinational corporations,[32]

30 The first colonial legislation on patents in India was enacted in 1856. The Act in force at the time of independence was the Indian Patents and Designs Act 1911. The purpose and effect of these laws was to protect British imports from local competition and imports from other countries: Janice Mueller, 'The Tiger Awakens: The Tumultuous Transformation of India's Patent System and the Rise of Indian Pharmaceutical Innovation', *University of Pittsburgh Law Review* 68, 2007, 491, 505–8.

31 See Patents Act 1970 (India) (as enacted); N. Rajagopala Ayyangar, *Report on the Revision of the Patents Law*, New Delhi: Government of India, 1959.

32 See Peter Drahos, 'Global Property Rights in Information: The Story of TRIPS at the GATT', *Prometheus* 13, p. 6; Susan K. Sell, *Power and Ideas: North-South Politics of Intellectual Property and Anti-Trust*, New York: State University of New York Press, 1998, pp. 221–4; Sudip Chaudhuri, *The WTO and India's Pharmaceuticals Industry: Patent Protection, TRIPS and Developing Countries*, New Delhi: Oxford University Press, 2005, pp. 314–16.

and against the wishes of India.[33] Moreover, the content of TRIPS ultimately reflected the intellectual property laws of the United States and Europe and, not accidentally, the interests of the corporations which lobbied for its inclusion in the WTO agreements.[34] As a result of the content of TRIPS, India was required to reverse many of the features of its patent law which it enacted following independence. It is thus possible to present the case that India, under the take-it-or-leave-it approach of the single undertaking system of WTO membership, was required to agree to TRIPS in order to join the WTO and consequently give up its 'sovereign' patent law,[35] which had served it so well, in place of patent laws designed to serve the interests of rich states and powerful multi-national corporations. In this story, the Indian state becomes beholden to the WTO, itself beholden to the interests of a few powerful states and corporations.[36]

I would agree with proponents of this story that the differences between Indian patent law before and after TRIPS, and India's opposition to TRIPS itself during the Uruguay Round, provide substantial grounds for questioning the legitimacy of the WTO's influence over Indian law. However, to the extent that such questioning uses the conventional conception of sovereignty as its chief analytical tool, its cogency dissipates. The key problem with characterising the WTO as an illegitimate intruder on state sovereignty is that the WTO's authority is, again following the conventional view, wholly derived from the sovereignty of the states whose agreement brought it into being. On this view, it is precisely the sovereignty of states which enables them to enter into agreements with other states and bind themselves (and one another) to common standards. Indeed, one of the core criteria

33 George Foster, 'Opposing Forces in a Revolution in International Patent Protection: The US and India in the Uruguay Round and its Aftermath', *U.C.L.A. Journal of International Law and Foreign Affairs* 3, 1998, 283, 311–12.

34 Peter Drahos, 'Developing Countries and Intellectual Property Standard-Setting', *Journal of World Intellectual Property* 5, 2002, 765, 772; Drahos, 'Global Property Rights', pp. 7–9.

35 Vandana Shiva, *Patents: Myths and Reality*, New Delhi: Penguin, 2001, p. 7.

36 Iyer, 'Doha-Delhi'.

specified by international law for the recognition of states is the capacity to enter into relations (which would necessarily include undertaking obligations) with other states.[37]

In the famous *Wimbledon Case*, the Permanent Court of International Justice was faced with the dilemma of whether a state's treaty obligation could be avoided because it constituted an imposition on that state's sovereignty. The decision it reached was the only one consistent with the view that states are sovereign and exist within a functioning international community. The Court held that it:

> declines to see in the conclusion of any Treaty by which a State undertakes to perform or refrain from performing a particular act an abandonment of its sovereignty. No doubt any convention creating an obligation of this kind places a restriction upon the exercise of the sovereign rights of the State, in the sense that it requires them to be exercised in a certain way. But the right of entering into international engagements is an attribute of State sovereignty.[38]

To find that state sovereignty could be relied on to avoid treaty obligations would have been to deny any force to the binding nature of those obligations and deny the operation of one of the key sources of international law.[39]

As such, the conventional view of sovereignty asks us either to wholly reject all intrusion on a state's legislative freedom by treaty making (thereby making any international agreement-making impossible), or to accept it (at least in terms of authority, if not content) without question. Rendered in terms of the WTO, the conventional view of sovereignty allows either outright rejection or a reduction of all questions of the legitimacy of the WTO's

37 See Montevideo Convention on Rights and Duties of States (1933), art 1.

38 *S.S. Wimbledon (United Kingdom v Germany)* (1923) PCIJ, Ser. A, No. 1, [35].

39 See Statute of the Permanent Court of International Justice (1920), art 38.1; Statute of the International Court of Justice (1945), art 38(a). See also Vienna Convention on the Law of Treaties (1969), art 26.

authority to the formal question of sovereign consent. As such, holding onto the state as the sole locus of sovereignty prevents us from thinking seriously and in a nuanced way about the WTO's influence in terms of sovereignty – that is, in terms of the source and legitimacy of its authority. What remains for opponents of TRIPS is to use the notion of sovereignty to attack the content of the treaty.

But sovereignty is a weak tool to use to resist the content of what an international treaty (or organisation formed by treaty) requires of a state party to it. Much of the argument about India's sovereignty focuses on the terms of TRIPS not being in India's national interest. It is true that at the time of its imposition, India was opposed to the treaty and tried actively to resist its inclusion in the WTO agreements. Nonetheless, the questions of whether its membership of the WTO as a whole is in its interests, or of how best to balance the interests of those within India who would benefit from stricter intellectual property laws and those who would suffer, are contested.

Indeed, rather than being a paradigm of a treaty whose content inherently involves a denial of state sovereignty, TRIPS provides a paradigm of how difficult it is to determine the point at which the content of a treaty can be said to violate state sovereignty. For example, despite the fact that parties to TRIPS are required to make medicines patentable, the treaty also contains various permitted exceptions to patentability and other provisions which enable member states to legislate (admittedly in limited circumstances) to preserve public health. The most significant is the ability to grant compulsory licences. Relying on these provisions, as we will see in Chapter 4 in more detail, India has legislated for compulsory licences to be available, among other circumstances, where the producer fails to make an invention available to the public at a reasonably affordable price.[40]

One can argue about whether the permissible exceptions to patentability in TRIPS and the compulsory licensing provisions allow sufficient scope for protecting public health. Even Iyer

40 Patents Act 1970 (India), s 84.

argued in 2000 that it was possible to interpret TRIPS in a way which would 'salvage a substantial portion of our existing statute.'[41] One can also argue about the appropriate balance to be struck between the incentive to invent new medicines promised by the availability of patents and their effect in raising prices, each of which may affect public health.[42] But the fact that these conflicting arguments are possible shows that it is not easy to draw a line between measures which would appear to violate a state's sovereign right or duty to protect public health and those which merely impact on the ways in which this can be done. Moreover, once we move beyond the question of whether a state should be absolutely free to determine its law without any restriction (even that which is self-imposed), and begin to consider the specific content of a particular restriction, the question quickly shifts from being about legislative freedom and becomes a substantive question about what policy is actually in the national interest. Given the diversity of interests within a national polity, this question will always be contested.

The main impediment to those using sovereignty to argue about substantive policy content is that there is no necessary link between the locus of a decision and the content of that decision. To argue for the ultimate authority of a particular collective body (a nation-state, for example) to decide a point of policy involves abandoning oneself to the decision of that body, whatever it may be. Similarly, maintaining determined opposition to particular policies promoted at the international level (such as those reflected in the patent requirements in TRIPS), requires an ambivalent position towards the question of national authority – since there is no settled content to the interests of national polities nor indeed

41 Iyer, 'Human Health'.

42 See World Trade Organisation, 'Declaration on the TRIPS Agreement and Public Health', Ministerial Conference, 14 November 2001, WT/MIN(01)/DEC/2, at: http://www.wto.org/English/thewto_e/minist_e/min01_e/mindecl_trips_e.htm (last accessed 6 December 2011) ('Doha TRIPS Declaration'), para 3.

those which might be pursued with success at the international level.

Finally, as we will see in more detail in Chapter 4, the same mechanisms which are said to deny India's sovereignty (membership of international organisations and the undertaking of treaty obligations), are the very same mechanisms which India uses to pursue its intellectual property policies on the international stage and which its government uses to project its authority domestically. This reveals a symmetry between the story in which TRIPS constitutes a denial of India's sovereignty and the story in which India's sovereignty is effected through its participation in international organisations. The concept of sovereignty is able to be used on both sides of each argument. The overarching reason for this is that the state and the WTO share the same ground of authority – the sovereign state. If state sovereignty is called into question, the basis for the WTO's authority falls away. Similarly, each nation-state relies on its capacity to enter into relations with other states and to participate in international institutions like the WTO. Not only is this a necessary element of the recognition of states at international law, but it provides a forum in which a government's domestic authority – its ability to speak for its people – can be played out. The conventional view of state sovereignty does not operate simply to oppose the authority of international organisations but instead grounds it. It thus offers little in the way of a framework for critique of the authority of such organisations.

As such, despite clear and significant concerns about the process by which India's patent law was amended to comply with TRIPS and the content of those changes, it is difficult to argue with rigour that by such a process India's sovereignty was denied. The mechanisms and techniques by which that purported denial occurred are the same ones by which its sovereignty is claimed and exercised. At the same time, it is also unsatisfactory to understand treaty-making in simply formal terms. Such an approach would find that the WTO is merely the product of a delegation of national authority and therefore account for everything that it does as flowing from an original exercise of state sovereignty. Marked by its attachment to purely formal notions of state authority and consent, this approach prevents proper analysis of the nature, source and legitimacy of the authority of the WTO. What is needed is a conception of sovereignty in which its ability to support both sides of various arguments is understood, accepted and worked through. This requires more than a bland acknowledgement that the compromises involved in treaty-making and in international negotiations involve both an exercise and restriction of sovereignty. Instead, it requires us to examine not only the way competing sovereign claims interact but how they constitute each other. Only then can we properly appreciate the dynamic between competing claims to authority to determine law without being required to ignore the complexity of national interests, the strategic use of decision-making fora and the inequalities marking the international political economy.

The theory of sovereign autopositioning advanced in this book provides space for such thinking. It allows us to recognise that the Indian state and the WTO each make competing claims to authority over Indian patent law (claims which intersect and overlap, but not entirely), and that no common higher authority exists to sort out any dispute between them. As such, the boundaries between their respective spheres of authority can only be determined (for the time being) by the relation between them. This approach emphasises not only the complexity of their relation but also the mutual constitution of these claims to authority. In so doing it accommodates the apparent contradictions within state sovereignty itself. It enables us to work, I will argue, towards a more nuanced understanding of the responsibility of both the WTO and the Indian state for the content of Indian patent law.

2.2 Sovereignty and traditional knowledge holders: a clash of incommensurable grounds of law

In the case of traditional knowledge holders, it is not a coincidence of grounds which demonstrates the limitations attending the conventional view of sovereignty, but rather an incommensurability of grounds. The groups in question do not aspire to statehood or otherwise fit the frame of self-determination as it is understood in international law. These are not claims which somehow fail to meet the requirements of self-determination, but ones which are not even made in terms which could meet those requirements. For while self-determination seems to provide a mode by which self-grounded communities could assert sovereignty, it remains tightly bound to the concept of the integrity of states.[43] Indeed, even in its most dynamic phase (decolonisation) self-determination only ever conceived of the 'self' as an incipiently 'national' self and one apt for statehood. Groups within states are left with what are generally termed as rights to 'internal' self-determination – obligations placed on states to respect minorities within the national frame, but not such as to disturb the comfortable completeness of the national sovereign claim itself.[44] The confinement of self-determination to existing territorial borders (which in the classic case of decolonisation is most often those of a coloniser) is acknowledged to be an arbitrary restriction on the concept, but it is usually defended on pragmatic grounds.[45] Its confinement to the national form itself is rarely put into question.[46]

The claims of local and indigenous communities in India to sovereignty over their traditional knowledge are, quite simply, incommensurable with the sovereignty of the state. If, in modernity, sovereignty is something which can be vested solely in

43 James Crawford, *The Creation of States in International Law*, 2nd ed., Oxford: Clarendon Press, 2006, pp. 108–31.

44 See, e.g.: the Declaration on the Rights of Indigenous Peoples (2007); article 27 of the International Covenant on Civil and Political Rights (1966); the Declaration on the Rights of Persons Belonging to National or Ethnic, Religious and Linguistic Minorities (1992). Crawford argues that while measures to protect the rights of national minorities and indigenous peoples are beginning to broaden the notion of what constitutes a 'people' for the purposes of self-determination, such 'developments are still tentative (*de lege ferenda*), and they do not affect the established rules and practices with respect to self-determination and the territorial integrity of States': ibid., p. 121.

45 See, e.g., Rosalyn Higgins, *The Development of International Law through the Political Organs of the UN*, London: Oxford University Press, 1963, pp. 104–5. See Crawford, *Creation of States*, p. 125.

46 An exception to this is Karen Knop, *Diversity and Self-Determination in International Law*, Cambridge: Cambridge University Press, 2002.

nation-states, and can be claimed only by nation-states or those communities with some hope or expectation of being recognised as such, it would appear that modern law has no place for the claims to sovereignty by local communities over traditional knowledge.

And yet, these claims seem to have a purchase and vitality that is not easily denied. There is broad consensus among policy makers that traditional knowledge should be protected and that local communities should have a say in its protection.[47] Of its fellow nation-states, India would be among the most receptive to (and indeed actively supportive of) this approach. But attempts to engage with the question of how traditional knowledge should be protected invariably involve a tension between national and international laws, and the laws of local and indigenous communities themselves.[48] Optimistic engagements would suggest that this tension can be overcome by the recognition or accommodation of the content of local rights within national and international law. And much that is aimed at supporting the substantive interests of traditional knowledge holders has been achieved through intense and difficult political action by and on behalf of local groups within the framework of national and international law.[49] Yet, as I will seek to show, the incommensurability of the claims would deny any full or final resolution of them. They are not just

47 See, e.g., the work of the Intergovernmental Committee on Intellectual Property and Genetic Resources, Traditional Knowledge and Folklore, World Intellectual Property Organisation, at: http://www.wipo.int/tk/en (last accessed 20 April 2012).

48 This tension can be observed in the numerous iterations of the draft articles for the protection of traditional knowledge drafted by the IGC. A full collection of documents for each committee session is available at http://www.wipo.int/meetings/en/topic.jsp?group_id=110 (last accessed 20 April 2012).

49 One example would be the efforts of Gene Campaign (among other groups) to successfully lobby the Indian Parliament to provide rights for farmers in its legislation on the protection of plant varieties (the *Protection of Plant Varieties and Farmers' Rights Act 2001* (India)): see Gene Campaign, 'Farmers' Rights and IPR' at: http://www.genecampaign.org/Sub%20pages/wws-ID9.htm (last accessed 6 December 2011).

about the protection of intellectual property, but are in substance about a clash between different ways of life.

The frame of reference for the protection of traditional knowledge under Indian national law is much narrower than the frame of reference within which local and indigenous communities make their claims. While it is no exaggeration to say that India's attempts to protect traditional knowledge and give effect to local community rights are at or near the forefront of global practice, they nonetheless focus on the protection of knowledge as a commodity. These attempts are geared towards enabling local communities to obtain some economic benefit from the commercial exploitation of their knowledge. They allow traditional knowledge to fit neatly within a national and international intellectual property system in which knowledge can be subject to private rights, assigned and exploited. This is incompatible with a view of traditional knowledge as an integral part of traditional ways of life embedded in cultural and legal practices which do not fit within the frame of national law.

For example, under the main piece of Indian legislation aimed at protecting the rights of local communities over traditional knowledge concerning genetic resources (such as plants with medicinal properties), those rights are conceived solely in economic terms. The Biological Diversity Act 2002 seeks to ensure that the economic benefits derived from the exploitation of traditional knowledge are shared equitably with the local custodians of that knowledge. The concept of equitable benefit sharing rests entirely on the premise that traditional knowledge can be licensed by its traditional custodians for commercial use outside the traditional context. That depends on it being alienable and having an asset value derived from the protection that will be afforded to it by patent law once 'inventions' are developed by those to whom it is licensed. This reduces traditional knowledge to a right to receive a royalty, with the role of local communities beyond this likely limited to the cultivation and sale of raw materials.[50]

50 This indeed is what happened in one of the early and most famous cases of 'equitable benefit sharing' of knowledge developed by the Kani tribe in Kerala

As such, whatever their intent, the measures enacted by India remain trapped within a conceptual framework in which knowledge exists as a commodity for commercial exploitation, detached from the way of life in which it has been created and developed. Such detachment and commodification is incompatible with the way the knowledge is understood in the traditional context, that is, as something integral to that context. As Sahai, Pavithran and Barpujari note, traditional knowledge

> has no association with the concept of private ownership. Acquired and developed as a community effort, it is usually held collectively, although specific individuals or families within the community may hold certain types of knowledge, and use it for the benefit of the community. Access to and use of [this knowledge] is governed by a wide variety of unwritten customary laws.[51]

The role played by customary laws in the access and use of traditional knowledge is a reflection of the way it is integrated into the

over the properties of the *arogyapaacha* plant. Despite the very best of intentions the scheme disrupted the social structure of the tribe by bestowing financial rewards unevenly and led to the further marginalising within the group of those members (the Plathi) who had the traditional authority to use tribal medical knowledge and a responsibility to do so for the benefit of the tribe. For details of the scheme, see P. Pushpangadan *et al.*, '"Arogyapacha" (Trichophus Zeylanicus Gaertn.): The "Ginseng" of Kani Tribes of Agasthyar Hills (Kerala) for Ever Green Health and Vitality', *Ancient Science of Life* 8, 1988, 13–16; Anil Gupta, *WIPO-UNEP Study on the Role of Intellectual Property Rights in the Sharing of Benefits Arising from the Use of Biological Resources and Associated Traditional Knowledge*, WIPO-UNEP, 2004, at: http://www.wipo.int/tk/en/publications/769e_unep_tk.pdf (last accessed 6 December 2011), 111–12. For analysis of the scheme's successes and failings, see Sachin Chaturvedi, 'Kani Case: A Report for GenBenefit', 2007, at: http://www.uclan.ac.uk/schools/school_of_health/research_projects/files/health_genbeneift_kani_case.pdf (last accessed 6 December 2011). See also Ka Shaji, 'Herbal Wars', *Tehelka Magazine* 5(38), 27 September 2008, at: http://www.tehelka.com/story_main40.asp?filename=Ne270908herbalwars.asp (last accessed 6 December 2011).

51 Suman Sahai, Prasmi Pavithran and Indrani Barpujari, *Biopiracy: Imitations Not Innovations*, New Delhi: Gene Campaign, 2007, p. 6.

way of life of the community. Providing for collective ownership of traditional knowledge might be simple enough,[52] but it would not take into account the complexity of these laws and their significance in the creation and development of traditional knowledge. Moreover, it would assume that every member of the community has equal rights to the knowledge, thus failing to take into account the nuance and complexity of the relations within the community itself.[53]

Something closer to the protection of traditional practices can be observed in the key piece of Indian legislation aimed at protecting farmers' rights, and yet a similar dissonance between existing modes of protection and the wider claims of local communities can be observed. Under the Protection of Plant Varieties and Farmers' Rights Act 2001, farmers have the right to save, share and sell seed even where it is subject to private rights created by the Act.[54] These are significant rights and came as a result of extensive lobbying on behalf of local farmers and communities.[55] Nonetheless, they operate as limited exceptions to a general rule that privileges private rights over seeds and plant varieties. This situation may be exacerbated by the Seeds Bill 2010. When first introduced in 2004, that bill contained clauses which would have placed hurdles in the way of the exercise of farmers' rights and may have implicitly undermined them by way of requiring that seeds sold comply with standards for quality and homogeneity.[56]

52 See, e.g., Daniel Gervais, 'Traditional Knowledge and Intellectual Property: A TRIPS-Compatible Approach', *Michigan State Law Review* Spring 2005, 137, 149: 'To recognize a community as owner of a patent is not a particularly difficult conceptual jump.'

53 See, e.g., Marilyn Strathern, 'Introduction: Rationales of Ownership' in Lawrence Kalinoe and James Leach (eds), *Rationales of Ownership: Transactions and Claims to Ownership in Contemporary Papua New Guinea*, Wantage: Sean Kingston, 2004, pp. 3–5; see also Peter Fitzpatrick and Richard Joyce, 'Copying Right: Cultural Property and the Limits of (Occidental) Law', in Fiona Macmillan (ed.), *New Directions in Copyright Law: Volume 4: Protection of Traditional Knowledge and Culture*, Cheltenham: Edward Elgar, 2007, pp. 187–8.

54 Protection of Plant Varieties and Farmers' Rights Act 2001 (India), s 39.

55 See Gene Campaign, 'Farmers' Rights and IPR'.

56 Clauses 6 and 25 of the Seeds Bill 2004 (India).

Recently proposed amendments to the bill seek to retain the exception for farmers' practices,[57] but nonetheless it is based on a model of agriculture in which farmers are predominantly consumers of seeds rather than being actively involved in their production. Such laws are based on a model of large-scale agriculture whose main goal is to produce products for international trade. As such, farmers promised higher yields from patented and protected seeds are not only faced with higher costs to buy the seeds and restrictions on the use of seeds derived from harvest, but find themselves increasingly at the mercy of fluctuating prices on world markets.[58]

When one looks at the kinds of claims by local farmers in India who develop and practise traditional knowledge in the field of agriculture, and the groups that work with them, one frequently finds a concept of traditional knowledge which cannot be reduced to a simple, transferrable right. Rather, the knowledge is intimately connected with a way of life incompatible with large-scale commercial monopolisation and exploitation. For example, agricultural knowledge in the traditional context in India has involved the collective development of innovation.[59] The sharing, exchange and sale of seeds was an integral part of that innovation, not an exception to a private right embodying it. The goal which this law sought to achieve was the continued diversity of crops suited to different climatic and soil conditions and the continued sustainability of local agriculture.[60] This was not simply a matter of

57 Clauses 1 and 2 of the Seeds Bill 2010 (India).

58 'The Great Unravelling: Is Globalisation Killing India's Cotton Farmers?' *Economist* 382, 20 January 2007, p. 34; cf Guillame Gruère, Purvi Metha-Bhatt and Deblotta Sengupta, 'Bt Cotton and Farmer Suicides', IFPRI Discussion Paper 00808, International Food Policy Research Institute, October 2008, p. 1.

59 Shiva, Jafri, Bedi and Holla-Bhar, *Enclosure and Recovery of the Commons*, pp. 3, 9, 21–5.

60 Campaign for Community Control over Biodiversity, 'Laws and Flaws: Farmers' Questions, Farmers' Answers', Report of a Workshop in Zaheerabad, Medak District, Andhra Pradesh, 14–16 January 2007, at: http://www.kalpavriksh.org/f1/f1.1/bdbdcamp (last accessed 15 May 2009, copy on file with author), p. 10.

agricultural production, but of a way of life. As prominent activist Vandana Shiva and her colleagues argue, there

> exists a very intricate relationship between the local communities [of India] and biological diversity…. Communities have developed knowledge and found ways to derive their livelihood from the bounties of nature's diversity, in wild and domesticated forms. Hunting and gathering communities use thousands of plants and animals for food, medicine and shelter. Pastoral, peasant and fishing communities have also evolved knowledge and skills to derive sustainable livelihoods from living diversity on the land, in the rivers, lakes and seas. So, there exists a symbiotic relationship whereby people have lived off nature while helping to sustain it. The life of communities was enhanced spiritually, culturally and economically as the communities enriched [the] earth's biodiversity.[61]

While this may seem a romanticised view of rural life, Shiva and her colleagues point out that such knowledge and its sustainable application are a simple matter of life and death for over two-thirds of India's population. They argue that 70 per cent of Indians depend on traditional agriculture and have their health care needs met by traditional systems of medicine.[62] The move towards the use of commercially produced seeds has had, in many cases, devastating effect. With higher prices, farmers have needed to take on additional debt which they have frequently been unable to repay when yields have fallen short of what was promised or expected.[63] Many thousands of farmers have, as a result, become trapped in a cycle of debt which has driven them to selling kidneys to repay debt and even to suicide. Shiva and Jalees report

61 Shiva, Jafri, Bedi and Holla-Bhar, *Enclosure and Recovery of the Commons*, p. 21.
62 Ibid.
63 Vandana Shiva and Kunwar Jalees, *Seeds of Suicide: The Ecological and Human Costs of Seed Monopolies and Globalisation of Agriculture*, 4th ed., New Delhi: Navdanya, 2006, pp. 56–62.

that over 40,000 Indian farmers committed suicide in the decade to 2004 with the inability to repay debt and acquire fresh credit 'widely accepted as the most significant proximate cause'.[64] Other estimates place the figure as high as 120,000.[65]

The incompatibility between the way of life supported by traditional laws on agricultural knowledge and that supported by private rights is clearly evident from the responses at a workshop soliciting farmers' perspectives on laws concerning plant varieties, seed exchange and intellectual property organised by the Campaign for Community Control over Biological Diversity in 2007. In the session on customary practices, Vijay Jardhari argued that agriculture is not an invention but rather 'is part of our evolution' and spoke of how farmers have traditionally regarded the 'soil as our Mother.'[66] Other participants noted that seeds should be regarded as 'life forms' not 'life-less products',[67] and 'as Nature's gift.'[68] It was argued that farmers are 'a part of and not above the natural process'.[69] That is, the innovations generated through farming practice are not regarded as the property of farmers but as something created and to be shared in collaboration with each

64 Ibid., pp. 56, 59. Cf Gruère, Metha-Bhatt and Sengupta, 'Bt Cotton and Farmer Suicides', p. 25. This report disputes the argument that there is evidence to support a direct correlation between Monsanto's genetically engineered Bt Cotton, a product which features heavily in Shiva and Jalees' analysis. However, it nonetheless argues that the higher price of seeds has contributed to increased indebtedness, which in turn is a key cause of the increase in suicides. As such, Monsanto's endorsement of the report as absolving it of responsibility may have been somewhat rash: see Monsanto, 'Latest Evidence on True Causes of Indian Farmer Suicides', at: http://www.monsanto.co.uk/news/ukshowlib.php?uid=13478 (last accessed 6 December 2011). In turn, Vandana Shiva disputes the conclusion of the Gruère, Metha-Bhatt and Sengupta report that there is no direct correlation between Bt Cotton and farmer suicides: see Tinku Ray, 'Indian GM Crops Battle Heats Up', BBC News, 18 December 2008, at: http://news.bbc.co.uk/2/hi/business/7785212.stm (last accessed 6 December 2011).

65 Campaign for Community Control over Biodiversity, 'Laws and Flaws', p. 12.

66 Ibid., p. 10.

67 Ibid., p. 7.

68 Ibid., p. 14.

69 Ibid.

other and with nature. It was further argued that the 'only way by which our sovereignty would survive' was to 'revive traditional practices and crop patterns.'[70] Some participants acknowledged that the pervasiveness of private rights in agriculture through the world-wide adoption of strict intellectual property rights under TRIPS meant that strategies aimed at securing private rights for farmers would be easier to achieve.[71] However, other participants argued that the attempt to create rights in individuals was counter-productive since it played into a system in which the use and exchange of seeds and associated knowledge is a matter of private right.[72] Indeed, the notion of reserving rights to farmers to save, exchange and sell seeds as limited exceptions to private rights was, in the words of one participant, 'equivalent to providing the right to breathe'.[73] It was argued that the issue is not simply that seeds and knowledge should be saved from unfair exploitation, but that they should be saved 'from these laws'[74] which would treat them as commodities.

Whatever the limitations of the efforts to protect traditional knowledge by legislation in India, it should be noted that by contrast to practices in which traditional knowledge was treated as part of the public domain and ripe for exploitation without any compensation to the communities responsible for generating, preserving and developing that knowledge, laws establishing a scheme of prior informed consent and equitable benefit sharing are a major advance. They have the potential to make fairer the process by which traditional knowledge is commercially exploited. But they do not challenge the idea that the knowledge exists, or can be appropriated, for the purpose of commercial exploitation. 'Protecting' traditional knowledge by turning it into a property right (even one vested in the community itself) changes the nature of that knowledge and the culture that has supported it. In short,

70 Ibid., p. 10.
71 Ibid., p. 14.
72 Ibid., p. 10.
73 Ibid., p. 8.
74 Ibid., p. 14.

it turns a complex cultural system into a commodity and may actually contribute to the destruction of the cultural and legal infrastructure in which that knowledge has been developed and on which it depends.[75]

75 It should be noted that much depends on how one characterises 'property' in this context. The use I make of it in this book is in keeping with Western intellectual property forms which underlie Indian patent law and the benefit-sharing scheme under the Biological Diversity Act 2002 (India), and in which rights in knowledge are treated as commodities. Property can have other meanings, however. For example Drahos, drawing on Hegel, argues that there is an essential link between property and personality, and in so doing pays careful attention to the way in which particular forms of property might promote the expression of individual or community personality, while others (depending on their content and the manner of their creation or imposition) may destroy it. From this perspective, he argues that while there 'are very good reasons to be critical of western intellectual property forms', there are also 'reasons for seriously considering the possibility that indigenous intellectual property forms might be a viable strategy of emancipation from present dominant western forms.' Drahos's approach, then, is not to reject 'property' as a way of dealing with traditional knowledge, but ask 'whether we can devise regulatory forms that will allow indigenous people to pursue their own economic interests in the use of their cultures in ways that are consistent with their aspirations for the preservation and evolution of those cultures', a task he would leave to 'indigenous people and the positive law of individual states': Peter Drahos, 'Indigenous Knowledge and the Duties of Intellectual Property Owners', *Intellectual Property Journal* 11, 1997, 179, 191–3, 196–8. However, a less nuanced approach to the question of the malleability of the concept of property can lead towards finding a superficial correspondence between the content of Western intellectual property and local customary law. In addressing the question of 'customary law' in the summary of its fact-finding mission on traditional knowledge, the World Intellectual Property Organisation stressed that concepts like 'property' and 'ownership' should not be thought to be 'inappropriate for delineating rights and duties with respect to [traditional knowledge]' since its findings revealed that 'such concepts – or at least close equivalents to them – also exist in most if not all traditional societies.' From there, WIPO suggested that 'patents, copyrights, trade secrets and trademarks' might not be 'entirely alien or incompatible concepts to all indigenous and traditional rural communities.' But it is one thing to note some general sense of 'property' or 'ownership' exists in traditional communities and quite another to suggest that this creates conditions for compatibility with Western intellectual property forms (which have very particular characteristics). At least WIPO was circumspect enough to note that while '[p]roprietary systems do

If we are to take seriously the notion that the cultural and legal system in which particular traditional knowledge has been created is important to its ongoing development (and therefore take seriously the possibility that the knowledge is better 'protected' by such a system than by Western notions of science and intellectual property law), then we would have to recognise that in order to protect traditional knowledge, we need to create conditions of possibility for traditional ways of life to continue and to develop on their own terms.[76] As such, conceiving of traditional knowledge as a commodity is not equal to the task of protecting it. Something more is required. And so, we should not be surprised that claims by local communities over traditional knowledge have gone beyond mere assertions of property rights and are phrased in terms of a sovereign right to determine the law applicable to the use of traditional knowledge and other resources. These claims reveal that debates over traditional knowledge are not just questions about the allocation of rights, but about how different forms of life and law can exist together. In this way, the example of traditional knowledge in India puts in focus an issue which lies at the heart of relations between nation-states and indigenous populations all over the world.

exist in many traditional societies ... any assumption that there is a generic form of collective community [intellectual property rights] ignores the intricacies and sheer diversity of indigenous and traditional proprietary systems:' World Intellectual Property Organisation, *Intellectual Property Needs and Expectations of Traditional Knowledge Holders: WIPO Report on Fact-Finding Missions on Intellectual Property and Traditional Knowledge (1998–1999)*, Geneva: WIPO, 2001, at: http://www.wipo.int/tk/en/tk/ffm/report/final/index.html (last accessed 6 December 2011), pp. 220–1.

76 As Drahos notes, 'the "embeddedness" of [traditional knowledge] in group life has many important implications, including the fact that the continued existence of [traditional knowledge] is bound up with the continued existence of the groups that generate it:' Peter Drahos, 'Towards an International Framework for the Protection of Traditional Group Knowledge and Practice', paper prepared for the *UNCTAD-Commonwealth Secretariat Workshop on Elements of National Sui Generis Systems for the Preservation, Protection and Promotion of Traditional Knowledge, Innovations and Practices and Options for an International Framework*, Geneva, 4–6 February 2004, p. 7.

The claims of traditional knowledge holders are not just about the content of particular laws, but about the question of who gets to determine them. In short, they concern the question of sovereignty. But if sovereignty is what local communities claim, then the tension between this claim and the sovereignty normally claimed for the state (ultimate, exclusive and originary) can only ever be resolved by complete concession or utter denial. In the Indian context, as we will see in more detail in Chapter 5, neither extreme seems to be in play. Instead, one can observe that irresolution is the operative dynamic of the politics concerning sovereignty and traditional knowledge. In this context, adherence to the view that all legal authority flows from the state at worst fails to give any credence to the claims and at best simply ignores much which is important about the relationship between these sites of authority. What is required, and what the theory of sovereign autopositioning advanced in this book seeks to provide, is a framework in which one can understand and work with the ongoing, irresolvable tension between these incommensurable sites of authority.

3 Constituent Qualities of Sovereignty

Having established that modern sovereignty demands critique, the next task is to explain the form that the critique in this book will take. My approach will be to critique sovereignty from the inside out by focusing on modern sovereignty's constituent qualities. Contrary to the standard view, however, I will argue that these qualities are not exclusive to the state and can also be seen to exist, for example, in the WTO and in local communities in India. As such, the WTO and local communities can be seen not simply as forces which challenge the sovereignty of the state, but as alternative sites of sovereignty themselves to which state sovereignty necessarily relates. By focusing on the constituent qualities of modern sovereignty, I hope to show that the challenges posed by the WTO and local communities do not reveal the sovereignty of the state to be in decline, but instead reveal that it was never what it was commonly supposed to be. Moreover, exploring these alternative sites of sovereignty will be seen to be crucial to an understanding of what modern sovereignty 'is'.

Displacing the nation-state as the sole form of sovereignty in modernity necessarily requires a departure from the standard usage of the term, where sovereignty is taken to mean the ultimate legal power of and in a state. It cannot be denied that the great writers of modern sovereignty such as Bodin, Hobbes and Rousseau all had the idea of the authority of the state in mind when they wrote about sovereignty. It cannot be argued that they thought their conceptions of sovereignty could or should be applied beyond the form of the state. As Jens Bartleson explains, Bodin's sovereignty 'stands in a relation of mutual implication to the state; to be sovereign means to be sovereign *over* a state'.[77] Scholarship on the question of legal and political sovereignty has largely followed this approach.[78]

There is, however, another usage of the term which is not restricted to the state. That is the philosophical usage where sovereignty denotes, in Peter Fitzpatrick's phrase, 'the formative condition of any ipseity.'[79] In this usage, the main concern is not the authority of the state but the question of how to account for the singular self in a way which does not presume (as modern

77 Jens Bartleson, *A Genealogy of Sovereignty*, Cambridge: Cambridge University Press, 1995, p. 141 (original emphasis). Bodin went so far as to declare that his devotion to legal scholarship came from a desire to contribute 'to the state, to which, after immortal God, we owe all things.' Jean Bodin, *Method for the Easy Comprehension of History*, tr. Beatrice Reynolds, New York: Columbia University Press: 1945, p. 1.

78 Even diverse treatments of sovereignty have the authority of the state in mind: see, e.g., Bartleson, *Genealogy*; F. H. Hinsley, *Sovereignty*, Cambridge: Cambridge University Press, 1986; Stephen Krasner, *Sovereignty: Organized Hypocrisy*, Princeton: Princeton University Press, 1999; Carl Schmitt, *Political Theology: Four Chapters on the Concept of Sovereignty*, tr. George Schwab, Chicago: University of Chicago Press, 2005.

79 Peter Fitzpatrick, 'Surpassing Sovereignty', in Julie Evans *et al.* (eds), *New Worlds, New Sovereignties: Frontiers of Possibility in the Emerging Global Order*, Honolulu: University of Hawai'i Press, forthcoming. 'Ipseity' is defined in the Oxford English Dictionary as: 'Personal identity and individuality; selfhood' and derives from the Latin *ipse* meaning 'self': *Oxford English Dictionary*, 2nd ed., Oxford: Oxford University Press, 1989. As we will see in Chapter 2, Jacques Derrida uses this term and gives it a particular meaning in the context of law and sovereignty.

Enlightenment thought would tend to do) that the individual is the irreducible starting point of all social being and of political life. Thought along these lines tends to find that we cannot find a stable ground for our selfhood in some solid notion of individuality.[80] And yet, together with its impossibility comes a certain imperativeness. It might be the case that the complexity of social life means that it is impossible to isolate what we are, as singular beings, from the social context in which we live. That would challenge the Enlightenment notion of the individual as irreducible and originary. But having made this point, we would then need to account for the fact that we are not simply adrift and without any sense of individuality, of identity, or of singularity. As such, we need to account not only for the impossibility of assured singularity, but also for a certain imperative towards it. And so, for Bataille, sovereignty 'eludes us all' and yet we remain 'doomed to seek it';[81] for Nancy, explicitly drawing on Bataille, it 'cannot stop haunting us'.[82]

But Bataille, for example, wrote that the 'sovereignty of which I speak has little to do with the sovereignty of States, as international law defines it.'[83] One should pause then, before taking the broader notion of sovereignty I have just outlined and relating it to the standard usage.[84] If sovereignty, as the 'formative condition of any ipseity', supplies the quality necessary for the being singular of the self, it is a quality that inheres in all of us. And if all of us possess a certain sovereignty in order to exist as singular

80 See Jean-Luc Nancy, *Being Singular Plural*, trs Robert Richardson and Anne O'Byrne, Stanford: Stanford University Press, 2000.

81 Georges Bataille, *Literature and Evil*, tr. Alastair Hamilton, London: Marion Boyars, 1973, pp. 193–4.

82 Nancy, *Being Singular Plural*, p. 132.

83 Georges Bataille, *The Accursed Share: Volumes II and III*, tr. Robert Hurley, New York: Zone Books, 1991, p. 197.

84 Indeed, in a book which will draw so heavily on Jacques Derrida, it would seem especially irresponsible to ignore his injunction to show 'mistrust for analogies and hasty transpositions': Jacques Derrida, 'Force of Law: The Mystical Foundation of Authority', tr. Mary Quaintance, in Jacques Derrida, *Acts of Religion*, ed. Gil Anidjar, New York: Routledge, 2002, p. 237.

beings, then are we not all 'sovereign'? Fitzpatrick, in his consideration of the distinction between these two usages of sovereignty invokes by way of illustration the exchange between Diotima and Socrates in Plato's *Symposium.* There, Diotima considers the term 'composition'. Of 'composition', Diotima says that it 'forms a general class. When anything comes into being which did not exist before, the cause of this is always composition.'[85] So Diotima asks Socrates whether this means that 'the products of all the crafts are compositions and the craftsmen who make them are all composers.'[86] Socrates says that is does, but Diotima responds:

> But you know that they aren't called composers but have different names. Out of the whole class of composition we pick one part, the one related to music and verse, and call that by the name of the class as a whole. It's only this that's called composition and those who have this subdivision of skill are called composers.[87]

A similar distinction could be made between the broader philosophical notion of sovereignty and the narrower meaning given to it by Bodin and others and which has taken on such force over such a long period of time. It might be that in the creation of singular identities, we all share a certain quality of 'sovereignty'. But it does not simply follow that we are 'sovereign' in a sense which corresponds to the question of legal and political authority, just as someone who makes a chair is not a 'composer' in a sense which corresponds to music and verse just because they have brought the chair into being. As such, in arguing that the WTO and local communities in India should be regarded as alternative sites of sovereignty which relate to the sovereignty of the state,

85 Plato, *Symposium*, tr. Christopher Gill, London: Penguin Books, 1999, p. 42; see Peter Fitzpatrick, 'Leveraging Leviathan' in Charles Barbour and George Pavlich (eds), *After Sovereignty: On the Question of Political Beginnings*, Abingdon: Routledge, 2010, p. 19.

86 Plato, *Symposium*, p. 42.

87 Ibid.

I will need to do more than simply show that these entities have the general quality of sovereignty that we all share.

I will have to show two additional things. First, I will have to show that consideration of the broader notion of sovereignty is necessary to understand the narrower class of entity to which the name 'sovereign' has been given in modernity – the nation-state. This I hope to achieve by showing that the conventional focus on the sovereignty of the nation-state has led to the characteristics it shares with the general class being overlooked. That is, I will argue that the qualities which apply to ipseity in general are also constituent qualities of the sovereignty of the nation-state. These qualities include the tension intimated above between impossibility and imperativeness. Just as the 'sovereignty' of the singular self is both impossible and imperative, so too is it with the nation-state, and, I would argue, other forms of political community. But the key feature which I argue is a constituent quality of modern sovereignty (in its legal and political, as well as its broader philosophical sense) is what Derrida refers to as 'autopositioning'.[88] The term 'autopositioning' refers to the ability of an entity to designate both its own identity and the scope of its authority. For Derrida, and for this book, such a quality is a necessary feature of sovereignty simply by virtue of the fact that modern sovereignty is a form of ipseity, and autopositioning is a necessary feature of ipseity.[89] Derrida quite explicitly develops his theory of sovereign autopositioning in the context of considering the authority of the state.[90] As such, his work provides a starting point for connecting the broader philosophical usage with the standard usage.

Second, I will have to show that there is some quality in modern legal and political sovereignty which is not present in all of us. Only then will I be able to argue that the WTO and local communities in India share with the nation-state the characteristics of that certain form of sovereignty which concerns legal and political authority. In order to make out this argument, I will focus on the type of claim made (or put into action) by the state, the

88 Derrida, *Rogues*, p. 12.
89 Ibid.
90 See, e.g., ibid.

WTO and local communities. I will show how each of these particular entities makes a claim to ultimate authority to determine the law of a community. That is not something that just anyone does, or that anyone can do. At this early stage, it might appear that law and community are very general and convenient concepts on which to base a connection between a general notion of sovereignty and a politico-legal variety. However, I will be developing more than just a superficial link between these concepts and sovereignty. I will argue that the concept of sovereignty developed in this book is an essential component of modern law and of community.

4 Outline of Chapters

The success of the theory advanced in this book depends first on overcoming the presumption that the nation-state is the sole ground of sovereignty in modernity. As such, the first chapter will be devoted to a detailed examination of the question of what grounds sovereignty in modern law. This I characterise as a question of 'position'. Staying close to the key source on which the theory of modern sovereignty has been built, Jean Bodin's *Six Books of the Commonwealth*, I will examine the characteristics he ascribes to the sovereign and consider what they reveal about the positioning of sovereignty.[91] For Bodin, sovereignty is the absolute, perpetual and indivisible power over law in a commonwealth.[92] I will argue that each of these characteristics

91 Jean Bodin, *On Sovereignty*; Jean Bodin, *Six Books of the Commonwealth*, tr. R. Knolles, London: Bishop, 1606. A note on these sources: the first is a clear and scholarly translation of the four chapters of Bodin's *Six Books of the Commonwealth* which deal most directly with the question of sovereignty. The second is a translation of the whole of the *Six Books* first published in 1606. Where the reference I wish to make to the *Six Books* falls within the four chapters in Franklin's collection, I will cite that source. However, where the reference falls outside these four chapters (and in a very few instances where Knolles's translation carries a flavour missing from Franklin's drier, if clearer, rendition), I will cite the second source.

92 Jean Bodin, *On Sovereignty*, pp. 1–4, 46–50.

provides an insight into the way in which modern sovereignty is positioned, but that this positioning relies essentially on irresolutions within these concepts rather than their apparent solidity. I will then consider whether 'nation' resolves the irresolutions within Bodin's concepts such that it could provide the exclusive 'position' of modern sovereignty. Arguing that 'nation' fails to do so, I will suggest that Bodin's characteristics of sovereignty actually require an 'autopositioned' claim to authority which cannot be guaranteed by any external authority nor located in any one form of community. Through this analysis I will attempt to expose the essential groundlessness of state sovereignty and open at least the possibility that the state is not the exclusive site of sovereignty in modernity.

In Chapter 2, I will set out in more detail Derrida's notion of autopositioning. I will argue that 'autopositioning' provides the groundless ground of modern sovereignty. I will expand on a simple notion of 'autopositioning' to show how the position of modern sovereignty arises through a dynamic relation between it and the concepts of law and community. Each concept will be found to be necessary to the constitution of the others without any of them being originary or prime. I will argue that the relation between sovereignty, law and community shows that the position of sovereignty is not to be found in a model which avoids or seeks to resolve the irresolutions in Bodin's conception of sovereignty, but rather in one which embraces them. I will then set out how the authority of the WTO, and the claims made by local and indigenous communities over traditional knowledge demonstrate this quality of sovereign autopositioning in their relation to law and community.

In Chapters 1 and 2, the focus will be on the constituent qualities of sovereignty that might be regarded, initially, as 'internal' to the community for which a particular entity is sovereign. That is only one part of Derrida's notion of autopositioning. The other concerns the relation of that sovereign position (and the community for which it speaks and whose law it claims to determine) and what might be regarded as 'external'. For Derrida, sovereignty is indeed 'autopositioned', but he is quick to point out that this autopositioning, this 'gathering of the self' necessarily occurs 'in the simultaneity of an assemblage or assembly, being together or "living together"'.[93] This quality of 'being together' is not just something that positioned sovereigns 'do', but it is something which is important for the way they are positioned. This I characterise as a question of 'relation'. And so, in Chapter 3, I will examine in more detail the way in which sovereign positions relate, and the constitutive function of this relation. Through this analysis, the standard conception of what is 'internal' and 'external' to the positioning of sovereignty will be thoroughly complicated. This complication will turn out to be very useful in Chapters 4 and 5, when I consider the complex and messy 'boundaries' which exist between the authority claimed and exercised by the WTO, the Indian state and local groups over patent law and traditional knowledge in India.

The discussion of 'relation' in Chapter 3 will focus on Jean-Luc Nancy's work on the question of singularity.[94] For Nancy, a completely isolated and self-contained singular being is impossible; or at least it is a contradiction in terms.[95] That is because, for Nancy, we cannot escape our being-with each other.[96] Even being alone requires something else that one could be alone from.[97] As such, an attempt to mark out even so lonely and singular position as that of a sovereign requires a relation to other forces and sites of authority. This analysis will further show that the concept of a sovereignty exclusively and originarily located in the nation-state, which is commonly taken as the starting point for international law, is impossible.

I will begin Chapter 3 by setting out the conventional account of international law which proceeds from the self-evident 'reality' of nation-statehood and finds that international law 'is the child

93 Derrida, *Rogues*, p. 11.

94 In particular, Jean-Luc Nancy, *The Inoperative Community*, ed. and tr. Peter Connor, Minneapolis: University of Minnesota Press, 1991, pp. 1–42; and Nancy, *Being Singular Plural*.

95 Nancy, *Inoperative Community*, p. 4.

96 See Nancy, *Being Singular Plural*, p. 3; ibid.

97 Nancy, *Inoperative Community*, p. 4.

and not the parent of states'.[98] We will see that support for this conventional view can be found in classic texts on sovereignty and international law by Bodin, Vitoria, Grotius, Pufendorf, Vattel and Rousseau. I will then briefly show how this claim to absolute self-containment is a feature of the sovereign claims made by and on behalf of the WTO and traditional knowledge holders. With help from Nancy, I will then demonstrate how this claim to self-containment is impossible. Having established this impossibility in the philosophical terms provided by Nancy, I will go on to show how this impossibility can be glimpsed in the work of those very theorists of international law most commonly called on to support the conventional view. Moreover, I will find that this impossibility is also evident in the historical 'event' most commonly cited as the origin of the singular modern nation-state: the Peace of Westphalia.

Having combined then the insight from Chapters 1 and 2: that sovereignty is 'autopositioned' and cannot be located in any one site or form of community, with the insight from Chapter 3: that all claims to sovereignty can only exist in the context of a relation with rival sites of authority, we will then be able to think about the complex interaction between states and between the WTO, the Indian state and local communities in a more nuanced way than would be possible if we were to adhere to the conventional view of modern sovereignty. This possibility will be explored in Chapters 4 and 5.

In Chapter 4, I will argue that the interaction between the WTO and the Indian state over patent law can be understood as a relation between rival sovereign positions: each of which makes a self-grounded or 'autopositioned' claim to determine patent law in India, but neither of which have the ultimate capacity to do so exclusively. The content of India's Patents Act 1970 will be presented as the result of the dynamic interaction between the sovereign authority claimed by the state and that claimed by the WTO rather than the product of the exclusive authority of one or

98 Robert Jackson, *Quasi-states: Sovereignty, International Relations and the Third World*, Cambridge: Cambridge University Press, 1990, p. 53.

the other. I will argue that viewing the content of the law in this way enables us to arrive at a better understanding of the responsibility which exists for the law that results from this interaction than a perspective in which the sovereignty of the state is thought to be exclusive yet somehow under threat.

In Chapter 5, the focus will shift to the interaction between the national and the local through an investigation of claims to authority over traditional knowledge in India. The task of this chapter will be to uncover the basis of the vitality of traditional knowledge holders' claims and what it reveals about the sovereignty of the state. Relating the claims set out in Chapter 2 to the provision made for local community autonomy under Indian national law (in particular, under the Indian Constitution), this chapter will show that local communities rely on their relation with the Indian state in order to constitute their own sovereignty. However this does not compromise the sovereign character of their claims. As I will have shown in Chapter 3, a reliance on a relation with rival sites of authority is consistent with the nature of modern sovereignty. Indeed, inverting the perspective, I will proceed to consider the Indian state's reliance on its relation with local communities in constituting its own sovereignty. This analysis will show that like the relation between the Indian state and the WTO, the relation between the Indian state and local communities is one in which rival sovereign positions converge on an area of law which neither has the capacity to determine completely. Rather, the law that exists is the result of the dynamic relation between them; a relation which cannot be resolved.[99] Finally, this irresolution will be shown to be productive, in that it demonstrates that despite its seemingly pervasive and complete hold, modern sovereignty actually carries within it a continuing openness to new possibilities of community, of law, and of life.

99 Or to be more precise, it can only be made subject to a re-solution for the time being. The *Oxford English Dictionary* defines 're-solution' as '[r]enewed or repeated solution.' The effect of the hyphen is further amplified by the definitions of 'resoluble' as 'capable of being resolved' and 're-soluble' as 'capable of being dissolved again'. Thanks to Peter Fitzpatrick for suggesting this term.

Part I

Position

Chapter 1

Modern Sovereignty and the Nation-State

A Failure of Grounds

> 'The sharing of the world is the law of the world. The world has nothing other; it is not subject to any authority; it does not have a sovereign.'[1]

Introduction

Nancy may be correct in asserting that the modern world does not have a sovereign. But we do not share the world in some general way. In French (the original language of Nancy's text), the word for sharing, *partage*, refers also to dividing or sharing out.[2] Thus 'sharing', as the law of the world, refers not only to the inescapability of our being with each other in the world and a commonality which arises from its joint use or enjoyment. It also refers to a certain inescapable division. This 'law of the world' prescribes a marking out of distinctions, of difference, of inclusion and exclusion, of positions and of borders. As such, our shared world, lacking a sovereign, is not short of entities claiming sovereignty. But what happens when such claims conflict, or when they have different grounds? In the absence of a singular overarching sovereign guaranteeing all others, how can we determine the validity of competing claims to sovereign authority? In its most familiar guise, the question might seem to pose the

1 Jean-Luc Nancy, *Being Singular Plural*, trs Robert Richardson and Anne O'Byrne, Stanford: Stanford University Press, 2000, p. 185.
2 Ibid., p. 194 (translators' note).

standard conundrum of international law – the problem of a legal system made up of sovereign states with no overarching power to determine disputes. But posing the question in this way nonetheless presupposes that states are sovereign, and that only states are sovereign. Taken in a broader sense, the question also puts in issue this very presupposition. It suggests that we need some way of establishing whether or not the nation-state is the sole occupant of the sovereign position in modernity. If the state's claim to exclusive sovereignty can be displaced, there emerges a capacity to think anew the relationship between states and international organisations, and between states and indigenous and local communities.

The approach of this chapter and the one which follows will be to take a very simple, perhaps self-evident, proposition about sovereignty and push it to its limits. That proposition is that sovereignty is the highest legal authority within a certain space and that this authority is not derived from or subject to any other. I will argue that pushing this simple proposition forces us to question our most common assumption about sovereignty – that it is a trait held only by nation-states. In working through this problem, I will specifically seek to avoid working 'around' it. I will not try to construct a new conception of sovereignty with different features and characteristics than those which have been classically ascribed to the state. In particular, I will not begin with features of alternative claims to authority (like those of the WTO and traditional knowledge holders) in order to generate a conception of sovereignty which accommodates them comfortably. If I were to do that, it would come as no surprise if the object of my construction was not bound by any limitations – especially those linking sovereignty to the state.

Indeed, in order to maintain a rigorous focus on the claim made for national sovereignty, this chapter will keep at a distance the context of alternative claims to sovereignty in India. In a sense, the goal is to clear the ground of existing assumptions in order to sow a more compelling and convincing account of sovereignty in modernity in subsequent chapters. My approach will be to take the classic constituent characteristics of modern sovereignty and consider whether they can be reconciled with the limitations we commonly place on the concept. I will, therefore, attempt a rigorous and thorough critique of sovereignty which is at once without limits and yet seeks to be faithful to the concept. A guide, and inspiration, for such an approach, can be found in the work of Jacques Derrida. As his meditations on the concepts of forgiveness[3] and hospitality[4] (not to mention law and justice[5]) show, Derrida's 'deconstructive' technique provides a way of reading which seeks to defy the limits we place on our understanding of concepts precisely through a rigorous fidelity to them. This fidelity requires the reader not to shy away from aporia or paradox, nor seek to suppress the things about these concepts which would destabilise or complicate them.[6]

In his later work, Derrida himself took some steps towards applying this approach to the question of sovereignty.[7] But well before doing so directly, Derrida had sought to apply deconstructive techniques to questions concerning the foundations of law and politics.[8] Indeed, in 'Force of Law', he went as far as to venture that it was 'normal, foreseeable, and desirable that studies of deconstructive style should culminate in the problematic of right,

3 Giovanna Borradori, *Philosophy in a Time of Terror: Dialogues with Jurgen Habermas and Jacques Derrida*, Chicago: University of Chicago Press, 2003, pp. 85–136.

4 Jacques Derrida and Anne Dufourmantelle, *Of Hospitality (Cultural Memory in the Present)*, tr. Rachel Bowlby, Stanford: Stanford University Press, 2000.

5 Jacques Derrida, 'Force of Law: The Mystical Foundation of Authority', tr. Mary Quaintance, in Jacques Derrida, *Acts of Religion*, ed. Gil Anidjar, New York: Routledge, 2002, pp. 230–98.

6 Ibid., pp. 235, 248.

7 See Jacques Derrida, *Rogues: Two Essays on Reason*, trs Pascale-Anne Brault and Michael Naas, Stanford: Stanford University Press, 2005; Borradori, *Philosophy*, pp. 85–136; Jacques Derrida, *Without Alibi*, tr. Peggy Kamuf, Stanford: Stanford University Press, 2002, pp. xv–xxxv, 202–80; Jacques Derrida, *The Beast and the Sovereign (Volume I)*, tr. Geoffrey Bennington, Chicago: University of Chicago Press, 2009.

8 See Jacques Derrida, 'Declarations of Independence', *New Political Science* 7, 1986, 7–15; Jacques Derrida, 'The Laws of Reflection: Nelson Mandela, In Admiration', trs M. Caws and I. Loenz in Jacques Derrida and Mustapha Tlili (eds), *For Nelson Mandela*, New York: Seaver Books, 1987; Derrida, 'Force of Law'.

of law [*loi*] and justice.'[9] He continued that 'deconstructive questioning' of

> values like those of the proper and of property in all their registers, of the subject, and thus of the responsible subject, of the subject of right, the subject of law, and the subject of morality, of the juridical or moral person, of intentionality, and so forth, and of all that follows from these ... is through and through a questioning of law and justice, a questioning of the foundations of law, morality and politics.[10]

With questions of legal and political foundation being so significant for Derrida, his later turn towards the question of sovereignty comes as no surprise. Of sovereignty itself, Derrida writes that it is

> no doubt necessary, in the name of reason, to call into question and to limit a logic of nation-state sovereignty. It is no doubt necessary to erode not only its principle of indivisibility but its right to the exception, its right to suspend rights and law, along with the undeniable ontotheology that founds it, even in what are called democratic regimes.[11]

But, no nihilist, he also warns that this questioning should not compromise too much. For Derrida, '[o]ne cannot combat, *head-on, all* sovereignty, sovereignty *in general*, without threatening at the same time, beyond the nation-state figure of sovereignty, the classical principles of freedom and self-determination.'[12] He argues that sovereignty's deconstruction must occur while 'recognising that all the fundamental axiomatics of responsibility or decision ... are grounded on the sovereignty of the subject,

9 Derrida, 'Force of Law', p. 235.
10 Ibid.
11 Derrida, *Rogues*, p. 157.
12 Ibid., p. 158 (original emphasis).

that is, the intentional auto-determination of the conscious self.'[13] Derrida writes that even the nation-state, under certain conditions, can be an 'indispensable bulwark against certain international powers.'[14] The challenge of thinking about sovereignty, for Derrida, is to think about 'sovereignty legitimately deconstructed here, but claimed there'; of the 'necessity of a strategy that, without relativism, does battle here against a sovereignty to support it elsewhere'.[15] In addressing himself to this challenge, Derrida focuses on what he described as sovereignty's 'autopositioning'.[16] This concept seeks to capture that simple quality of sovereignty I described above – that if a sovereign is the highest, underived authority, then in a modern world which forbids recourse to the divine, it can only rely on itself to ground that authority.

In taking up Derrida's challenge, the aim of this chapter is not simply to undermine the sovereignty of the state. Rather, it is to better understand its grounds and consider whether its claims to exclusivity can be sustained. I will seek to go beyond the limits commonly ascribed to modern sovereignty by suspending the assumption that the state is the only entity capable of holding that position, while attempting to remain faithful to modern sovereignty's constituent characteristics. In order to do this, I will focus on the work of Jean Bodin. Bodin is the 'standard source for the modern idea of sovereignty.'[17] He famously pronounced that '[s]overeignty is the absolute and perpetual power of a commonwealth.'[18] For Bodin, sovereignty is 'not limited either in power, or in function, or in length of time'[19] and 'he is absolutely sovereign who recognises nothing, after God, that is greater

13 Derrida, *Without Alibi*, p. xix.

14 Derrida, *Rogues*, p. 158; Derrida, *Beast and the Sovereign I*, p. 76.

15 Derrida, *Without Alibi*, xix; Derrida, *Beast and the Sovereign I*, p. 76.

16 Derrida, *Rogues*, p. 142.

17 Peter Fitzpatrick, 'What are the Gods to Us Now?: Secular Theology and the Modernity of Law', *Theoretical Inquiries in Law* 8, 2007, 161, 168.

18 Jean Bodin, *On Sovereignty: Four Chapters from the Six Books of the Commonwealth*, ed. and tr. Julian Franklin, Cambridge: Cambridge University Press, 1992, p. 1.

19 Ibid., p. 3.

than himself.'[20] Such absolute power, modelled on the image of God, cannot be shared; it is singular and indivisible.[21] Moreover, it is a power to determine the content of law.[22] With these characteristics, Bodin is taken to have established a theory of sovereign absolutism and one which, once shed of its reliance on divine power, provides the theoretical basis for the sovereignty of the modern nation-state. If these characteristics can provide a stable ground for modern sovereignty and can be found only in the nation-state, then it could be argued that the state is the exclusive site of modern sovereignty. If, however, the reverse is true of these characteristics, then it would seem possible that modern sovereignty could reside in places other than the state.

In part one of this chapter, I will take Bodin's characteristics of sovereignty in turn. I will argue that each gives some clue to the positioning of modern sovereignty, but that this positioning occurs not by virtue of the seemingly robust and assured terms of Bodin's definition, but by virtue of irresolutions within these characteristics. More precisely, we will find that these characteristics are necessary and impossible elements of Bodin's conception of sovereignty. More precisely again, we will find that they must be claimed by entities seeking to exercise sovereign authority, but that this claim can never ultimately be realised. In other words, in order to be what it is, a sovereign must claim to be more than it can actually be. Thus, we will find that a sovereign must claim to be an absolute authority, but is in fact dependent on a transcendent source of power. It must also claim to be perpetual, but is in fact, and must be, vulnerable. The sovereign must also claim an indivisible authority, and yet we will find that this same sovereign depends essentially on its relation to other rival powers. It must claim to hold authority over law, and yet is dependent on law for its position and finally, while it may appear to be grounded in 'the commonwealth', that entity is itself dependent on sovereignty and thus fails to provide a solid grounding for it. Indeed, to

20 Ibid., p. 4.
21 Ibid., p. 50.
22 Ibid., p. 55.

borrow Bataille's evocative phrase, 'sovereignty must inhabit the realm of failure.'[23]

In part two, I will analyse whether 'nation' is able to resolve the tensions in Bodin's conception of sovereignty such that it could claim to be the ultimate realisation of modern sovereignty and thus its exclusive site. I will argue that despite the claims made for it, 'nation' spectacularly fails to resolve these tensions. Rather its success lies in how effective it has been in working with them. But since the tensions themselves remain – tensions which make an unquestionable claim to sovereignty impossible – this effectiveness should not be confused with exclusivity. In Chapter 2, I will build on this analysis to show how sovereignty is positioned not in a fixed and stable ground, but is, using Derrida's term, 'autopositioned'. But this does not mean that just anyone can make and sustain a sovereign claim. I will argue that the autopositioning of modern sovereignty occurs in a dynamic relation with law and community. As such, the sovereign position will be found to be one open to any entity capable of speaking for a community and determining its law. This analysis will open the possibility that the WTO and local communities in India might, in addition to the Indian state, hold a sovereign position.

1 Bodin and the Characteristics of Sovereignty

1.1 Sovereignty is absolute

For Bodin, sovereignty exists only where it is absolute. By absolute, Bodin means that the sovereign is not subject to the command of any other person and that its exercise of power carries no obligations or conditions.[24] For Bodin, if an entity in which power is vested is answerable to any other, then no matter how great the extent of the power vested in it, that entity does not

23 Georges Bataille, *Literature and Evil*, tr. Alastair Hamilton, London: Marion Boyars, 1973, p. 194.
24 Bodin, *On Sovereignty*, pp. 8, 11.

hold sovereignty.[25] Similarly, if power is given by one entity to another on condition that it may be reclaimed, then sovereignty remains with that first entity.[26] And while, as we will see, Bodin's sovereign has a complex relation to law, there are passages in Bodin's work in which this relation is shown to reflect the sovereign's quality of absoluteness. Bodin writes that the sovereign is not bound by his own laws or those of his predecessors.[27] Rather, law depends on, but does not bind the sovereign.[28] At its most basic, Bodin's argument is that sovereign power primarily involves the sole capacity to make laws binding on all subjects, and that this power is located in the entity which is not subject to the authority of any other. Taking these points at face value, we might be led to the quick conclusion that an absolute sovereign need go no further than its own authority to find its grounds.

And yet, despite law's seeming dependence on an absolute sovereign power, Bodin does not find that the existence of an absolute sovereign is an inevitable condition of political community. Here he would contrast with Austin, who concluded that the existence of an entity which is subject to the authority of another implies the existence of an entity at the top of the chain which is not.[29] Bodin gives as examples of bodies he would consider to

25 Ibid., pp. 6–7, 49.
26 Ibid., pp. 1–8 (esp. 6–7).
27 Ibid., p. 14.
28 Ibid., p. 15.
29 John Austin, *Province of Jurisprudence Determined*, ed. Wilfred Rumble, Cambridge: Cambridge University Press, 1995, pp. 179–81. This argument is reflected in Austin's observation about independent political society, of which sovereignty is the 'essential or necessary property:' p. 179. Austin wrote that 'a political society which is not independent is a member or constituent parcel of a political society which is. Or (changing the expression) the powers or rights of subordinate political superiors are merely emanations of sovereignty:' pp. 180–1. It should be noted, however, that a close reading of Austin reveals him to be less than consistent on this score, especially when it came to accounting for the continued sovereignty of the French government and the continued existence of the French nation despite Allied occupation in 1815 (at pp. 167–8): see Peter Fitzpatrick, *Modernism and the Grounds of Law*, Cambridge: Cambridge University Press, 2001, pp. 95–6.

possess absolute sovereignty the 'genuine monarchs of France, Spain, England, Scotland, Ethiopia, Turkey, Persia, and Moscovy – whose power has never been called into question and whose sovereignty has never been shared with subjects'.[30] He contrasts this with the 'kingdoms of Poland, Denmark and Sweden, where the nobility makes claims to sovereignty [and] the kings can undertake a war [one of the powers Bodin reserves to the sovereign] only if it is decreed by the Estates.'[31] In these kingdoms, writes Bodin, the 'form of the state is uncertain and changeable, according to whether the prince or the nobility is stronger.'[32] Accordingly, Bodin is able to find examples of political communities which evidently have law but lack an absolute sovereign.

Nonetheless, the presence of imperfect or contested sovereignties would not go to disprove Bodin's theory as to what true sovereignty involves. Bodin would agree that entities claiming sovereignty could, in practice, be less than absolute. He would simply say that despite their claims they are not truly sovereign in his terms. However, there is a more fundamental limitation on the purported absoluteness of Bodin's sovereign which sits squarely within his ideal theory. That limitation is that the sovereign is bound to follow divine and natural law. Writes Bodin: 'For if we say that to have absolute power is not to be subject to any law at all, no prince of this world will be sovereign, since every earthly prince is subject to the laws of God and of nature.'[33] Bodin adds another category of laws to which the sovereign is bound, these being 'the various human laws that are common to all peoples.'[34] I will return to this last category later; my immediate concern is with divine law.

The sovereign's subjection to divine law is the price it pays for the scope of its earthly power. Sovereigns are 'established by

30 Bodin, *On Sovereignty*, p. 115.
31 Ibid., p. 61.
32 Ibid., p. 63.
33 Ibid., p. 10.
34 Ibid.

[God] as His lieutenants for commanding other men.'[35] Because of this, the sovereign is entitled to respect, reverence and obedience as if to God.[36] But it also means that the sovereign owes its position to God and His laws.[37] It could be argued that since the sovereign is only answerable to God and is also in a position (vis a vis its subjects) to decide what God's demands are,[38] this subjection has no real effect on its absolute temporal authority. However, the authority of the Church, for one, would at least be the cause of some restraint on the sovereign's absolute capacity to determine the will of God.

Another argument against the significance of this restriction would be that whatever its effect in Bodin's time, it does not survive modernity's destruction of the concept of rule by divine right. However, Bodin's subjection of the sovereign to God reveals something about the condition of modern sovereignty that survives the death of God. That is, sovereignty does not operate without a transcendent ground. Bodin's sovereign is not absolute in and of itself. It relies on something other to it, in this case God, to justify its power. As we will see, in modernity, sovereign power remains grounded in transcendent concepts even when the idea of divine right passes in favour of government by the people or the nation.

Thus Bodin's sovereign is absolute and not absolute. It is absolute in the sense that it is subject to no other earthly authority. However, by virtue of its reliance on God's authority and its subjection to divine law, the sovereign's authority is grounded in a concept outside of itself – albeit a transcendent one.

1.2 Sovereignty is perpetual

Of itself, the quality of perpetuity answers nothing about the grounds of sovereignty. But if perpetuity is a characteristic of

35 Ibid., p. 46.
36 Ibid., pp. 46, 50.
37 Ibid., p. 10.
38 See Thomas Hobbes, *Leviathan*, London: Penguin, 1968, p. 333 (Ch 26).

sovereignty, then it might at least provide a ground for accepting the authority of an incumbent sovereign, even if we can't be sure of the legitimacy of its origin. However, despite its prominence in Bodin's oft-quoted formula, Bodin was not attempting to make such a substantial point out of his reference to sovereignty's perpetuity. When Bodin refers to sovereignty as being a 'perpetual power', he meant to make the basic point that there can be no specified time limit on a sovereign entity's occupation of that position. Such a limit would make the occupant of a position of authority a mere trustee or borrower of that position on behalf of another sovereign entity to whom power must be returned.[39] For Bodin, the absence of a specified limit is sufficient to show perpetuity; sovereignty need not be eternal but rather 'for the life of him who has the power.'[40] For Bodin, if it were otherwise, sovereignty could only exist in aristocracies and democracies, which, because of their corporate nature, 'never die'.[41] Bodin was aware of the maxim that the 'the king never dies', but did not find it very convincing.[42] For Bodin, the idea that a monarch's sovereignty could be made eternal by rules of hereditary succession was not convincing, given that on his count, few monarchs were in fact hereditary.[43] Thus Bodin had a much more limited conception of the perpetuity of sovereignty than would first appear from the grandiose phrase in which he uses the term.

Thus Bodin's conception of perpetuity fails to account for the acceptance of the status quo and also fails the more basic task of

39 Bodin, *On Sovereignty*, pp. 1–2.
40 Ibid., p. 6.
41 Ibid.
42 Ibid., p. 44. As Kantorowicz shows, the development of the theory that the king never dies was a long and complex process, based as it was not only on the corporate nature of the polity but also on the king himself, distinct from the polity, having a natural body (which could die) but also an invisible body representing the royal dignity (a sort of distillation of divine appointment and a representation of the polity itself – but distinct from both), which could not die: see Ernst Kantorowicz, *The King's Two Bodies: A Study in Medieval Political Theology*, Princeton: Princeton University Press, 1957, pp. 314–450. These fine distinctions do not appear to have interested Bodin.
43 Bodin, *On Sovereignty*, p. 6.

accounting for the continuity of legal authority in a commonwealth. Nonetheless, his view has one key advantage in that it takes seriously the possibility that an entity's sovereignty can end and that end does not retrospectively make a lie of its former sovereign status. It thus allows for a certain flexibility and pragmatism in determining, at any one time, who the sovereign is, since there is no need to root sovereign title in an ancient path of succession. Moreover, as Bodin wrote, the 'greatest Commonwealths oftentimes fall' by 'reason of the changes of worldly things, which are so mutable and uncertain.'[44] Since no entity can guarantee its own perpetual survival in a constantly changing world, any theory of sovereignty, must, like Bodin's, have some way of accounting for the end of a particular sovereign condition and the beginning, not fully determined in advance, of a new one.

1.3 Sovereignty is indivisible

Bodin's argument that sovereignty is indivisible is one of his most famous contributions to the theory of sovereignty. It is also the one which most clearly lends itself to the conclusion that within a particular space (a national space, for example) sovereignty can exist in only one position. For Bodin, the prerogatives of sovereignty cannot be shared, for once the 'sovereign prince does share them with a subject, he would make a companion of his servant and, in so doing, would cease to be sovereign.'[45] This cannot be so, writes Bodin, because:

> Just as God, the great sovereign, cannot make a God equal to Himself because he is infinite and by logical necessity … two infinities cannot exist, so we can say that the prince, whom we have taken as the image of God, cannot make a subject equal to himself without annihilation of his power.'[46]

44 Jean Bodin, *Six Books of the Commonwealth*, tr. R. Knolles, London: Bishop, 1606, p. 406 (Book 4, Ch 1).
45 Bodin, *On Sovereignty*, p. 50.
46 Ibid.

Thomas Hobbes agrees with Bodin. In *The Elements of Law Natural and Politic*, he writes that 'if there were a commonwealth, wherein the rights of sovereignty were divided, we must confess with Bodin ... that they are not rightly to be called commonwealths, but the corruption of commonwealths.'[47] This view carries through to *Leviathan* where we find the rights 'which make the Essence of Soveraignty ... are incommunicable, and inseparable.'[48] For Hobbes, the ambiguity of written law, and the passions which lead people to distort their understanding of natural law, necessitate a sovereign who can be identified and relied on as the sole determiner of meaning.[49]

Bodin's concern is with the possibility that the 'marks' or 'prerogatives' of sovereignty could be divided between different entities within one state structure. These marks include the power to give laws,[50] decide cases by way of final appeal,[51] grant pardons,[52] impose taxes,[53] declare war or make peace[54] and institute the death penalty.[55] All of these, argues Bodin, can be collapsed into the category of making and repealing law, 'so that strictly speaking, we can say that there is only this one prerogative of sovereignty.'[56] For Bodin, it is inconceivable that the law-making power could be shared. The result would be inconsistent commands. Bodin draws two different conclusions from the hypothetical case of a state in which it was not possible to determine which of a number of different entities held the sole law-making (and thus sovereign) power in a state. The first, offered by Bodin in the French version of his treatise in 1576, is that the people must be sovereign and any authorities within that state must hold

47 Thomas Hobbes, *The Elements of Law Natural and Politic*, Whitefish: Kessinger Publishing, 2004, p. 118, para 7.
48 Hobbes, *Leviathan*, p. 236.
49 Ibid., pp. 319–20.
50 Bodin, *On Sovereignty*, p. 92.
51 Ibid., p. 67.
52 Ibid., p. 73.
53 Ibid., p. 59.
54 Ibid., p. 58.
55 Ibid., p. 56.
56 Ibid., p. 58.

their position on trust and at danger of being removed by popular action.[57] By the time of his Latin version in 1586, Bodin conceived another, more terrible possibility. Taking more seriously the possibility of conflicting commands, Bodin now finds that this situation would be 'anarchy … which is worse than the cruellest tyranny.'[58]

Julian Franklin argues that Bodin's thought on indivisibility was based on a concern that it was impossible for more than one entity to hold all of the state's law-making functions.[59] This meant that he thought it was not possible for different functions within a state's law-making apparatus to be located in different bodies, with no overlap between them. For this reason, Bodin has been accused of paying insufficient attention to the realities of mixed constitutions which existed in the societies he uses as examples, both in ancient Rome and (then) contemporary Europe.[60]

Because of his focus on the impossibility of sovereign prerogatives being exercised by multiple entities within the one state structure, Bodin did not consider indivisibility in terms of two rival authority structures contesting influence in a single territorial space. As Franklin argues, 'when Bodin spoke about the unity of sovereignty, the power he had in mind was not the constituent authority of the general community … but the power, rather, of the ordinary agencies of government.'[61] With a Christian God being the sole source of sovereign authority, and his analysis restricted to European examples, Bodin did not contemplate the possibility of two rivals claiming sovereignty based on incommensurable grounds. As such, by contrast to Francisco de Vitoria, his analysis does not deal with the problem of the grounds of the authority of coloniser and colonised in the territory of the New World.[62] Nonetheless, even if Bodin did not expressly consider

57 Ibid., p. 92.
58 See Franklin, 'Introduction', in ibid., p. xviii.
59 Ibid.
60 Ibid., p. xx–xxiii.
61 Ibid., p. xiii.
62 I will return to this question in Chapter 3.

indivisibility in relation to questions of constituent authority, he surely would have found it to be applicable to that problem. If, for Bodin, sovereign prerogatives cannot be shared within a state 'because two infinities cannot exist', then it must follow in a single territorial space there can be only one constituent ground of authority which grounds a single constituted sovereign power.

Taking up Bodin's thought on these lines, Carl Schmitt advanced a theory of sovereignty in which the concept of indivisibility provides the basis for the location of all constituent legal authority and decision-making power in a single site.[63] The position of Schmitt's sovereign is not a site guaranteed by anything other than its own effectiveness. Hence its singularity, if it could be sustained, would suffice to ground it. Importantly, Schmitt applies his theory to a liberal constitutional order in which, in the normal situation, functions of government are divided between different bodies. For Schmitt, in exceptional situations which threaten the life of the state, these bodies give way to a sovereign able to transcend the constitutional order so as to defend it. Thus Schmitt manages to hold to what appears to be a rigorous conception of

63 The Schmitt presented here is that of Carl Schmitt, *Political Theology: Four Chapters on the Concept of Sovereignty*, tr. George Schwab, Chicago: University of Chicago Press, 2005. This text is not presented as a full representation of Schmitt's whole body of work on the questions of law, authority and constitutional theory (nor even of that increasing portion of his work that has been translated into English), though it is arguably his most famous contribution to the question of sovereignty (especially in English-speaking countries). A more detailed account of his thoughts on constitutional law and practice is contained in Carl Schmitt, *Constitutional Theory*, ed. and tr. Jeffrey Seitzer, Durham: Duke University Press, 2008. My reason for focusing on *Political Theology* is that Schmitt's theory of the sovereign exception (and the inconsistencies within it) serve as a useful counterpoint both to Bodin's work and that of Derrida. Moreover, it has recently received a lot of attention, partly as a result of the so-called exceptionalism of the United States in its war on terror, and partly through debates around Giorgio Agamben's *State of Exception*, tr. Keven Attel, Chicago: University of Chicago Press, 2005. As such, the critique of it presented here may serve as a contribution to those debates; for a more direct contribution, see Peter Fitzpatrick and Richard Joyce, 'The Normality of the Exception in Democracy's Empire', *Journal of Law and Society* 34, 2007, 64.

sovereign indivisibility even within a modern liberal constitutional order.

For Schmitt, famously, '[s]overeign is he who decides on the exception.'[64] His view is that the constitutional state relies on what is beyond the constitution itself: a singular power capable of doing whatever is necessary to protect the state. According to Schmitt, the sovereign's position flows from its capacity to decide on the exception in terms of both its existence and what should be done about it.[65] For Schmitt, '[w]hat characterises the exception is principally unlimited authority, which means the suspension of the entire existing order.'[66] It 'cannot be circumscribed factually or made to conform to a preformed law.'[67] The decision about and in the exception suspends the monotonous regularity of the normal situation; it 'frees itself from all normative ties,' it 'departs ... from the legal norm.'[68] In the moment of the exception, then, sovereignty in a constitutional state is revealed as intensely personal and singular.

Whether or not one agrees with Schwab that Schmitt is the 'Hobbes of the twentieth century,'[69] it is clear that one thing Schmitt shares with Hobbes is his admiration for Bodin's theory of sovereign indivisibility. Schmitt writes that 'what is truly impressive in [Bodin's] definition of sovereignty [is that] by considering sovereignty to be indivisible, he finally settled the question of power in the state. His scholarly accomplishment and the basis for his success thus reside in his having incorporated the decision into the concept of sovereignty.'[70] Schmitt argues that at the heart of Bodin's theory of sovereignty was the question: '[t]o what extent is the sovereign bound to laws and to what extent is he responsible to the estates?'[71] For Schmitt, Bodin's concern here

64 Schmitt, *Political Theology*, p. 5.
65 Ibid., pp. 5–7.
66 Ibid., p. 12.
67 Ibid., p. 6.
68 Ibid., pp. 12, 13.
69 George Schwab, 'Introduction', in ibid., p. lii.
70 Schmitt, *Political Theology*, p. 8.
71 Ibid., p. 8.

was whether 'the commitments of the prince to the estates or the people dissolve his sovereignty.'[72] And for Schmitt, Bodin's answer came by his 'referring to the case in which it becomes necessary to violate such commitments, to change laws or to suspend them entirely according to the requirements of a situation, a time and a people.'[73] Schmitt's argument leads to the conclusion that by leaving the sovereign free to break its promises to its people in circumstances of 'urgent necessity', Bodin gave rise to a theory of sovereignty which recognised both its singular, indivisible nature and its ability to transcend any purported limitation on its power.

However, while Schmitt could argue that his work has some basis in Bodin's, Schmitt draws more from Bodin than is actually there. In particular, in discussing the 'case' that Schmitt cites, Bodin does not deal with specific emergencies at all, but rather the fact that over time and due to changing circumstances, laws have to be changed. Because of the weight Schmitt places on it, and because he paraphrases it without referencing it, despite himself lamenting that 'nowhere does one find cited [this] core quote'[74] it is necessary to set it out in full:

> the prince that sweareth to keep the laws of his country, must either not have the sovereignty; or else become a perjured man, if he shall abrogate but one law, contrary unto his oath: whereas it is not only profitable that a sovereign prince should sometimes abrogate some such laws, but also necessary for him to alter or correct them, *as the infinite variety of places, times, and persons shall require.* Or if we shall say the prince to be still a sovereign, and yet nevertheless with such condition, as that he can make no law without the advice of his counsel or people; he must also be dispensed with by his subjects, for the oath that he hath made for the inviolate observation of the laws; and the subjects again which are obliged and

72 Ibid., pp. 8–9.
73 Ibid., p. 9.
74 Ibid., p. 8.

> bound unto the laws, be it in particular, or in general, have also need to be dispensed withal by their prince, for fear they should be perjured: so shall it come to pass that the majesty of the Commonwealth inclining now to this side, now to that side, sometimes the prince, sometimes the people bearing sway; shall have no certainty to rest upon: which are notable absurdities, and altogether incompatible with the majesty of absolute sovereignty, and contrary both to law and reason.[75]

Contrary to Schmitt's reading, in this passage Bodin does not deal with the question of the circumstances in which it is proper for a sovereign to break a promise to maintain, in general, the laws in place. Bodin's point here is that such a promise is inconsistent with sovereignty itself. Moreover, Bodin is not referring to the 'suspension of the entire legal order' but merely to the need, as the case arises, to change the ordinary laws of the land. There are other sections where Bodin does deal directly with the question of when it becomes permissible for the sovereign to break promises to maintain particular laws. I will deal with these in the next section on Bodin's view of the relationship between sovereignty and law. It suffices to say for now that 'urgent necessity' is not given by Bodin as a reason for a sovereign breaking promises to maintain particular laws.

Schmitt would have been better to rely on Bodin's discussion of the dangers of changing laws within a commonwealth in chapter 3 of book 4. Having discussed ordinary laws (which, for Bodin, should be changed infrequently and as little as possible, so as not to impair the people's confidence in the law itself), Bodin turns to the question 'not of laws concerning ordinary policy, but of such as concern the very state itself.'[76] Here, at last, we appear to be on Schmitt's terrain. Bodin writes:

> 'I would … wish, if possibly it might be, that they should still be most *firm and immutable* … for the Commonwealth's sake. For why, the first and chief law of all Commonwealths, is this,

75 Bodin, *Six Books*, pp. 100–1 (Book 1, Ch 8) (spelling changed, my emphasis).
76 Ibid., p. 471 (Book 4, Ch 3).

> *Salus populi suprema lex esto*, The welfare of the people, let that be the last law.'[77]

He adds that 'no law is so sacred, but that upon urgent necessity it is to be changed.'[78] One could conclude that Bodin's emphasis here on the maintenance of the existing order, the appeal to a general law concerning the welfare of the people, and a recognition that any law must be able to be changed in a circumstance of urgent necessity, implicitly supports Schmitt's view that sovereign power involves the capacity (and the responsibility) to take whatever measures are necessary (even those that violate the constitutional order) in order to protect the constitutional order.

And yet, the opposite conclusion would seem at least as likely. Bodin writes that while 'laws could never be made immutable, neither were [they] to be all at once together changed.'[79] Rather 'where of new laws must of necessity be devised: which must yet for all that by little and little be done, and not violently all at once.'[80] This does not seem like a setting in which a sovereign may suspend the entire legal order, even to protect it. Moreover, as we will see below, for Bodin, the sovereign cannot detract from 'the laws which concern the state of the kingdom and its basic form'.[81] And in chapter 3 of book 4, the section which appears to give most support to Schmitt, we find numerous warnings to sovereigns against changing too much, too quickly. Bodin writes that 'to change the laws which concern the state is dangerous, as to remove the foundation or corner stones which uphold the whole weight or burden of [a building].'[82] Further, as we will see in the next section, the relationship of Bodin's sovereign to law is more intimate and complicated than one which is amenable to the idea that a sovereign power could suspend the legal order and rule by exceptional decrees. It is impossible to know what Bodin would

77 Ibid. (my emphasis).
78 Ibid.
79 Ibid.
80 Ibid.
81 Bodin, *On Sovereignty*, p. 18.
82 Bodin, *Six Books*, p. 470 (Book 4, Ch 3).

have thought of Schmitt's theory of the sovereign exception and his reliance on (and extension of) Bodin's idea of sovereign indivisibility. As the analysis above has shown, however, there is much in Bodin which would counter the reduction of an entire constitutional order to the singular decision of a sovereign.

While indivisibility is an important element in Bodin's theory of sovereignty, the difficulty he has in finding examples which actually fit that theory and the consequent elevation of a sovereign's responsiveness to other powers (like the Estates in France) as being dictates of natural law, reveals something of the impossibility of sovereign indivisibility. This impossibility is in turn reflected in Schmitt's having to rely on a misreading of Bodin's work to support his theory of singular sovereign exceptionality. In the sovereign's relation to its subjects, to law and to God (each of which are necessary to, and thus constitutive elements of, Bodin's sovereign), its purported indivisibility is constantly exposed. But at the same time, without the characteristic of indivisibility – without, as Hobbes would have it, the capacity to be known as the sole authority – a sovereign could not render determinate decisions (exceptional or otherwise). Indivisibility thus appears as a necessary and impossible characteristic of sovereignty. The challenge left by Bodin is not, as Schmitt argues, to conceive of a sovereign elevated such that the entire order is guaranteed by its singular capacity to decide on the exception. Rather, the challenge is to conceive of sovereignty which is at once indivisible and yet able to be shared – singular and yet in relation.[83] The sovereignty of an entity must, therefore, be grounded not by its own singular decision-making capacity, but in its relation to law, to the transcendent ground it seeks to represent, and to other sites of power.

1.4 Sovereignty is a power over law

As we have seen, Bodin is widely thought to have established a theory of sovereignty in which the sovereign holds absolute

83 See Derrida, *Without Alibi*, p. xix; Derrida, *Beast and the Sovereign I*, pp. 76–7.

determining power over law. For Bodin, 'the power of the law lies in him who has the sovereignty',[84] law being 'nothing but the command of a sovereign making use of his power.'[85] This point will be made again, of course, most famously by Austin.[86] For Bodin, this power to give law to subjects is the 'first prerogative of sovereignty'[87] and one which, as we saw above, encompasses all the others. In this section I want to consider whether the characteristic of authority over law might provide a position which grounds sovereignty.

Of course, we have already seen how Bodin's sovereign is 'established by [God]'[88] and is thus constituted by divine law. Bodin is also clear that the sovereign is subject to, and its authority does not extend over, divine and natural law.[89] As such, Bodin positions the sovereign between natural or divine law (whose content is determined by God), and 'civil' law (whose content is determined by the sovereign). This is neatly shown by what seems at first to be a circular statement. Bodin concludes a discussion of the sovereign's exclusive ability to determine the content of law by stating that 'the law says that the prince is not subject to the law'.[90] This only makes sense if we read it that *natural or divine* law says that the sovereign prince is not subject to (its own) *civil* laws. Thus when Bodin makes claims for the exclusive capacity of the sovereign to determine the content of law, it is clear that he must be referring to 'civil' law, or what would become known as positive law – law posited from a sovereign position.[91]

While the structure seems simple enough: God determines divine and natural law and the sovereign determines positive law (being bound only to the former), it is not always easy to know

84 Bodin, *On Sovereignty*, p. 55.
85 Ibid., p. 38.
86 Austin, *Province*, p. 165.
87 Bodin, *On Sovereignty*, p. 92.
88 Ibid., p. 46.
89 Ibid., pp. 13, 46. Cf for Hobbes, the sovereign power obliges men to obey natural law: Hobbes, *Leviathan*, p. 314.
90 Bodin, *On Sovereignty*, p. 11.
91 See Fitzpatrick, *Modernism*, p. 130.

whether a law is divine, natural, or positive. Some clues can be found in Bodin's analysis of whether a sovereign is bound to maintain laws which it has promised to keep. For Bodin, to the extent laws are its own creation, the sovereign may change them at any time, or excuse itself from compliance.[92] But to the extent that the sovereign has *promised* to keep a law, it is bound to maintain and follow the law, seemingly on the basis of a law of contract which exists as natural or divine law and which binds the sovereign just as much as its subjects. Indeed, it may bind the sovereign even more strictly, since by his good faith he is 'the formal guarantor to all his subjects of good faith among themselves.'[93] Breaking this promise contravenes this natural law unless, on the basis of what seems to be a higher natural law, the particular law promised to be maintained '*ceases to be just*'.[94] But 'if there is no just cause to set aside a law that he has promised to maintain, the prince ought not and cannot [justly] contravene it.'[95] As noted above, and contrary to Schmitt's reading of Bodin, no exception is given for cases of 'urgent necessity'. Neither does that exception seem to apply for other substantive restrictions on Bodin's sovereign imposed by natural law, including rules against the sovereign appropriating property without compensation,[96] preventing presentations of petitions,[97] and revoking promises of predecessors that concern the state and bring it profit.[98] As such, the sovereign's authority over law seems much more restricted than it first appears and seems to provide an unstable ground for sovereignty.

92 Bodin, *On Sovereignty*, p. 12. Cf Hobbes, *Leviathan*, p. 313, where Hobbes justifies greater freedom for the sovereign to change the law than Bodin. Vitoria, on the other hand, justifies less: Francisco de Vitoria, *Political Writings*, eds and trs Anthony Pagden and Jeremy Lawrence, Cambridge: Cambridge University Press, 1991, pp. 181–5.
93 Bodin, *On Sovereignty*, p. 35.
94 Ibid., p. 15 (my emphasis).
95 Ibid., p. 14 ('justly' appears in the text in square brackets).
96 Ibid., p. 40.
97 Ibid., p. 70.
98 Ibid., p. 44.

There is another aspect of law which binds the sovereign which is not reducible to the distinction between natural or divine law, and positive law. As we saw above, Bodin's seemingly absolute sovereign is also bound to act in accordance with 'the various human laws that are common to all peoples.'[99] For Bodin, these 'are different from the laws of nature and of God'.[100] Nor are they custom. While custom arises from the course of common interaction between people rather than sovereign decree, it is local and in any event has legal force only 'by sufferance' and may be repealed by the sovereign at any time.[101] Bodin does not expand on what he means by the laws 'common to all peoples' or how they come to be binding on sovereigns. It could be read simply as the commonality between the laws created by a number of different sovereigns in various places.[102] Such a reading would at least preserve the place of the sovereign, in general, as the creator of law, even if it means that a particular sovereign has to abide by what his predecessors and counterparts around the world have previously set in place.[103]

99 Ibid., p. 10.
100 Ibid., p. 129.
101 Ibid., pp. 57–8.
102 It is not clear that Bodin would have been referring to sovereigns being bound by international law as we would understand it. In the Latin, the phrase Bodin used for laws 'common to all peoples' is *ius gentium*, which to modern readers would suggest the 'law of nations' or international law – particularly those parts having the status of *jus cogens*. But according to Franklin, for readers of Bodin's time, and earlier, the phrase used, *lex omnium gentium communis* meant 'law common to all peoples'. See Bodin, *On Sovereignty*, p. 129. This fits with Franklin's interpretation of Bodin's method as comparative (hence he would have been attuned to finding what was common between states' legal systems without necessarily relating this to an overarching (international) legal framework): see Julian Franklin, *Jean Bodin and the Sixteenth Century Revolution in the Methodology of Law and History*, New York: Columbia University Press, 1963. Interestingly, Bodin's translator in 1606 preferred law 'of nations': see Bodin, *Six Books*, p. 91 (Book 1, Ch 8).
103 Indeed, taking this approach, even international laws having the status of *jus cogens* would have begun life as laws created by individual sovereigns in various places.

An alternative reading would have it that these laws are so fundamental they exist without the need for, and indeed govern, all sovereigns. In this mode, the people are the creators of the law that binds them. Supplementing this thought with that of the social contract, one finds resonances with Hobbes's creative incipient multitude. Not only do 'men', for Hobbes, create the 'Artificial Man, which we call a Common-wealth' for their preservation and peace, but so also do they make:

> Artificial Chains, called Civill Laws, which they themselves, by mutuall covenants, have fastned at one end, to the lips of that Man, or Assembly, to whome they have given the Soveraigne Power; and at the other end to their own Ears.[104]

This passage from Hobbes could be read such that it is the people that have the first word and last word on the laws which bind them, even if this power is mediated by the sovereign they create.[105] If that is the case, then it is much more extensive than Bodin's category of 'laws common to all people'. Nevertheless, even if the category is small, the possibility that certain laws might spring from the relations between people and bind the sovereign introduces a relationship between the sovereign and the polity which involves a certain mutual regard – a sociality that exists through and because of law.

This relationship between subject and sovereign goes some way to explaining Bodin's insistence that the sovereign governs through law. Law, in this way, is not something which merely exists for the sovereign's pleasure, a useful technique of governing which the sovereign uses to supplement to some other power. Rather it is the mode by which a sovereign must govern. Were the sovereign to govern, in the manner of Schmitt's exceptional power, 'without any law, leaving all to the discretion of the magistrates, or else of themselves' such a government could not 'be of any continuance, or assurance, for that it hath not in it any bond

104 Hobbes, *Leviathan*, pp. 263–4. See Fitzpatrick, *Modernism*, p. 95.
105 Fitzpatrick, *Modernism*, p. 95.

wherewith to bind the greater unto the lesser, nor by consequence any accord at all.'[106] As such, Bodin's sovereign does not sit wholly above the law. It is constituted by law and is bound to govern through it, by virtue of a necessary sociality which exists not simply among its subjects, but also between it and them. In this way, the relationship of Bodin's sovereign to law is much more complex and constraining than might appear at first.

1.5 Sovereignty is 'of a commonwealth'

Bodin refers to the sovereign as being the absolute and perpetual power *of a commonwealth*. In this, the existence of a commonwealth that the sovereign would be sovereign over is taken as a pre-existing form – the form of the state. Bartleson cites Bodin as among the first to place sovereignty as a 'mark of the individuality of the state'.[107] As we saw in the Introduction, for Bartleson, Bodin's sovereignty 'stands in a relation of mutual implication to the state; to be sovereign means to be sovereign *over* a state.'[108] In Bodin's theory, the sovereign exists as the sole authority within certain territorial limits. Sovereign power is thus defined by its exclusive relation to a commonwealth defined in terms of a community inhabiting a certain territorial space.

For Bodin, the idea of the commonwealth places and grounds the sovereign's rule and is thus crucial to its constitution. Without the commonwealth, sovereignty falls away. Hence, for Bodin, even the sovereign cannot detract from 'the laws which concern the state of the kingdom and its basic form, since these are annexed to the crown' and constitute 'the royal laws on which the sovereign majesty is founded and supported.'[109] If the sovereign cannot question the basic form of the state, such questioning is

106 Bodin, *Six Books*, pp. 760–1 (Book 6, Ch 6) (spelling changed).
107 Jens Bartleson, *A Genealogy of Sovereignty*, Cambridge: Cambridge University Press 1995, p. 141.
108 Ibid. (original emphasis). See also F. H. Hinsley, *Sovereignty*, 2nd ed., Cambridge: Cambridge University Press, 1986, pp. 1–26.
109 Bodin, *On Sovereignty*, p. 18.

clearly beyond the power of its subjects.[110] And so it is not just because of its divine authority that the sovereign's power cannot be called into question, but because of the immutability of the form of the state on which this authority also rests. Thus the commonwealth or the state provides what seems to be a solid foundation for Bodin's sovereign. However, the idea of the commonwealth has contrary dimensions. It at once grounds Bodin's sovereign and exposes it as groundless.

That aspect of the commonwealth which may be described as 'community' – clearly evokes these contrary dimensions. The question of community will be dealt with in greater detail in later chapters. But for present purposes it is necessary only to introduce the idea that community, as evoked by Bodin in his references to the commonwealth, both constitutes and is constituted by the sovereign. It constitutes or grounds the sovereign because there can be no sovereign without subjects. The sovereign must have a body of people over which to rule, or else its authority has nothing to act on.

In his writings which relate specifically to sovereignty, Bodin seems to assume that this body of people simply exists in the territorial space governed by the sovereign. But elsewhere Bodin directly addresses the question of the origin of the commonwealth. For Bodin, the commonwealth either grows gradually from a single family, or else arises all 'at once' because a multitude of people, cast out from one city or commonwealth, take root in another place and establish a new commonwealth.[111] In both cases, it would seem that some form of sovereign power establishes the commonwealth. Bodin writes that the commonwealth is always established by the strength of someone stronger than the people, or by the power of someone to whom they have voluntarily subjected themselves.[112] This voluntary subjection

110 For Bodin, even the opinion that France might be anything other than a monarchy (by virtue of the role of the aristocracy and the Estates) was 'not only absurd but punishable by death': ibid., p. 100.

111 Bodin, *Six Books*, p. 406 (Book 4, Ch 1).

112 Ibid.

may be to the power and pleasure of a 'sovereign power without any law at all', or else to a sovereign power 'upon certain laws and conditions betwixt them agreed upon.'[113] Bodin's reference to a subjection to sovereign power 'without any law' would seem to conflict with the statements we just encountered to the effect that it is impossible for the sovereign to rule without law. This apparent conflict could perhaps be reconciled if we read Bodin to be arguing that the voluntary subjection might occur without any pre-existing or fixed conditions; not that law itself would be absent in the foundation of the order arising in and through that subjection.[114] But nonetheless, in both cases envisaged by Bodin, sovereign power is the mode by which the commonwealth is constituted. But if it is the commonwealth on which sovereign majesty is 'founded and supported', then sovereignty constitutes that which constitutes it.

That sovereign power constitutes Bodin's commonwealth is most obvious where this occurs simply by the strength of the sovereign. But it is also true where the sovereign's power comes into being through a social contract. For Hobbes, the community that constitutes the sovereign by a social contract comes into existence only in relation with and by virtue of that sovereign. On one telling, the community comes together in the process of forming the sovereign. For Hobbes, the reduction of multiple wills to one sovereign will involves 'more than Consent, or Concord; it is a *reall Unitie* of them all, in one and the same Person, made by a Convenant of every man with every man.'[115] This 'real unity' is something greater than the sum of various agreements. He writes that 'the Multitude so united in one Person, is called a

113 Ibid.

114 Law must be present since the foundation of a legal order, though not determined in advance, would necessarily involve a claim to exercise 'a normative hold on futurity', to borrow the phrase from Peter Fitzpatrick, 'Is Humanity Enough? The Secular Theology of Human Rights', *Law, Social Justice and Global Development* 1, 2007, at: http://www2.warwick.ac.uk/fac/soc/law/elj/lgd/2007_1/fitzpatrick (last accessed 6 December 2011).

115 Hobbes, *Leviathan*, p. 227 (my emphasis).

Commonwealth.'[116] As such, the commonwealth, as a community of people, does not exist prior to the formation of the sovereign.

On another telling, the primal role of the sovereign in constituting the community becomes even more pronounced. In *Elements*, Hobbes seeks to refute the error that 'the people is a distinct body from him or them that have the sovereignty over them.'[117] For Hobbes, 'when the people claimeth anything otherwise than by the voice of the sovereign power, it is not the claim of the people, but only of those particular men, that claim in their own persons.'[118] Thus for Hobbes 'the people' has neither body nor voice prior to the sovereign bringing it into being. Vitoria, by contrast, finds that by divine law, authority in a commonwealth is 'vested in the community, which must be able to provide for itself.'[119] And it is only because it is 'im-[possible] for this power to be administered by the commonwealth itself, that is to say, the multitude' that power becomes vested in a sovereign.[120] It is because the 'commonwealth as such cannot frame laws, propose policies, judge disputes, punish transgressions, or generally impose laws on the individual [that] it must necessarily entrust all this business to a single man.'[121] Thus for Vitoria, the authority of, and thus by extension the existence of, the community or commonwealth pre-exists the sovereign who comes to rule it.

However, if we combine Hobbes's view that 'the people' is not a distinct body from the sovereign with Vitoria's view that the multitude is incapable of actually doing anything, we could, moving quickly with some additional help from Derrida, go further and find that 'the people' invoked by the instituting declaration 'We the people', to take the exemplary instance of the

116 Ibid.
117 Hobbes, *Elements*, p. 119, para 9.
118 Ibid.
119 Vitoria, *Political Writings*, p. 11.
120 Ibid., p. 14. Note that the 'im-[possible]' is in the text, chosen by the translators as the most likely word used here by Vitoria – which was lost on the original text.
121 Ibid.

Declaration of Independence, does 'not exist as an entity, it does not exist, *before* this declaration, not *as such*.'[122] The people is declared into being by a signature which authorises itself 'in a sort of fabulous retroactivity.'[123] That is, the declaration is never said first, in unison, by the people. It is always the words of a representative, claiming, in a sovereign fashion, the right to speak and act for the community. This is because despite the generative capacities they ascribe to the multitude, even for Vitoria and Hobbes it cannot act as a pure collectivity. And if the impossiblity of the multitude acting as a pure collectivity is also applied to its generative capacities, then we would find, with Lindahl, that the constitution of political community comes when a power arises which can '*seize the initiative* to determine what interests are shared by the collective and who belongs to it.'[124] Thus the commonwealth over which the sovereign rules does not pre-exist it and thus at best is mutually constituted with the sovereign. It thus cannot, of itself, provide solid ground for sovereign authority.

Indeed, the people's reliance on the sovereign in order to constitute it as a 'people' or a 'commonwealth' is that which, for Kant, requires it to eschew the search for solid grounds of authority. For Kant, a 'people should not *inquire* with any practical aim in view into the origin of the supreme authority to which it is subject.'[125] Kant writes that 'a people already subject to civil law,' must be 'regarded as already united under a general legislative will' and as such, 'may not judge otherwise than as the present head of state (*summus imperans*) wills it to.'[126] Since 'the act by which a people forms itself into a state,' the 'original contract', is '[p]roperly speaking ... only the idea of this act,' 'subtle reasonings' about whether

122 Derrida, 'Declarations', p. 10 (original emphasis).

123 Ibid.

124 Hans Lindahl, 'Constituent Power and Reflexive Identity: Towards an Ontology of Collective Selfhood', in Martin Loughlin and Neil Walker (eds), *The Paradox of Constitutionalism: Constituent Power and Constitutional Form*, Oxford: Oxford University Press, 2007, p. 22 (my emphasis).

125 Immanuel Kant, *The Metaphysics of Morals*, ed. and tr. Mary Gregor, Cambridge: Cambridge University Press, 1996, p. 95 (original emphasis).

126 Ibid.

the origins of legal authority within a state are legitimate 'are altogether pointless and, moreover, threaten a state with danger.'[127] Instead, as a principle of practical reason, the 'presently existing legislative authority ought to be obeyed, whatever its origin.'[128] This authority must be 'thought *as if* it must have arisen not from human beings but from some highest, flawless lawgiver,' namely God.[129]

More, perhaps, could be expected of territory. It might be regarded as axiomatic that claims to sovereign authority are rooted in a relationship between the sovereign and the physical territory it rules. Moreover, the very singularity of a territorial space is one of the key reasons why, for Bodin, sovereignty must be indivisible. But in grounding sovereign authority in a territorial space, Bodin leaves open the question of whether that particular sovereign has good title to the territorial state over which it purports to rule. For Vitoria, this question falls within Aristotle's category of subjects whose deliberation, were it to be undertaken, would 'have to go on *ad infinitum*.'[130] Vitoria adds: '[i]f the titles to rule had always to be proved by going back to the seeds of time, no tenure could ever be fully established.'[131] Sovereign title to territory must therefore be taken *as if* it is legitimate. And consequently, the sovereignty it grounds must be taken *as if* it is legitimate. As such, we find that the physical territory of the state, the seemingly solid foundation of sovereign power, is precisely that thing which necessitates the polity closing its eyes to questions concerning the legitimacy of sovereign power. And so, trying to ground sovereignty in the territory of the commonwealth leads us back towards Kant's 'flawless lawgiver';[132] towards a finding that sovereignty is not grounded in the earth, but in the sky.

127 Ibid., pp. 92–3, 95.

128 Ibid., p. 95.

129 Ibid. (my emphasis). On the question of the 'as if' see Derrida, *Without Alibi*, Chs 4 and 5.

130 Vitoria, *Political Writings*, p. 234. See Aristotle, *The Nicomachean Ethics*, New York: Oxford University Press, 1980, pp. 55–8.

131 Vitoria, *Political Writings*, p. 234.

132 Kant, *Metaphysics of Morals*, p. 95.

2 Nation and the Characteristics of Sovereignty

It could be argued that the irresolution embedded in the characteristics of Bodin's sovereign arises because Bodin's thought exists between the medieval and the modern. That is, its incipient modern character remains tainted and confused by certain medieval examples, principles and concerns. Taking this line, it would be argued that it is not until the institution of the great modern nation that the characteristics described by Bodin are realised in the form which resolves the tensions which linger in his work. Apparently freed from the divine and the personal, the modern nation is taken to have and to bring to sovereignty all of the characteristics Bodin ascribed to his sovereign. In short, nation is taken to be absolute, perpetual, indivisible, the source of all legal authority and the ultimate expression of the 'commonwealth'. If nation could realise the characteristics of Bodin's conception of sovereignty by resolving within itself their tensions, there would be a good argument that national sovereignty does provide the exclusive ground of sovereignty in modernity. This would also provide good grounds for arguing that the sovereignty of nation could be put beyond question. However, in this section I will show that nation fails to resolve the tensions in Bodin's conception of sovereignty and therefore cannot put the issue of sovereignty's position beyond question by casting itself as its exclusive occupant.

2.1 The absolute nation?

In modernity we neither have the comfort nor the restriction of resorting to divine sources of power to justify earthly rule. Something apparently more tangible and within the realm of human determination is seemingly required to ground legal authority. Modernity's answer is 'nation'. No stronger statement of nation's absoluteness could be made than Sieyès's view that the 'nation exists prior to everything; it is the origin of everything.... A nation is all that it can be simply by being what it is.'[133] And so, the 'principle of sovereignty', we learn from article 3 of the Declaration of the Rights of Man and Citizen 'resides *essentially* in the nation.'[134] Article 3 goes on to state that '[n]o body nor individual may exercise any authority which does not proceed directly from the nation.'[135] Could nation, then, achieve the absolute self-positing that evaded Bodin's sovereign?

We need look no further than Sieyès for some doubts about this. Despite his elevation of nation, something intangible, though not divine, lingers above it. Sieyès writes that '[p]rior to the nation and above the nation there is only natural law.... A nation is formed solely by *natural* law.'[136] Alas, even for something which is 'the origin of everything' there is a hint of its dependence on something else. And yet, it is not the dependence on natural law which exposes nation's inability to embody within itself and actualise the quality of absolute sovereignty. It is the fact that like Vitoria's multitude, a 'nation' cannot actually do anything and yet, if it is to be sovereign, must be able to do everything. When the divine entity relied on by Bodin vacates the field, it leaves behind quite a lot of work to the concept of nation. And nation cannot perform this work unless it possesses some of the qualities of the divine being it replaces.[137] In particular it must have some mode of earthly efficacy and yet at the same time be able to exceed whatever limitations accompany any single incumbent. That means it can only operate through a representative. This representative exercises sovereign power in the name of nation but is not the nation itself and cannot enduringly contain what it is.

In this way, nation becomes itself a transcendent concept; a secular divinity.[138] While it is possible, and often done, to speak

133 Emmanuel Sieyès, *Political Writings*, ed. and tr. Michael Sonenscher, Indianapolis: Hackett Publishing Company, 2003, pp. 136–7.

134 Declaration of the Rights of Man and Citizen, National Assembly of France, 1789, art 3 (my emphasis).

135 Ibid.; Fitzpatrick, 'Secular Theology', pp. 180–1.

136 Sieyès, *Political Writings*, pp. 136, 137 (original emphasis).

137 Fitzpatrick, *Modernism*, p. 121; Fitzpatrick, 'Secular Theology'.

138 See Fitzpatrick, 'Secular Theology'.

in general terms of the nation itself being sovereign, this authority is no more tangible than Bodin's 'God, the great sovereign'.[139] The representative of the sovereign nation has the same relation to the 'nation' that the monarch used to have in relation to God. Like God, nation gives the entity occupying the position of earthly sovereignty qualities that entity would otherwise lack.[140] Later in this chapter and again in Chapter 3, I will come to another way in which nation's lack of absoluteness is exposed, by way of analysis of the way in which it is defined, and thus dependent on, what is other and in relation to it. For now, it suffices to point out that even in terms of the modern nation-state, the purportedly absolute grounding force behind sovereignty and the exercise of sovereignty itself is not fused in one immanent entity. Rather, sovereignty remains grounded in a transcendent concept which necessarily exists apart from its earthly manifestation.

Three important points can be drawn from this observation, each of which will animate much of the analysis which follows. First, it is impossible for a sovereign to position itself as sovereign solely on the basis of its own immanent qualities. A sovereignty grounded solely within itself could not survive beyond the life of its immediate incumbent, if it lasted even that long. This is because it would have no mode of exceeding its own limitations. Accordingly, all sovereign claims rely on some transcendent concept. Secondly, in order to maintain supremacy over all earthly rivals, a sovereign has to claim the exclusive ability to represent that transcendent concept. Thus Bodin's sovereign would have been, as God's representative on earth, the entity with the sole capacity to speak for God when it came to questions of rule (if not religion).[141] And the sovereign in a nation-state claims the capacity to represent and speak for that nation. Neither God nor the nation can speak for themselves. As such, since its authority cannot be determined in advance by the transcendent concept on which it relies, it is still up to the sovereign to declare itself to be

139 Bodin, *On Sovereignty*, p. 50.
140 Fitzpatrick, *Modernism*, p. 121.
141 See Hobbes, *Leviathan*, p. 333.

the representative of that concept. As such, the sovereign's authority still retains the quality of self-position. The difference between this and a 'pure' or 'absolute' self-position is that no matter how great their power, no incumbent sovereign can completely contain or determine what else might be claimed in the name of that transcendent concept. The third point brings us somewhere close to the first. That is, if sovereignty is grounded in a transcendent concept for which the sovereign claims the exclusive capacity to speak, then no other entity can be called on to determine rival claims to sovereign authority. We have no mode, then, of authoritatively determining the merits of the claims of a rival sovereign who does not believe in the incumbent's claim, or worse still, in the incumbent's god. This problem seems to direct us again towards Kant's injunction that we should not inquire into the grounds of sovereignty, but rather should act as if we are subject to a divine flawless lawgiver.[142] It hardly provides a solid ground for modern sovereignty.

2.2 The perpetual nation?

The corporate nature of the modern nation-state would seem to suggest that Bodin's limited concept of perpetuity as meaning 'for the life of the sovereign' need not limit the sovereignty of the nation. The democratic state would, in Bodin's terms, be a body that never dies and whose sovereignty could actually be perpetual. Modern sovereignty must, it is true, have some mode of going beyond any single instantiation and democracy is the exemplary mode by which this is achieved. Democracy supplies both the practical means of moving from one representative of a nation's sovereignty to another and also a link to the symbolic placement of 'the people', or indeed 'nation' as sovereign.[143] Of course, there are

142 Kant, *Metaphysics of Morals*, p. 95 (see above notes 125–9 and accompanying text).

143 Kantorowicz's analysis of the question of sovereign perpetuity in medieval times would show that this quality rested not only on the corporate nature of the polity, but in the combination of real, mortal qualities in the body of the

many examples of modern sovereigns who have not relied on democratic, specifically electoral, means, although as Derrida points out, very few regimes '*do not present themselves* as democratic'.[144] If all of this can be achieved, and national sovereignty is perpetual, then perhaps this answers our question as to the grounds of the sovereignty of the form of the nation-state which has so comprehensively swept the world. Once established, it continues perpetually and cannot be challenged.

But examining the democratic nation-state as an example of such a sovereign polity reveals a close link between perpetuity and vulnerability. One cannot come without the other. Since there is no specified limit on a nation's existence, it may be regarded as perpetual. But it is equally true that nations come and go; they are vulnerable to outside forces and internal friction. This tension between perpetuity and vulnerability is, however, a productive one for rulers claiming to represent that nation's sovereignty, since it enables them to call on the sacrifice of citizens for the defence of the nation and its sovereignty. If the nation was truly and inevitably perpetual, it would not need defending. On the other hand, without some sense of perpetuity it would be very difficult to justify the extreme sacrifice nation can demand of its citizens in its defence. As such, the characteristic of perpetuity bestowed on Bodin's sovereign means that, in modernity, sovereign authority must have no end in sight. It must have a mode of going beyond any singular instantiation and believe itself to be perpetual. This mode and this belief does not make national sovereignty eternal. It is also vulnerable. Thus the sovereignty of the nation-state both is and is not perpetual. Again, we see a gap between what the sovereign must claim and what it can actually be.

King and a transcendent, immortal quality in the figure of the King: see Kantorowicz, *King's Two Bodies*. As discussed in the previous section, nation can be shown to be the inheritor of these qualities – combining the determinate and transcendent, but this would not distinguish it from all other forms of community. In any event, the analysis below would show that even the perpetuity of the corporate body of the national polity itself cannot be guaranteed.

144 Derrida, *Rogues*, p. 28 (original emphasis).

Democracy and the modern nation-state do not resolve the tension between the need for a sovereign to be perpetual and a recognition that sovereignties can end and new ones can begin.

2.3 The indivisible nation?

Indivisibility is one characteristic most often claimed for the nation-state. The United States of America, we learn from its official pledge of allegiance, is 'one Nation, under God, indivisible.'[145] A more recent example can be drawn from Australia. In October 2007, dealing with an issue which strikes at the heart of the modern nation's claim to completeness and to which I will return – that of the place of indigenous peoples – the then Prime Minister raised the prospect of a constitutional amendment to formally recognise Indigenous Australians and in particular 'their special (but not separate) place within a reconciled, indivisible nation.'[146] But do these claims show that nation somehow resolves the tension between the necessity and impossibility of sovereign indivisibility we observed in Bodin?

For something so commonplace, the idea of the indivisible nation seems to require tenacious, even anxious affirmation. This is because despite all the powers attributed to it, nation lacks a settled content of its own. As Fitzpatrick writes, '[n]ation seems fated to remain tied to the very criteria – of common language, territory, history and so on – which repeatedly fail to mark it definitively.'[147] One influential conclusion is that it must be imagined.[148] And yet, its existence as imagined would still fail to mark it as distinct, and not least fail to accommodate those tangible,

145 United States of America, *Pledge of Allegiance*, at: http://www.sos.wa.gov/flag/pledge.aspx (last accessed 6 December 2011).

146 John Howard, 'The Right Time', Address to the Sydney Institute, 11 October 2007, printed in *The Age*, 11 October 2007, at: http://www.theage.com.au/articles/2007/10/11/1191696077007.html (last accessed 6 December 2011).

147 Fitzpatrick, *Modernism*, p. 112.

148 See Benedict Anderson, *Imagined Communities*, London: Verso, 1991; see Fitzpatrick, *Modernism*, pp. 111–14.

if insufficient, characteristics it tends to have.[149] The absence of positive qualities has meant that nation has come to be defined by what it opposes.[150] Most conspicuously, the opposition is one where the civilised character of nation is cast against those designated as savages and barbarians.[151] This would prove to have at least two useful consequences. The first would be that the 'irredeemably' fixed and particular characteristics of the savage could be used to ground the nation's identity through negation, without nation needing to have any substance or content of its own.[152] The second would be that as colonisation expanded from the eighteenth century, European nationhood could retain its character as 'universal' simply by expanding the number of peoples thought to be 'savage' or 'backward'.[153] These oppositional forces, therefore, go to constitute nation. This is true not just in the case of a colonial other, but of that which within nation always seems to pose a threat to it. These 'projected characters', the 'particular and lawless, the chaotic, static and backward … remain in the site of their generation, within European identity, where they are recognised as having been suppressed but as still dangerous.'[154] Nation thus affirms itself in and is constituted by opposition to those fragmentary and fragmenting forces that would challenge its claims to surpassing singularity. It is not indivisible in and of itself but can only affirm itself as such in a continual and dynamic opposition to all that would oppose and divide it. Unable to ground itself except in opposition to what divides it, nation cannot ground unequivocally an indivisible sovereignty.

Moreover, and in a related vein, despite its claims, powers based on the concept of nation have never existed as the sole source of legal authority. It is true that national governments

149 Fitzpatrick, *Modernism*, p. 119.
150 Ibid., pp. 120–9.
151 Ibid., p. 122.
152 Ibid., p. 122.
153 Ibid., p. 157.
154 Ibid., p. 125.

claim surpassing, singular authority within their territories (and sometimes outside them). It is also true that something like this claim is necessary in order to operate a legal system in which decisions can be regarded as final. And yet, national governments have always had to have regard to other forces with which they relate – most significantly those falling under the term 'international'. I will return to this in Chapter 3. For now, it may be concluded that the modern nation does not overcome the tension in Bodin's theory of sovereignty between the necessity for a claim of singular, indivisible power, and the reality of the relations within which the sovereign is embedded.

In addition, the constitutional form of the modern nation-state also militates against a resolution of the problems in Bodin's theory of sovereign indivisibility. In the modern constitutional state, the marks of sovereignty, as Bodin would call them, are divided between the legislature, executive and judiciary. However, as we saw above, divisions of powers within single governing structures were already commonplace in Bodin's time. Bodin resolved this by describing these divisions as dictates of natural law – thus expanding the content of natural law binding the sovereign and in turn dividing sovereignty in a different way (by way of a relation to God and law). Franklin argues that 'Bodin would have done better ... to have defined the ruler's sovereignty as absolute (except with respect to the law of nature and fundamental law more narrowly defined), and have conceded that its functions were divided among the king, the Parlements, and the Estates.'[155] This would have left a theory of sovereignty much more easily adaptable to modern conditions, but it would still have left the question of ultimate legal authority unresolved.

Again, one seems drawn to Carl Schmitt's theory of the sovereign exception. We have already seen above that Schmitt's theory is not supported by Bodin's work to the extent that he argues it is. But it remains the theory which seems best placed to allow for sovereign indivisibility within a liberal constitutional order. If Schmitt's theory of sovereign exceptionality accurately describes

155 Franklin, 'Introduction', in Bodin, *On Sovereignty*, p. xxii.

the condition of modern sovereignty in nation-states, then nation could, it seems, embody this quality, despite the separation of powers in constitutional states. Moreover, if the sovereign within a nation-state has the kind of power Schmitt describes, then it would also appear that the sovereign of a nation-state could not only transcend the separation of powers in a constitutional order, but also transcend the relation to God and law which, as we saw above, exposed the failure of Bodin's sovereign to be truly indivisible. However, for the sovereign of a nation to be able to suspend the entire order and rule by exceptional decrees, that sovereign would also have to transcend 'nation'. And this is impossible since, as we saw above, nation itself is the transcendent concept which grounds the exercise of powers of modern sovereignty. The incumbent sovereign cannot transcend that which, in its transcendence, constitutes its sovereignty. Moreover, nation cannot be contained in any enduring sense by a single determining power, no matter how powerful it may seem. The same, we will see, applies to law.

2.4 Law and nation

We saw above that Bodin's sovereign was dependent on law (in particular, though not limited to, divine and natural law) even as the key mark of its sovereignty was the power to determine law. In modernity, as we saw above from article 3 of the Declaration of the Rights of Man and Citizen, the 'principle of all sovereignty resides essentially in the nation' and '[n]o body nor individual may exercise any authority which does not proceed directly from the nation.'[156] Thus nation appears to resolve Bodin's problem by, once and for all, elevating itself above law. At first glance, this appears to accord with Sieyès' view, also noted above, that nation is the 'origin of everything'.[157] That nation is the origin of law became the standard modernist assumption underlying the legitimacy of both national and international law; an assumption

156 See above note 134 and accompanying text.
157 See above note 133 and accompanying text.

conveniently maintained simply by refusing to entertain any question about the origin or legitimacy of the nation itself.

But for Sieyès, there is more to it. For him, nation does not merely precede the law, 'it is the law itself'.[158] Understood in this way, nation resolves the problem of how the sovereign relates to law (and in particular, the question of whether the sovereign depends on law or whether law depends on the sovereign) not by elevating itself above law, but by bringing law within itself and thus ceasing any such relation.[159] Rather than a relation, nation has, on this reading of Sieyès, an identity with law. Only understood in these terms could nation provide law with a capacity of pure, yet emplaced, self-generation. Law could not have this capacity if nation was ultimately set above it. And it is because of this perceived capacity that citizens of a nation can take themselves to be ruled by law, even if they are subject to an authority which is expressly national.

The immediate difficulty with this line of thought is that law and nation are clearly different things. Law has characteristics that nation does not have; and vice versa. Bearing in mind the difficulty we encountered earlier of trying to determine the characteristics of nation, we need go no further than to venture the suggestion that nations are particular institutional and territorial entities, even if the form of the 'national' is taken to be a universal condition and marker of modern society. If anything, it is even harder to determine what law 'is' than nation. Again, treading lightly, we could at least say that law is not a particular institutional and territorial entity. We might even venture to say that it has something to do with the conditions on which entities within a social space relate to each other; a description which could not apply to nation (at best nation could be understood as a mode by which these conditions take a particular form). But while they are different, they are intimately connected. Both modern law and nation make claims to universality and yet are

158 Sieyès, *Political Writings*, p. 136.

159 Fitzpatrick, *Modernism*, p. 130: 'the completeness of nation would then paradoxically contain "its own" relatedness to law.'

instanced particularly.[160] In doing so, each borrows from the other. Modern law requires nation to provide a place of particular grounding. Nation requires modern law as a particular mode of governing. Moreover, the universal orientation of each supplies the other with the capacity to exceed any fixed condition.[161] All this depends on a relation between law and nation. If they were the same then there would be no relation between them. And if there was no relation, nation and law could not draw on each other to overcome their limitations and thus could not play the roles modernity assigns to them. It is perhaps for this reason that despite his elevation of nation and his equation of it with law, Sieyès also asserts that natural law is prior to, above and constitutive of the nation.[162]

As Fitzpatrick shows, an analysis of the 'complementary relation between them shows law to be a creature of nation and nation to be a creature of law.'[163] In so far as law is a creature of nation, this would fit with the view of nation as elevated over law (if that were all there was to it). In this dimension, nation's particular territorial location provides law with a position – a place from which, and in which, it can act on the world.[164] It also provides a population for which, and over which, that law operates; a population conceived in national terms. And in this vein, nation also generates a history through which that population and all manner of its characteristics: language, place, culture, and (not least) law, can be conceived in national terms. The concept of the English common law deriving from 'time immemorial' provides one telling example of the power of historical memory (even if it is one attuned to forgetting) to ground law.[165] Any characteristic which pre-dates the national can be rendered in terms of moving towards it, and thus be ultimately of the nation even if the nation

160 Ibid., pp. 129–30.
161 Ibid.
162 Sieyès, *Political Writings*, pp. 136, 137 (original emphasis).
163 Fitzpatrick, *Modernism*, p. 136.
164 Ibid., p. 130.
165 Ibid., pp. 92–3, 133.

itself comes later.[166] Moreover, rather than weakening its perceived hold on law, nation's failure to be marked definitively by its characteristics and its constituent dependence on what is other to it actually helps to strengthen that hold. Of all the things nation is defined in opposition to, the most conspicuous is 'savagery'; a condition in which (we are told) there is either no law or some form of arbitrary rule or simplistic custom.[167] In defining itself in opposition to savagery, nation asserts 'homogeneity of population, boundedness of territory, and centrality of rule', conditions in which law can flourish and by which it 'takes on a concentrated and pervasive "strength"' by contrast to the lawless (or only faintly legal) condition of the savage.[168] Nation's lack of definitive characteristics assists law in another way. It means that its content (and that of any of its particular instantiations) can never be stilled or finally determined. This means that not only does nation provide a 'place' or position for law, it provides a place whose characteristics are capable of infinite change. This quality is necessary for nation to continue to ground a law which must, as we will see, be capable of ever-adapting to the infinitely changing circumstances of the life it seeks to rule.

In so far as nation is a creation of law, it cannot be elevated over law. Here we find that nation (and its sovereignty) is dependent on law, perhaps even more so than Bodin's sovereign. As Fitzpatrick argues, 'law was not simply the formal and consequential marker of national sovereignty but was, rather, prerequisite and instrumental in the formation of modern nation.'[169] Nation's dependence on law takes a variety of forms; three will suffice for now. First, law provides a means of national identification. In these terms, a nation's existence is bound up with, and consequent upon, its having 'its own' law; a capacity supposedly denied all other bodies politic in modernity. Identification operates on another level too, as law provides the mode by which the

166 Ibid., p. 130.
167 See Ibid., p. 131.
168 Ibid.
169 Ibid., p. 132.

'citizens' of a nation identify as such and with each other – a mode therefore by which a population becomes 'national'.[170] As Fitzpatrick argues, to 'the extent that citizens have an operative common existence within the order of the nation, it is law which constitutes that existence.'[171] In effecting this mode of identification, the law of citizenship also operates to exclude that which is outside the nation, such that 'nation is bounded ... by law and by its designating who can and cannot enter it legally.'[172] Nation's second mode of dependence on law comes from law's providing a way in which rule can be effected in a uniform manner throughout the whole of a (national) territorial space. This uniform law, in 'transcend[ing] the diverse and particular within that territory'[173] may indeed be one of the very few things within that territorial space that can actually be said to be common to the nation itself. Third, the mode by which this uniformity is achieved is one which remains attuned to nation's illimitable possibilities. That is, law does not occupy the national territory like a fixed or thick mass which would constrict nation's capacity for change. Rather, law applies uniformly by 'hovering ubiquitously over and incipiently occupying all finitudes.'[174] Law thus provides nation with a means of maintaining a consistent basis of rule which is at once emplaced and capable of infinite change. This is, of course, very useful for nation, but it betrays a dependence on law which shows that nation is not capable of transcending law so as to ground its own authority over law.

2.5 Commonwealth and nation

The question here is whether nation is such a peculiar embodiment of the concept of a 'commonwealth' that it surpasses these

170 Ibid., p. 135. See Sieyès, *Political Writings*, p. 97: a nation is 'a body of associates living under a common law.'

171 Fitzpatrick, *Modernism*, p. 135.

172 Ibid., p. 136.

173 Ibid., p. 133.

174 Ibid.

limitations and for this reason can provide the exclusive ground of sovereignty in modernity. On the commonwealth's first dimension, community, it follows from the analysis above that the national community is incapable of a pure origin from which it could ground its own existence and that of an operative sovereign authority. As Derrida's analysis of the Declaration of Independence shows, the founding of a national community is precisely an instance in which the community comes to be constituted by a self-authorised claim to represent it.[175] In another context, Derrida writes that it

> is probable … [that] a coup de force always marks the founding of a nation, state or nation-state. In the event of founding or institution, the properly *performative* act must produce (proclaim) what in the form of a *constative* act it merely claims, declares, assures it is describing.[176]

A nation is formed, therefore, by 'a violent act [which] at once produce[s] and presuppose[s] the unity of [that] nation.'[177] Thus nation shares with all forms of political community the impossibility of its being present to itself or capable of some operative capacity unmediated by a self-authorised representative claim. Here, the national community, like Bodin's commonwealth, is dependent on some form of sovereign claim and thus cannot stand apart from sovereignty in order to ground it.

But if it is not capable of a pure origin, could nation nonetheless be capable of transcending the limitations of any constituted form – of breaking free of its dependence on some limited 'founding' moment? For Sieyès, the answer would be yes. He writes, the 'Nation is always the master of every reform to its constitution' and the right to decide anything in relation to a constitution

> belongs to the Nation alone, independently, as we keep repeating, of all forms and all conditions…. A nation cannot

175 See above notes 122–3 and accompanying text.
176 Derrida, 'Laws of Reflection', p. 8 (original emphasis).
177 Ibid., p. 19; See also Derrida, 'Declarations', pp. 8–10.

> decide not to be the nation it is or choose to be itself in only one particular way, simply because this would amount to saying that it could not be a nation in any other way.[178]

On this basis, any condition on political form – any sovereign decision which attempts to set limits on the character and interests of the nation – would always remain subject to the nation's overarching authority to decide otherwise. This ability to exceed all fixed forms[179] and conditions is crucial if nation is to be able to sustain the operation of sovereignty and law in a constantly changing world. It is the reason why nation must occupy a transcendent position in relation to sovereignty, as we have seen. But it also raises the problem, again already encountered, as to how the 'nation' might actually go about making a decision about its constitution. For Sieyès, the answer comes through an identity of nation with the 'the totality of its members', but he does not argue that the nation can be made present to itself and act as a pure collectivity. Rather, he argues that a means of representation can be established which gives effect to the will of this totality.[180] Sieyès writes: 'To do what it has to do, a representative body always has to stand in for the Nation itself.'[181] Thus representatives are needed, but who can choose them in advance of the nation's formation?

For Sieyès, the answer comes by the seemingly simple measure that the national community is simply that which inhabits the territory in question. He writes that the nation comprises 'the forty thousand parishes covering the whole territory, in all the inhabitants and all the contributions to the public establishment.'[182]

178 Sieyès, *Political Writings*, p. 141 (my emphasis).

179 Other than, one might suppose, the form of 'nation' (whatever that is).

180 Sieyès, *Political Writings*, pp. 141, 142–4. Note: Sieyès's concern was to distinguish a system of representation of all inhabitants from one which gave disproportionate representation to the privileged orders. His plan was that there would be a meeting of extraordinary representatives (who would then not have a personal interest in the form of government which was to follow) to determine the constitution (pp. 140–4).

181 Ibid., p. 142.

182 Ibid., p. 140.

This turn towards territory appears to make things simpler. Unlike community, territory is not confronted with the problem of the impossibility of being present to itself and acting as a pure collectivity. It is tangible. It can be fought over, measured and mapped. It is this tangible quality which, as we saw above, enables nation to provide a 'place' for law in modernity.[183] It might be thought that it would, in a similar vein, provide a place for sovereignty. But we must bear in mind that territory is not simply a physical space, but denotes a relationship between a community and a place. A place is not territory until it is defined by way of the capacity of a person or group to exclude others from it.[184] As such, there must be some mode by which a group comes to identify itself as a community with a certain relationship to a particular space which it calls its territory. This means that we are still left with the problem of how this group comes to identify itself as a community in the first place and in addition need to contend with the basis on which it claims its right to the territory itself. In doing this, nation provides us with no better answer than the one arrived at by Vitoria and Kant: sovereign (and national) title to territory must be taken 'as if' it is legitimate. To this Sieyès can only add tautology. To the question 'where is the Nation?', Sieyès answers: 'Where it is.'[185] Accordingly, nation is simply another form of political community which depends on a sovereign decision to 'seize the initiative' to determine its interests and its character – even if that sovereign's authority is constituted in its relation to the community it brings into being.

183 Fitzpatrick, *Modernism*, pp. 129–31.

184 The 'unsettled' etymology of territory uncovered by the editors of the Oxford English Dictionary finds that it is usually taken as a derivative of *terra* ('earth, land') but that its original form suggests a derivation from *terrēré* ('to frighten') and *territorium* ('a place from which people are warned off'): *Oxford English Dictionary*, 2nd ed., Oxford: Oxford University Press, 1989.

185 Sieyès, *Political Writings*, p. 140. In using the capital 'N', Sieyès is referring to France in particular rather than nations in general, but the tautological aspect of the exercise (and its applicability elsewhere) remains.

Conclusion

The analysis so far shows that sovereignty holds an elusive position. It cannot be grounded solely in a conception of a 'commonwealth' and consequently not in the variant of the 'commonwealth' which we call 'nation' – since the commonwealth and 'nation' are shown to be dependent on sovereignty. Further, its characteristics betray points of irresolution. These points of irresolution reveal a gap between what sovereigns claim (and what is claimed for them) and what they can actually be. A sovereign claims to be absolute, but is in fact dependent on a transcendent authority for which it claims sole authority to speak but which it cannot fully contain. It claims to be perpetual, but is in fact vulnerable. It claims to be indivisible, but depends on that which would divide it. It claims authority over law and yet cannot escape its own dependence on law. 'Nation' fails to resolve these points of irresolution, even if it is able to make excellent use of them.

Modernity thus leaves us in a situation where sovereignty cannot be conclusively grounded in a divine being, on a natural law, in a commonwealth or in a nation. What, then, is sovereignty based on? As I suggested in the Introduction, if we take Bodin's definition of the sovereign as a person recognising 'nothing, after God, that is greater than himself,'[186] and seek to apply it in a modern world devoid of divine authority, we find that the sovereign is simply an entity which recognises no authority greater than itself with respect to that over which it claims authority. If the sovereign recognises no authority greater than itself, then it must rely on itself to justify its own authority. It is self-authorising and self-justifying – in Derrida's terms, autopositioned.[187]

We have already seen intimations of the nature of this autopositioning in the analysis above. In the section on 'absoluteness' we saw how in making a claim to sovereignty, the sovereign claims exclusive authority to speak in the name of a transcendent authority – a claim which must be self-authorised because that

186 Bodin, *On Sovereignty*, p. 4.
187 Derrida, *Rogues*, p. 142.

transcendent authority cannot speak for itself. We also saw how both the commonwealth and the nation depended for their very formation on a claim to say what they were which could not be guaranteed or determined in advance of that claim. If national sovereignty relies essentially on self-authorisation – if, indeed, there is nothing essential about it – one would have to question its privileged place in modern law. Such questioning appears especially urgent in situations where assertions of national sovereignty appear to be impotent or anachronistic (as some would see it in the face of economic 'globalisation'), or where national sovereignty seems to be an impenetrable barrier to the claims of indigenous communities in post-colonial settings. It leads to considering the possibility that the position of modern sovereignty is not exclusive to the nation-state and that modern law might find its origin in a plurality of positions. But the characteristic of self-authorisation or 'autopositioning' does not turn sovereignty to a meaningless claim. In the next chapter, I will examine in more detail the nature of sovereign 'autopositioning' by reference to its role in sustaining (and being sustained by) community and law. Then, using the example of claims over intellectual property law and traditional knowledge in India, I will show how the claims to legal authority made by the World Trade Organisation and by local communities can be understood as autopositioned sovereign claims.

Chapter 2

Autopositioning

The Groundless Ground of Modern Sovereignty

'[E]verything here gets played out at the limit between the calculable and the incalculable'.[1]

Introduction

If sovereign authority lacks solid grounding and in fact results from an autopositioned claim to authority, then the position of sovereign appears to be open to any entity capable of making and sustaining a self-grounded claim to legal authority. It cannot be tied to a particular person or a particular form (including the 'national' form). But while the legitimacy of a sovereign claim cannot be guaranteed in advance and while a sovereign must rely on itself to justify its own authority, this does not mean that the position of sovereignty is simply open to anyone who cares to declare themselves sovereign over some field of authority. If that were all there was to it, there would be nothing to stop anyone declaring themselves sovereign over whatever self-designated field of authority (a vegetable patch, perhaps) they thought

1 Jacques Derrida, *Rogues: Two Essays on Reason*, trs Pascale-Anne Brault and Michael Naas, Stanford: Stanford University Press, 2005, p. 122.

they had the strength to defend. Something more is required. As Rousseau writes:

> '[a]ny man can write on tablets of stone, or pay for an oracle, or pretend to be in secret communication with some divinity, or train a bird to speak in his ear, or find some other crude methods of deceiving the people. A man who knows no more than this may even, perhaps, be able to gather together a band of demented followers, but he will never found an empire, and his wild work will perish with him.'[2]

That something more is a relation to community and law. A sovereign is not a sovereign simply for itself. Rather, it is sovereign for the community for which it claims authority to speak. It is therefore dependent on a relation to community. Moreover, as we saw in Chapter 1, sovereignty does not involve a simple application of power, but rather is dependent on law for its mode of rule. The relation between sovereignty, law and community shows that the position of sovereignty is not to be found in a model which avoids or seeks to resolve the irresolutions in Bodin's conception of sovereignty. Rather, it is to be found in one which embraces them. What is required is a conception of sovereignty in which its quality of autopositioning is combined with its dependence on law and community and their dependence on it. In this chapter, I will show that it is precisely the lack of solid ground to each of these concepts which provides their 'position' and not only explains their characteristics but enables them to function in the way that they do.

1 Autopositioning

In one of his most sustained engagements with the concepts of sovereignty and democracy, Derrida returns repeatedly to the

2 Jean-Jacques Rousseau, *The Social Contract*, tr. Christopher Betts, Oxford: Oxford University Press, 1994, p. 79.

relation between selfhood and autonomy.[3] That is, the relation between a self's self-designation (what it is) and the authority it claims over itself (what it can authorise itself to do). This relation can be reduced to what is at stake whenever someone says, for themselves, the two words 'I can…'.[4] Referring to the concept of 'sovereign self-determination, of the autonomy of the self,'[5] Derrida reduces this relation to the concept of *ipseity*, by which he means, 'the power that *gives itself* its own law, its self-representation, the sovereign and reappropriating gathering of the self in the simultaneity of an assemblage or assembly, being together, or "living together", as we say.'[6] For Derrida, there is a 'power, potency, sovereignty, or possibility implied in every "I can," … [which refers] always to possession, property, and power, to the authority of the lord or seignior, of the sovereign'.[7] Here, one of Derrida's concerns is democracy, and the possibility of a singular entity which is capable of counting itself (and being counted) as a vote in a democracy – a singular entity that might be imagined (even if it could never be in practice) the foundation of a self-authorising polity. But he is also careful to point out that the concept of ipseity it is not restricted to (or indeed founded on) the concept of a 'person'. It is also applicable to the constitution of a collective political subject.

As we saw in Chapter 1, for Derrida, a collective political subject is always called into being by a self-authorised decision by an entity which both produces and presupposes the existence of the subject for which it claims authority to speak. Thus the principle of ipseity is not simply related to questions of personal freedom

3 Derrida, *Rogues*. The seminar series in which Derrida developed and refined many of the arguments subsequently pursued in *Rogues* has been published posthumously. It appears in the English translation as Jacques Derrida, *The Beast and the Sovereign (Volume I)*, tr. Geoffrey Bennington, Chicago: University of Chicago Press, 2009.

4 Derrida, *Rogues*, p. 11. See also Jacques Derrida, *Without Alibi*, tr. Peggy Kamuf, Stanford: Stanford University Press, 2002, p. 275.

5 Derrida, *Rogues*, p. 10.

6 Ibid., p. 11 (original emphasis); Derrida, *The Beast and the Sovereign I*, pp. 66–7.

7 Ibid., p. 11.

and autonomy, but also to political autonomy and authority. Derrida writes:

> Before any sovereignty of the state, of the nation-state, of the monarch, or, in democracy, of the people, ipseity names a principle of legitimate sovereignty, the accredited or recognized supremacy of a power or a force.... That is what is implied, posed, presupposed, but also imposed in the very position, in the very self- or autopositioning, of *ipseity itself*.[8]

Thus, for Derrida, the concept of ipseity grounds all claims to sovereignty. That is, legitimate sovereignty is grounded by self-authorisation, by autopositioning. This applies as much to the nation-state as to any other possible form of sovereignty. Its legitimacy flows from strength, from being 'the strongest,' from having the ability to decide, from having one's reason 'win out.'[9] And yet, there seems to be something more required. This legitimacy seems connected to a sovereign claim being accredited or recognised as such. Most significantly, there is a connection to law. A *right* is granted to the strongest (from where could it come, other than from law?); and strength gives force to law. Moreover, since ipseity does not involve a 'once-off' decision, but rather a continual 'reappropriation', a claim to speak for a community must have constant regard to the changing dynamics of that community – the dynamics of being together (both within and outside the community – as provisional as the determination of what is inside and outside must necessarily be). As such, Derrida's concept of autopositioning does not empty sovereignty of its connection to principles of legitimacy and responsibility, of its relation to community, or of its connection to law.

8 Derrida, *Rogues*, p. 12 (original emphasis).
9 Ibid., pp. 12–13.

2 The Constitutive Criteria of Autopositioned Sovereignty: Community and Law

2.1 Community

In the discussion of the 'commonwealth' in Chapter 1, we saw that sovereignty and community are mutually constitutive. In this section, I will relate that mutual constitution to the question of autopositioning. It will be seen that community grounds sovereignty by what it brings to sovereignty and by what it lacks – a lack that creates an imperative for autopositioned sovereignty.

2.1.1 Grounding sovereignty in what community brings

In Chapter 1 we saw that community was taken to constitute or ground the sovereign because there can be no sovereign without subjects; without some body of people over which to rule. Further, in the discussion of 'nation' as a particular embodiment of the 'commonwealth', we saw how important it was for the sovereign to be able to speak in the name of the community. The 'national' community thus became a transcendent concept for which the sovereign claimed exclusive authority to speak. Thus nation (or, more generally, community) can be seen to have replaced God in its grounding of sovereign authority. It gives the dual qualities of palpability and transcendence to the sovereign – enabling it to be emplaced but also capable of going beyond its own limitations. These are qualities that no wholly autopositioned claim can give itself. At the same time, only an autopositioned claim to speak for that community will do. If community is transcendent, then no immanent entity exists which can determine, in advance, the sovereign's right to speak for the community.

2.1.2 Grounding sovereignty in what community lacks

This necessity of an autopositioned claim can also be seen in the way in which community grounds sovereignty by what it lacks. Here, the work of Jean-Luc Nancy on the concept of community provides assistance.[10] Using Nancy in this way must be done with some care, as Derrida expressed reservations about Nancy's use of the term 'community', especially in so far as Derrida felt it was connected to Nancy's use of 'fraternity' in *The Experience of Freedom*.[11] For Derrida, the use of fraternity, for all its attractions, could not avoid certain problematic links between 'masculine authority', nature and birth which may lead (but certainly not straightforwardly) back to the received privileging of national sovereignty.[12] But looking at Derrida's sovereign autopositioning through the lens of Nancy's work on community illuminates much about it, particularly if one focuses on the restlessness of community which Nancy exposes in his earlier work, *The Inoperative Community*.[13] As we saw above, Derrida describes the autopositioning of sovereignty as occurring in the 'simultaneity of an assemblage or assembly, being together or "living together"'.[14] These concepts fit well with those which underlie Nancy's conception of community.

Analysis of the attempt by Bodin to locate sovereignty in the commonwealth showed community to be dependent on sovereignty to determine what it is for the time being. In Nancy's terms, this would be because community cannot be complete and present to itself. Community, for Nancy, is not a thing in itself, nor the distillation or representation of a common essence, nor the collective work of individual subjects.[15] Rather, community exists simply because of the fact that we are inescapably with each other in the world.[16] As the epigraph to Chapter 1 suggests, for Nancy, there is no highest authority or prior law which determines in advance the nature and character of any community.

10 Jean-Luc Nancy, *The Inoperative Community*, ed. and tr. Peter Connor, Minneapolis: University of Minnesota Press, 1991.

11 Derrida, *Rogues*, pp. 56–61. See Jean-Luc Nancy, *The Experience of Freedom*, tr. Bridget McDonald, Stanford: Stanford University Press, 1993.

12 Derrida, *Rogues*, pp. 56–61. See also, Jacques Derrida, *Politics of Friendship*, tr. George Collins, London: Verso, 2005, pp. 81–107.

13 Nancy, *Inoperative Community*, pp. 1–42.

14 Derrida, *Rogues*, p. 11.

15 Nancy, *Inoperative Community*, pp. 3–35.

16 Ibid., p. 28.

Nor can such a nature or character be enduringly set. Community is that which is constituted by our relations with each other as singular beings.[17] And if 'we' are always changing, then the communities that exist because of the fact of our relations with each other must also constantly be changing. Indeed, as opposed to being a 'work', for Nancy, community is an 'unworking' – inoperative and uncontainable.[18] It is something which works towards the unravelling of fixed positions and identities. As such, community 'assumes the impossibility of its own immanence.'[19] It thus lacks whatever it would need in order to assume determinate form.

At the same time, there are such things as communities. And such things cannot exist as complete vacuities of content.[20] A purely open community would dissipate into nothingness. And so, in order to take a determinate form, a community must have a mode of deciding, for the time being, what its content and characteristics are. We saw above, through Hobbes and Vitoria, that this is something a political community can only achieve via its representative, the sovereign. For this reason, community cannot provide a solid ground apart from sovereignty on which a sovereign claim could rest. But that very inability to act, to be present to itself and have a content of its own, creates an imperative for an autopositioned sovereign claim. It requires a claim based on no higher authority, again in Lindahl's terms, to '*seize the initiative* to determine what interests are shared by the collective and who belongs to it.'[21] What then sets a successful sovereign claim to

17 Much more on singularity, and on community, will follow in Chapter 3.

18 As the translator explains, the French word used in Nancy's original text, *désoeuvrement*, has no adequate translation in English. 'Unworking' is used by the translators in the text itself, but 'inoperative' is used in the title because it too captures something of the original and further, 'a title ought not to inflict upon the reader an 'unrecognisable' word: Nancy, *Inoperative Community*, p. 156 (translator's note).

19 Ibid., p. 15.

20 As Fitzpatrick shows in the case of law: Peter Fitzpatrick, *Modernism and the Grounds of Law*, Cambridge: Cambridge University Press, 2001, pp. 104–6.

21 Hans Lindahl, 'Constituent Power and Reflexive Identity: Towards an Ontology of Collective Selfhood', in Martin Loughlin and Neil Walker (eds),

speak for community from the mere fancy of Rousseau's charlatan is not the authority it brings to this determination, but how effectively its claim can be supported in retrospect – how effective it is in erasing its arbitrary origins by a process of 'fabulous retroactivity.'[22] At least part of this goes to how effectively the sovereign is able to reflect (as well as shape) the aspirations of the community for which it claims to speak – to be responsive and responsible.[23]

It should be noted, however, that the sovereign claim does not completely overcome the restless nature of community. Even in the case of the most successful sovereign claims to speak for community, the groundless origin of the initial claim is never completely erased. Community cannot be enduringly subordinated to a single site of power. In Nancy's terms, it is 'resistance itself: resistance to immanence.'[24] Since community resists predominant power – any instantiation of sovereignty must be open to challenge. This openness to challenge presents an opportunity for rivals to claim the authority to speak for the same community for which an incumbent sovereign claims to speak. But further, since community does not take a determinate form until it is brought into being by sovereign assertion, no particular form of community (such as the 'nation') could be the only one which could possibly ground sovereignty. This openness to challenge presents an opportunity for sovereign positions to emerge which claim to speak for communities other than the ones presently dominant.

Such possibility of challenge is not all bad news for incumbent sovereigns. It does necessitate the reassertion of sovereignty even in what appear to be stable sovereign positions (reassertions which, depending on how well that particular sovereign can

The Paradox of Constitutionalism: Constituent Power and Constitutional Form, Oxford: Oxford University Press, 2007, p. 22 (my emphasis).

22 Jacques Derrida, 'Declarations of Independence', *New Political Science* 7, 1986, 7–15, 10.

23 Or, to use an antique spelling evoking the *ability* to be responsive and responsible: 'responsable': *Oxford English Dictionary*, 2nd ed., Oxford: Oxford University Press, 1989.

24 Nancy, *Inoperative Community*, p. 35.

continue to reflect and shape the aspirations of its community, may or may not be successful). But it does not mean, necessarily, that the entity or person holding a sovereign position changes with the wind. Rather, it means that sovereigns must constantly be responsive to the unconditional quality of community and able to adapt to it. In grounding their authority in some form of 'community', sovereigns thus arrogate something of its unconditional quality and are thus able to go beyond their own limitations and adapt to the changing circumstances of life.[25] The uncontainability of community thus presents both a challenge to incumbent sovereign position but also the necessary means for its adaptation and persistence.

It is by this process that we can observe in a theory of autopositioned sovereignty the dynamic of an operative crisis – a sovereignty in which the capacity to call it into question is embedded in what it is. But this promise of questioning, openness and resistance is not (just) opposed to the ultimate claims to authority made by autopositioned sovereigns. It also welcomes, indeed demands, such claims. Since a community cannot be present to itself, then if it is to function in an operative sense, it continually needs a sovereign power to render its unconditional quality into some determinate form for the time being. By this process, community thus requires, even as it undermines, an autopositioned claim to absolute sovereign determining power.

2.2 *Law*

In Chapter 1, we saw elements of sovereignty's dependence on law in the sections on indivisibility and on the inability of Bodin's sovereign and the nation to rule without law. In this section, I will examine this dynamic in more detail. Like community, law grounds sovereignty by what it brings and by what it lacks.

25 Something it would need to do in order to persist for any length of time: see Fitzpatrick, *Modernism* p. 71.

2.2.1 Grounding sovereignty in what law brings

A sovereign claim is not concerned only with effective power. Rather, it involves a claim to a right to exercise that power. As Pascal states, 'right without might is helpless, might without right is tyrannical.'[26] Pascal's answer to this is that might must be made into right (since the reverse is impossible).[27] This seems to resonate with Derrida's conception of the sovereign as able to position itself as the 'supreme source of every "reason of the strongest" as the right [*droit*] granted to force or to the force granted to law [*droit*].'[28] But Derrida's conception subtly shows the mutual relation between force and right. As the translator's rendition of *droit* into both 'right' and 'law' in this sentence shows, what follows from the sovereign's claim to govern by right is a connection between sovereignty and law. And so, the sovereign brings force to law. But equally, law brings something to force. Law provides the only amenable form of effecting continuate rule in the name of right.[29] As we saw in Chapter 1, even Bodin's purportedly absolute sovereign could not govern 'without any law' since such rule would be without 'any continuance, or assurance, for that it hath not in it any bond wherewith to bind the greater unto the lesser, nor by consequence any accord at all.'[30] With law, therefore, the sovereign can make use of that bond to legitimise its rule and to adapt to the changing circumstances it encounters. Thus the claim to right elevates the sovereign's authority above the mere exercise of power and gives it a depth and endurance which is vital to its functioning.

26 Blaise Pascal, *Pensees*, tr. A. J. Krailsheimer, London: Penguin, 1995, p. 26.

27 Ibid., pp. 26–7.

28 Derrida, *Rogues*, p. 12. On *droit* and *loi* see Jean Bodin, *On Sovereignty: Four Chapters from the Six Books of the Commonwealth*, ed. and tr. Julian Franklin, Cambridge: Cambridge University Press, 1992, p. 38.

29 Peter Fitzpatrick, 'What are the Gods to Us Now?: Secular Theology and the Modernity of Law', *Theoretical Inquiries in Law* 8, 2007, 161, 186.

30 Jean Bodin, *Six Books of the Commonwealth*, tr. R. Knolles, London: Bishop, 1606, pp. 760–1 (Book 6, Ch 6). To this Grotius might add: 'The moment we recede from Right we depend on nothing:' Hugo Grotius, *The Rights of War and Peace*, ed. Richard Tuck, Indianapolis: Liberty Fund, 2004, vol 1, p. 97.

But at the same time, law's gift to sovereignty is treacherous. Bringing 'right' within 'might' undermines the self-sufficiency of might. For Derrida, the moment a sovereign seeks to justify itself, to claim a *right* to govern, the absolute nature of its claim to self-sufficiency and power is violated.[31] Law thus undermines the absolute claim to authority made by the sovereign. The full extent of this treachery will be explored shortly below where I will consider the relation between law and justice in the context of Schmitt's thought on the sovereignty and the exception. But for now I want to cast an image of law's simultaneous elevation and subjection of the sovereign, through the encounter with the law of Blanchot's narrator in the *Madness of the Day*.[32] If we substitute his narrator for the sovereign, the terms of this encounter evoke the dynamic I am endeavouring to explain. Blanchot's narrator encounters the 'silhouette of the law.'[33] Here Blanchot suggests that the law has a palpable form and presence yet is somehow hidden and obscure. To render it absolutely visible or determinate would destroy it. Hence the narrator tempts the law to reveal her face and then immediately castigates himself: 'It was a foolhardy appeal. What would I have done if she had answered?'[34] But it is still possible to encounter law's silhouette. There, Blanchot's narrator (our sovereign) finds a law which: 'absurdly credited me with her powers; she declared herself perpetually on her knees before me.'[35] This law presents itself as utterly reliant on the sovereign to determine its content and enforce it. And yet, the same law refuses to allow anything specific to be demanded of it; and then sets our sovereign to a particular (and in light of the discussion that will follow, a familiar) task: 'I knew that one of her aims was to make me "see justice done."'[36] Again, she is unable

31 Derrida, *Rogues*, p. 101.
32 Maurice Blanchot, 'The Madness of the Day' in Maurice Blanchot, *The Station Hill Blanchot Reader: Fiction and Literary Essays*, Barrytown: Station Hill Press, 1998, pp. 191–9. See Fitzpatrick, *Modernism*, pp. 83–4.
33 Blanchot, 'Madness of the Day', p. 193.
34 Ibid.
35 Ibid., p. 197.
36 Ibid.

to effect this herself, and requires the sovereign to do so. And so, 'she exalted me, but only to raise herself up in her turn.'[37]

Law thus provides sovereignty with an important characteristic: a claim to govern through right. As we have seen, sovereignty cannot operate without it. But at the same time, this does not provide sovereignty with something approximating a 'ground'. Indeed, it seems as much to undermine sovereignty as to elevate it. Reversing the orientation, I will now look at what sovereignty brings to law. Using this approach, I will find that law grounds sovereignty not by what it brings, but by what it lacks.

2.2.2 Grounding sovereignty in what law lacks

One of the reasons law fails to provide a solid ground for sovereignty is that it cannot function, by itself, as a ground for anything. As Fitzpatrick shows, law must be able to accommodate the infinity of our being-with each other – of the ceaseless changing circumstances and complexities of life.[38] Thus law can have no enduring content of its own; it is a vacuity.[39] But this vacuous quality does not undermine sovereignty. Rather, it creates an imperative for it. While law can have no enduring content of its own, it cannot exist without some determinate content for the time being. And so it relies on some power beyond it to endow it with that content. Similarly, law relies on some power apart to enforce it. As Nancy writes, 'law itself does not have a form for what would need to be its own sovereignty.'[40] And since, as Derrida argues, there can be no law without force, without the possibility of it being enforced,[41] law is dependent on some kind

37 Ibid., p. 198.

38 Fitzpatrick, 'Secular Theology', pp. 183–7; see Jacques Derrida, 'The Laws of Reflection: Nelson Mandela, In Admiration', trs M. Caws and I. Loenz in Jacques Derrida and Mustapha Tlili (eds), *For Nelson Mandela*, New York: Seaver Books, 1987, p. 22.

39 Fitzpatrick, 'Secular Theology', p. 185.

40 Jean-Luc Nancy, *Being Singular Plural*, trs Robert Richardson and Anne O'Byrne, Stanford: Stanford University Press, 2000, p. 131.

41 Jacques Derrida, 'Force of Law: The Mystical Foundation of Authority', tr. Mary Quaintance, in Jacques Derrida, *Acts of Religion*, ed. Gil Anidjar,

of determining power to render binding decisions. Without such a power, law's intrinsic openness would result in an endless negotiation in each and every situation. For Derrida, sovereignty is 'the power to decide, to be decisive, to prevail, to have reason over or to win out over ... and to give the force of law.'[42] He writes, '[i]n its very institution, and in the *instant* proper to it, the act of sovereignty must and can, by force, put an end in a single, indivisible stroke to the endless discussion.'[43] Indeed, it 'is by winning out over time, by putting an end to the infinite order of time, so to speak, that [Cronos] asserts his sovereignty.'[44] Thus rather than providing a stable ground for sovereignty, law itself is open to the sway of predominant power; to a power capable of making a decision which cuts through law's endless changefulness.

Thus the openness of law, its vacuity, invites, even demands, an autopositioned sovereign claim to authority. Since law cannot give itself its own content or enforce itself, the sovereign claim cannot be positioned wholly within law. And if that claim is to be ultimate and not derivative, it must be autopositioned. Moreover, the claim must be one to absolute determining power – to determine, in any instant, what the law is and to render enforceable, final, decisions. Sovereign claims must be made in absolute terms, or sovereignty cannot do the work law requires of it. Thus we can see that it is law's vacuity which actually goes to ground the authority of the autopositioned sovereign. But, consistent with the discussion above of sovereignty's dependence on law, law's vacuity does not elevate sovereignty wholly above law. It also means that no sovereign, however powerful, can completely contain law. As such, the sovereign claim can never be realised in an absolute and enduring sense. Law requires the sovereign to claim a capacity to contain and determine law absolutely – while at the same time making such a claim impossible. Like Blanchot's law,

New York: Routledge, 2002, p. 233. See also Bodin, *On Sovereignty*, p. 55 (although for Bodin, the sovereign's word is enough to give 'force' to law).

42 Derrida, *Rogues*, p. 13.

43 Ibid., p. 10 (my emphasis).

44 Ibid., p. 17.

this law elevates sovereignty only to raise itself up in its turn.[45] Law thus combines 'determination with what is beyond determination.'[46] And it is the sovereign which enables law to achieve this seemingly impossible dynamic.[47] Again, Schmitt's theory of sovereign exceptionalism, through its failures and contradictions, illustrates the point. The exception, we will find, lies within law, not in the hands of the sovereign.

Schmitt seeks to ground the legal order in the power of the sovereign to determine whether or not an exceptional situation exists and, if it does, what should be done about it. The legal order is dependent on this power because no legal order can set down rules in advance which could guarantee its survival in the face of an extraordinary threat to its own existence. Schmitt can only suggest at what might actually constitute an exception, since this can only ever be decided by a sovereign in a particular moment. Nevertheless, he writes that it can 'at best be characterised as a case of extreme peril, a danger to the existence of the state, or the like.'[48] For Schmitt, '[w]hat characterises the exception is principally unlimited authority, which means the suspension of the entire existing order.'[49] It 'cannot be circumscribed factually or made to conform to a preformed law.'[50] There is a dual determination in play here. Because the sovereign determines when the exception exists, it also 'definitively decides when [the] normal situation actually exists.'[51] Thus, for Schmitt, the legal order seems to be entirely dependent on the power of the sovereign. And yet, we also find that while the sovereign 'stands outside the normally valid legal system, he nevertheless

45 Blanchot, 'Madness of the Day', p. 198.

46 Fitzpatrick, *Modernism*, p. 76.

47 Blanchot, 'Madness of the Day', p. 198; See also Michel Foucault, 'Maurice Blanchot: The Thought from the Outside', tr. Brian Massumi, in Maurice Blanchot and Michel Foucault, *Foucault/Blanchot*, New York: Zone Books, 1987, pp. 34, 38.

48 Carl Schmitt, *Political Theology: Four Chapters on the Concept of Sovereignty*, tr. George Schwab, Chicago: University of Chicago Press, 2005, p. 6.

49 Ibid., p. 12.

50 Ibid., p. 6.

51 Ibid., p. 13.

belongs to it'.[52] Moreover, the exception, the decision as to which is constitutive of Schmitt's sovereign, remains 'accessible to jurisprudence because both elements, the norm as well as the decision, remain within the framework of the juristic.'[53] Suddenly the exception seems to be a creature not of the sovereign decision but of law. Indeed, we find that in the exception, 'law suspends itself.'[54] In this relation between norm and decision, the sovereign plays an important role, but it is a role cast by law; not by the sovereign itself.

It could be argued that in the exception, the sovereign steps wholly outside the law and suspends the relation between norm and decision. But law does not permit such a distancing. First, the exception depends on the norm to which it is exceptional. This perhaps explains why the decision of Schmitt's sovereign only suspends, rather than abolishes, the legal order. That order remains in the wings awaiting its inevitable return.[55] And so, even in Schmitt's terms, the relation between norm and decision is not suspended in the exception, even if the legal order itself is suspended. But even this suspension seems impossible. How could the sovereign stand outside the legal order so as to suspend it? As Foucault writes, 'the moment you believe that you can read its decrees from afar and that they apply only to other people is the moment you are closest to the law.'[56] Since law must encompass the infinity of our being with each other, it cannot be contained. And contained it would need to be if the sovereign could stand outside it and suspend it. This is impossible even, or especially, when the law is most threatened. For Foucault:

> the order of the law was never so sovereign than … when it envelops what had tried to overturn it. Anyone who attempts to oppose the law to found a new order, to organise a second

52 Ibid., p. 7.
53 Ibid., p. 12–13.
54 Ibid., p. 14.
55 See Peter Fitzpatrick and Richard Joyce, 'The Normality of the Exception in Democracy's Empire', *Journal of Law and Society* 34, 2007, 64, 66.
56 Foucault, 'Thought from the Outside', p. 34.

> police force, to institute a new state, will only encounter the infinitely accommodating welcome of the law.[57]

Law thus denies claims to ultimate containment and destruction while welcoming the new power's claim to endow it with content. And if an attempt to destroy the law results only in affirming sovereignty's dependence on law, then so must an attempt to suspend it.

That the exception, and the call for sovereign decision, is within law, can be gleaned not only from the big question of the decision which, for Schmitt, guarantees the legal order, but from the day to day operation of the normal legal order itself. By contrast to the fantastic exception, Schmitt's normal legal order appears at first to be a rather dull creature. The decision about and in the exception suspends the monotonous regularity of the normal situation; it 'frees itself from all normative ties,' it 'departs ... from the legal norm.'[58] For Schmitt, in 'the exception the power of real life breaks through the crust of a mechanism that has become torpid by repetition.'[59] Thus the normal legal order seems to be reduced to a calculating mechanism which operates day to day without any relation to 'real life'. This law thus has no mode of adapting to the changing circumstances of life and leaves no room for the legal decision itself. And yet, when Schmitt himself turns to the problem of the legal decision, things start to look more complex. There, we find that the norm does not operate completely without a moment of decision, rather, in the normal situation the 'autonomous moment of the decision recedes to a *minimum*.'[60] More specifically, Schmitt himself finds that there is something of the decision in every legal prescription, noting that:

> every concrete juristic decision contains a moment of indifference from the perspective of content, because the juristic deduction is not traceable in the last detail to its premises and

57 Ibid., p. 38.
58 Schmitt, *Political Theology*, pp. 12, 13.
59 Ibid., p. 15.
60 Ibid., p. 12 (my emphasis).

> because the circumstance that requires a decision remains an independently determining moment.[61]

Indeed, as Derrida points out, law cannot be reduced to 'applying a rule ... enacting a program or effecting a calculation,' since it would not involve any moment of decision.[62] There is, then, in every legal decision the impossibility of it being determined mechanically, of it escaping the need for an exceptional decision that would bring the abstract norm to bear on a specific situation. Law thus seems to invite and depend on a power outside of itself to ensure its normal operation. All of this could be seen to elevate further the power of the sovereign.

However, the space inevitably opened by the call for decision (and, by implication, the call to determine the content of law) is not filled simply by the force of a predominant power. Law does not call on the sovereign to make any decision; it calls for a decision made in the name of justice. As Blanchot's narrator discovered, law gives the sovereign a power of determination but in the same breath requires it to 'see justice done.'[63] Derrida's work on the relationship between law and justice bears this out. Derrida's conception of justice, and its relation to law, is, however, quite specific. As such, it is necessary to outline what Derrida means by justice. And by doing so, it will help to further explain the conception of law which I have been using up to now.

When we think about justice, particularly in its strict legal context (as opposed, let's say, to a general call for political or social justice), we tend to think of an outcome which has been reached fairly and could be justified on the basis of having followed particular determinate rules.[64] This is not Derrida's conception of justice. For Derrida, justice is unconditional; 'infinite, incalculable,

61 Ibid., p. 30.
62 Derrida, 'Force of Law', p. 251.
63 Blanchot, 'Madness of the Day', p. 197.
64 Such a meaning would fall broadly within the meanings given by the *Oxford English Dictionary* to the use of 'justice' that refers to 'judicial administration of law or equity:' see *Oxford English Dictionary*.

rebellious to rule and foreign to symmetry.'[65] Justice demands the impossible. Of a legal decision-maker for example, it would require adherence to a general rule and the freedom to depart from it – to take fully into account all specific circumstances, especially those which could not have been foreseen at the time of the rule's creation.[66] It would also require the decision to be made urgently: 'a just decision is always required *immediately*, right away, as quickly as possible' and yet to be fully just or justified it would need to be based on 'infinite information' and 'unlimited knowledge of all conditions, rules or hypothetical imperatives'.[67] Indeed, for Derrida, even if one could imagine such mastery, the decision would always mark an 'interruption of the process of ... deliberation that precedes it, that *must* [doit] precede it.'[68] A decision left until the point at which all deliberation is exhausted could not be just; indeed, since that point of exhaustion could never be reached, that decision would never arrive.[69] As such, justice is not something that can be done;[70] the appeal to justice is necessarily 'always unsatisfied'.[71]

In one sense, for Derrida, this conception of justice is a counterpoint to law; or at least a law conceived (for the moment) as embodying conditioned judgments or calculation.[72] In opposition to such a conception of law, justice is unconditional and incalculable.[73] But this opposition is not simple; it is not a 'true distinction, an opposition the functioning of which [is] logically

65 Derrida, 'Force of Law', p. 250.
66 Ibid., pp. 251–5.
67 Ibid., p. 255 (original emphasis).
68 Ibid. (original emphasis).
69 The experience of waiting for it would be familiar to Kafka's man from the country: Franz Kafka, *The Trial*, trs Willa and Edwin Muir, London: David Campbell, 1992, pp. 23–46.
70 Derrida, 'Force of Law', pp. 252–3.
71 Ibid., p. 249.
72 Ibid., p. 244. This is not the whole story, of course. We have already seen above that for Derrida, law cannot be reduced to the element of calculation: see above note 62 and accompanying text.
73 Ibid., p. 244.

regulated and masterable.'[74] Each carries within itself something of the other. Moreover, each needs the other. As Derrida writes, 'law claims to exercise itself in the name of justice and that justice demands for itself that it be established in the name of a law that must be put to work ... by force "enforced."'[75] It is by claiming the ability to exercise itself in the name of an unconditional justice that law carries the ability to go beyond any fixed determination and to respond to changing circumstances. As such, it is not simply that law happens to claim to exercise itself in the name of justice, but that it *must* claim to do so.

Similarly, justice *must* demand to be applied by a law 'put to work': 'incalculable justice *commands* calculation.'[76] It cannot wait or remain detached from life.[77] Indeed, left to itself, 'the incalculable and giving [*donatrice*] idea of justice is always very close to the bad, even to the worst for it can always be reappropriated by the most perverse calculation.'[78] Law offers no guarantee of avoiding perverse appropriations. As Derrida writes, an 'absolute assurance against this risk can only saturate or suture the opening of the call to justice' and seek to limit the illimitable.[79] But though it cannot guarantee the avoidance of perverse appropriations, any appropriation of justice through law would at the least demand a certain vigilance and a fidelity, based on a certain faith, to the notion of the social bond law enacts and seeks to serve.[80] As such, justice and law, though heterogeneous, cannot

74 Ibid., pp. 250–1.
75 Ibid., p. 251.
76 Ibid., p. 257 (original emphasis).
77 Ibid., p. 255.
78 Ibid., p. 257.
79 Ibid.
80 Such a passing reference to faith and the social bond is not unproblematic. Here, I want to give just a sense of the combination of the mystical, theological and social that underlies Derrida's conceptions of law and justice. Much more would need to be said to draw out the relation between these concepts. The best starting point after 'Force of Law' would be: Jacques Derrida, 'Faith and Knowledge: The Two Sources of "Religion" at the Limits of Reason Alone', tr. Samuel Weber, in Jacques Derrida, *Acts of Religion*, ed. Gil Anidjar, New York: Routledge, 2002, pp. 42–101 and Derrida, *Politics of Friendship*, pp. 74–111.

be dissociated.[81] For Derrida, the nature or order of this dual imperative (law *must*...; justice *must*...) does not 'belong either to justice or to law.' Rather, it 'belongs only to either realm by exceeding each in the direction of the other.'[82] The relationship between justice and law is one where each supplies a lack in the other.

These two orders meet in the moment of the sovereign decision – in the moment when law is put to work. For Derrida, justice requires the decision to be responsible and free. As we saw in Chapter 1, if law was simply the mechanistic application of pre-existing rules, it would involve no call for decision. Indeed, a legal decision must be, at least for a moment, absolutely without condition: undecidable. In Derrida's terms, a 'decision that would not go through the test and ordeal of the undecidable would not be a free decision.'[83] And so any application of a rule must necessarily pass through a moment where its outcome is not predetermined.[84] Again, this creates a call for a sovereign decision without conditions, which cannot be determined in advance; by a sovereign whose claim to authority cannot be derived from or beholden to any other power – in short, by an autopositioned sovereign. But the call for decision – this need to respond – cannot be filled solely by arbitrary sovereign determination. If that were the case, law would be reduced to an instrument of totalitarianism. Moreover, it would require sovereign power to contain law completely (which we have seen above it cannot do). Instead, that decision must be made with regard to an unconditional justice.

Thus it is through law's relation to unconditional justice that we glimpse the nature of law's responsive dimension; its vacuity; its capacity to go beyond any fixed determination or instantiation. As we have seen above, this combination of the determinate and responsive in law is dynamic and uneasy. For Fitzpatrick, what constitutes and impels law is 'the antinomy between these two dimensions combined with their necessity for each other.'[85]

81 Derrida, 'Force of Law', p. 257.
82 Ibid.
83 Ibid., p. 252.
84 Ibid., pp. 251–8.
85 Fitzpatrick, *Modernism*, p. 104.

The sovereign position can thus be seen as the position through which law becomes determinate and also the site which must be open to justice, or law's responsive dimension, and in turn the site through which the demands of justice return again to the determinate. Accordingly, the sovereign plays a crucial role in the dynamic oscillation of law between its determinate and responsive dimensions. But crucially, it cannot transcend this dynamic; it is caught – positioned even – within it.

3 Sovereignty Beyond the State

In a world which lacks a founding rule and a single overarching authority, claims to sovereignty will always be open to challenge. In order to be able to understand those challenges, it is therefore important to understand the bases on which existing claims rest. As we saw in the Introduction, the assumption that the nation-state provides the exclusive position of sovereignty in modernity arbitrarily constrains efforts to understand the complexity of the challenges posed by the World Trade Organisation and by local communities in India. Given the constraints it places on thought, that assumption should be tested and either proved or found to be false. My goal up to now has been to show that it is false. Even in the seemingly robust terms provided by Bodin, modern sovereignty is a creature of irresolution. It cannot be located solely in one position or in a particular form of community. As we have seen, nation does not resolve the irresolutions in Bodin's conception such that it provides a solid ground for modern sovereignty. Rather, it provides an example of its groundless nature. All sovereignty, even that of the nation-state, is autopositioned. It relies on a self-grounded claim to speak for a community and determine its law. Since nation is not the only form of community and national law is not the only form of law, sovereignty cannot be tied exclusively to the nation-state.

As such, the autopositioning of modern sovereignty reveals the possibility that it might lie beyond the nation-state. In the remainder of this chapter, I will show how the WTO and local communities in India make sovereign claims to legal authority which have the same characteristic of autopositioning that we have seen applies to the nation-state. I will argue that the international community and local communities in India can both be seen as communities of law. And since, as we have seen, law and community are dependent on sovereignty, then if law and community can be found in the local and the international, then we should expect also to find sovereignty there. But we should not expect to find an exact replica of the sovereignty claimed by or for nation-states. The vacuity of law and community is not always contained to the same degree by sovereign assertion. In short, in any given instance, there is as much community, law and sovereignty as there is.[86]

3.1 The autopositioned sovereignty of the WTO

At the heart of autopositioned sovereignty is the claim by an entity to ultimate authority to determine the law of a community, where that claim is based on no higher authority than that of the entity itself. In this section, I will argue that the WTO can be seen to make a sovereign claim in these terms in that it makes a self-grounded claim to speak for the community made up of its member states. I will argue that the WTO is an entity which has an identity and life of its own which is more than just the sum of the authority delegated to it by its member states. This is shown by the content of its constitutive documents (by which the WTO is established as an independent entity) and by the nature of its dispute settlement procedure (by which the WTO arrogates ultimate authority to determine the meaning of WTO law). These features apply to the WTO in general. Having set these out, I will then briefly note how the Agreement on Trade-Related Aspects of Intellectual Property Rights (TRIPS), the WTO treaty which deals, among other things, with patent law, fits into the institutional framework of the WTO. More on the detail of TRIPS and its relation to Indian patent law will follow in Chapter 4.

86 On there only ever being as much law as there is, see Peter Fitzpatrick, 'Access as Justice', *Windsor Yearbook of Access to Justice* 23, 2005, 3, 16. On there only ever being as much community as there is, see Nancy, *Inoperative Community*, p. 35.

3.1.1 The WTO's constitutive documents and its community of law

At first, it seems difficult to argue that the WTO makes a sovereign claim over the law of its member states. This is because the WTO self-consciously presents itself as nothing more than a negotiating forum for governments to agree on trade rules and as an administrative vehicle for implementing such agreements.[87] The WTO distinguishes itself from other entities such as the International Monetary Fund and the World Bank, where powers are delegated to an executive which has the power to influence a country's policy by withholding credit.[88] By contrast, all WTO decisions are made by consensus of its member states. The WTO website states:

> when WTO rules impose disciplines on countries' policies, that is the outcome of negotiations among WTO members. The rules are enforced by the members themselves under agreed procedures that they negotiated, including the possibility of trade sanctions. But those sanctions are imposed by member countries, and authorized by the membership as a whole.[89]

In this way, the WTO seems to go along with the view that all legal authority flows from nation-states. However, its constitutive documents and its operation show otherwise. Both in terms of its formal structure and its activity, the WTO exists as an entity independent of any of its members. The existence of the WTO as a distinct, independent legal entity is established by articles I and VIII of the Marrakesh Agreement Establishing the World Trade

87 See World Trade Organisation, 'What is the World Trade Organisation?', at: http://www.wto.org/english/thewto_e/whatis_e/tif_e/fact1_e.htm (last accessed 6 December 2011).

88 World Trade Organisation, 'Who's WTO is it anyway?' at: http://www.wto.org/english/thewto_e/whatis_e/tif_e/org1_e.htm (last accessed 6 December 2011).

89 Ibid.

Organisation (WTO Agreement).[90] This marks a distinct shift from the lack of a formal organisational structure which existed under the General Agreement on Tariffs and Trade (GATT).[91] Both formally and in practice, none of its constituent members, or any other entity, can speak for it.

The WTO thus claims ultimate authority to speak for the community made up of its member states. Its mode of speaking is through the agreements which constitute it and which it administers, declarations arising from Ministerial Conferences and decisions of the General Council, and decisions made under its dispute settlement procedure.[92] The authority thus claimed by the WTO is one exercised through law. It is based in the WTO agreements, which are treaties entered into by states under international law. These agreements are referred to by the WTO as 'legal texts'.[93] They 'provide the legal ground-rules for international commerce.'[94] The reverence attached to the agreements as the legal foundation for the WTO is reflected in the notice on the WTO website, where copies of the agreements appear, that the 'texts reproduced here do not have the legal standing of the original documents which are entrusted and kept at the WTO Secretariat in Geneva.'[95] Not only does the WTO base its claim on legal texts, but its process for determining disputes under its texts is a self-consciously legal process. As Macmillan argues, the WTO 'purports to establish something that looks very much like a self-contained system of law operating at the supra-national

90 Marrakesh Agreement Establishing the World Trade Organization (1994), arts I and VIII.

91 Rüdiger Wolfrum, Peter-Tobias Stoll and Karen Kaiser (eds), *WTO: Institutions and Dispute Settlement*, Leiden: Martinus Nijhoff, 2006, p. 29.

92 The Ministerial Conference is the highest decision-making body in the WTO structure. It is convened at least every two years and is constituted by representatives of all WTO members. Between Ministerial Conferences, the General Council meets regularly and has the power to carry out the functions of the Ministerial Conference. It too is constituted by representatives of all WTO members: WTO Agreement, art IV.

93 World Trade Organisation, 'WTO legal texts', at: http://www.wto.org/english/docs_e/legal_e/legal_e.htm (last accessed 6 December 2011).

94 World Trade Organisation, 'What is the World Trade Organisation'.

95 World Trade Organisation, 'WTO legal texts'.

level.'[96] The WTO arrogates a power over the law of its community which transcends the authority of any of its individual members and has a life of its own. The WTO's claim to authority thus carries the qualities of a self-grounded claim to determine the law of a community which we observed earlier in this chapter as the basis of autopositioned sovereignty.

The nature of the community over which the WTO claims authority bears some further consideration. In Chapter 1 and again earlier in this chapter, I argued that the community for which the sovereign speaks cannot be present to itself or do anything. Incapable of acting as a pure collectivity, it could only act through its representative, the sovereign. The community relied on the sovereign both in its formation and in its operation. Applying that argument to the WTO, we can observe in the formation of the WTO the creation of an entity which claims to speak for its members. But the idea that the WTO is a perfect representation of the collective (such that it could be seen as the collective itself in action), is perhaps harder to refute than in the case of communities like nation-states. In communities with many members, their sheer number makes its inability to act as a pure collectivity obvious. In the case of the WTO, this quality is perhaps less pronounced. It could be argued that while in the case of the state, a social contract must be imagined or presumed, the WTO's constitutive documents are in fact an operative social contract. On this basis, one could argue that the community of WTO member states is in fact a perfect community, constituted by documents reflecting pure consent.

However, the claim to an operative social contract is as fanciful in this context as it is in all the others to which it is commonly brought to bear. The formation of the WTO was not the creation of a perfect community, but the product of an ongoing relation though which its constituent members were also transformed. Just as Hobbes's commonwealth required the sovereign to bring it into existence, the community represented by the WTO did not

96 Fiona Macmillan, 'International Economic Law and Public International Law', *International Trade Law and Regulation* 6, 2004, 115, 121.

exist, as such, until the agreements which brought the WTO into existence were signed. Moreover, it is, like all other communities of law, subject to change. As we have seen, communities of law depend on an autopositioned sovereign to cut through the changefulness of both community and law in order to render, for the time being, binding, determinate decisions. In the case of the WTO, this occurs through its dispute settlement procedure – a procedure in which we see its claim to determine WTO law elevated to one of supreme authority.

3.1.2 The WTO's dispute settlement procedure

Article 64 of TRIPS provides that the full WTO dispute settlement procedure applies to disputes about compliance with TRIPS. It is the most comprehensive system for the settlement of disputes and enforcement of decisions that has ever been applied to a multilateral treaty concerning intellectual property. This procedure builds on the system which existed under GATT. The provisions which trigger the process are taken directly from GATT (articles XXII and XXIII) and decisions and practices under GATT also continue to have an influence on the current WTO procedure by virtue of article XV1:1 of the WTO Agreement. These provisions and practices are now supplemented by the Understanding on Rules and Procedures Governing the Settlement of Disputes (commonly referred to as the Dispute Settlement Understanding or DSU) which was negotiated during the Uruguay Round to remedy perceived weaknesses in the GATT system, particularly relating to enforcement.[97] The DSU applies to disputes arising under any of the multilateral WTO agreements.[98] The DSU contains rules on standing, the constitution of bodies and the selection of individuals to hear disputes and the implementation and enforcement of decisions.

97 Mitsuo Matsushita, Thomas Schoenbaum and Petros Mavroidis, *The World Trade Organisation*, Oxford: Oxford University Press, 2004, p. 22. The DSU is annex 2 to the WTO Agreement.

98 DSU, art 1.1. (The covered agreements are listed in appendix 1 to the DSU.)

The DSU contemplates five main stages to the settlement of a dispute. The first is consultation between the parties, the second is a hearing by the Panel, the third is an appeal to the Appellate Body, the fourth is formal approval by the Dispute Settlement Body (DSB) and the final stage is implementation and enforcement. For present purposes, the powers held by the DSB following a decision by the Appellate Body put into clearest view the nature of the claim of the WTO to ultimate authority to determine the meaning and effect of WTO law.

Appeals against Panel reports are heard by a standing Appellate Body consisting of seven individuals, three of whom sit on any one case. Appointments to the Appellate Body are made for four years and in addition to requiring expertise in law and international trade, appointees must be unaffiliated with any government.[99] The subject matter of an appeal is limited to issues and interpretations of law arising in the Panel report. The Appellate Body is empowered to uphold, modify or reverse the legal findings of the Panel.[100] An Appellate Body report is adopted by the DSB unless it decides by consensus not to do so.[101] If adopted, the report must be unconditionally accepted by the parties to the dispute.[102] This requires a complete submission to the authority of the appellate body on issues concerning whether a state is in compliance with its obligations under the WTO agreements, including TRIPS.

Accordingly, by virtue of the WTO's dispute settlement procedure, not only are states bound to the text of the treaties they have signed, but also the interpretation of those treaties by the primary WTO decision-making bodies, the Panel and Appellate Body.[103] However, article 3.2 of the DSU seems to elevate the

99 DSU, arts 17.2 and 17.3.
100 Ibid., art 17.13.
101 Ibid., art 17.14.
102 Ibid.
103 In strict terms, Member states are only bound to a particular determination if they are parties to the dispute in which it is delivered, but in practice a body of law is emerging in which prior decisions (particularly of the Appellate Body) are treated with respect: Matsushita, Schoenbaum and Mavroidis,

primacy of the agreements themselves and diminish the role of the decision-making bodies. It provides that '[r]ecommendations and rulings of the DSB cannot add to or diminish the rights and obligations' contained in the WTO agreements.[104] While this may appear to limit the reach of such decisions, the same article also provides that the dispute settlement system exists to 'clarify the existing provisions of [the WTO] agreements in accordance with customary rules of interpretation of public international law.'[105] Such clarification inevitably has an effect on the meaning of the underlying agreements, whether or not it can be understood as adding to or diminishing the rights and obligations of members. Moreover, as the interpretation of *legal* rights and obligations, such decisions are not immune from the demands of justice. They are not, despite article 3.2 of the DSU, the work of a calculating machine.

Given the binding nature of their decisions (via the DSB), states submit to the authority of the Panel and Appellate Body in a manner comparable to litigants in a domestic court. These bodies are independent from any of the WTO's individual member states. Moreover, they are placed to determine the limits of their own jurisdiction. As Sarooshi writes, the 'determination by an [international] organ of the scope of its powers will, in the absence of review by a body which has jurisdiction to decide such a matter, certainly prevail over the interpretation of States.'[106] An example of such determination occurred in a case brought by the United States against India in relation to the 'mailbox' requirements in TRIPS.[107] In this case, the WTO's dispute settlement

World Trade Organisation, p. 25; Jose Alvarez, *International Organizations as Law-makers*, Oxford: Oxford University Press, 2005, p. 469.

104 DSU, art 3.2.

105 Ibid.

106 See Dan Sarooshi, *International Organisations and their Exercise of Sovereign Powers*, Oxford: Oxford University Press, 2005, p. 22.

107 *India – Patent Protection for Pharmaceutical and Chemical Products*, Report of the Panel (WT/DS50/R), 5 September 1997; *India – Patent Protection for Pharmaceutical and Chemical Products*, Report of the Appellate Body, (WT/DS50/AB/R), 19 December 1997. The United States argued that India was in breach of articles 70.8 and 70.9 of TRIPS because it did not provide an

bodies affirmed their authority to make determinations about the effect of Indian law when considering whether it complied with the requirements of TRIPS.[108] To find otherwise, in the view of the Appellate Body, would 'be to say that only India can assess whether Indian law is consistent with India's obligations under the WTO Agreement ... [which] clearly, cannot be so.'[109] Accordingly, the Appellate Body found that the WTO's dispute settlement bodies have ultimate authority to determine a state's compliance with the WTO agreements, even to the extent of determining the effect of domestic law.[110] As such, despite its disavowal of separate existence, the WTO does make a claim to authority to determine the scope of its powers and the meaning of the laws it administers and applies. No other entity exists which can make a superior claim. The High Court of Madras has, for example, ruled that the question of whether Indian legislation complies with TRIPS cannot be determined in a domestic Indian court.[111]

effective 'means by which applications for patents' on pharmaceutical and agricultural products could be filed, and for exclusive marketing rights, pending later changes which would make these products patentable. Despite India's argument that its law included an administrative scheme to handle applications, both the Panel and Appellate Body found that Indian law was not in compliance with the obligations in articles 70.8 and 70.9 and recommended that India take steps to become compliant: see Report of the Appellate Body, para. 98. The European Community brought a similar complaint against India relying on the same facts: *India – Patent Protection for Pharmaceutical and Agricultural Chemical Products*, Report of the Panel, (WT/DS79/R), 24 August 1998.

108 *India – Patent Protection for Pharmaceutical and Chemical Products*, Report of the Appellate Body, (WT/DS50/AB/R), 19 December 1997.

109 Ibid., para 66 (original emphasis).

110 In so doing, the Appellate Body denied that this involves interpreting Indian law. Rather it sought to treat domestic law as a 'fact', relying on the Permanent Court of International Justice in *Certain German Interests in Polish Upper Silesia* [1926], PCIJ Rep., Series A, No. 7, 19: 'From the standpoint of International Law ... municipal laws are merely facts which express the will and constitute the activities of States.' Ibid., paras 65–66.

111 *Novartis AG v Union of India* (2007) High Court of Judicature at Madras, Case No 24759 and 24760 of 2006 (judgment delivered 6 August 2007). Thanks to Achal Prabhala for providing a copy of the judgment. We will return to this case in Chapter 4.

However, the dispute settlement procedure not only demonstrates the ultimate nature of the claim to authority to determine WTO law, it also exposes a significant limit on the scope of that claim. While the decisions of a Panel (if adopted) and the Appellate Body are final on the question of compliance, the question of what measures are required to be taken in order to achieve compliance is not finally determined by either body. In the first instance, it is up to the non-compliant member state to decide what measures it needs to take in order to comply with a panel or appellate body ruling. We will return to this question in Chapter 4 when we consider in more detail the relation between the WTO and India, and focus on the precise boundary between their sovereign positions.

3.1.3 The WTO's claim over the patent law of member states

India became a member of the WTO at its inception and was thus bound to the WTO Agreement when it entered into force on 1 January 1995.[112] Compliance with TRIPS is a mandatory condition of membership of the WTO.[113] No reservations may be entered in respect of any of the provisions of TRIPS without the consent of all other members.[114] TRIPS itself also includes a requirement that member states comply with it. Article 1 provides that 'Members shall give effect to the provisions of this Agreement.'[115]

112 World Trade Organisation, 'Members and Observers', at: http://www.wto.org/english/thewto_e/whatis_e/tif_e/org6_e.htm (last accessed 6 December 2011).

113 WTO Agreement, art II.

114 TRIPS, art 72.

115 Ibid., art 1. Under the implementation provisions of TRIPS, all members were given a period of one year from the date of the WTO Agreement within which to ensure that their intellectual property laws complied with TRIPS (art 65.1). 'Developing Country Members', a classification which included India, were given an additional four years to comply (except in relation to the provisions concerning national treatment (articles 3, 4 and 5 of TRIPS, where the one-year rule applied) (art 65.2). An additional delay of five years was allowed for Developing Country Members to change their laws to extend product patent

The WTO does not establish an institutional framework requiring that member states automatically incorporate the text of its agreements into their domestic law. Implementation is a matter for states themselves.[116] As such, the WTO's sovereign claim operates by making demands on national legislative bodies to enact and enforce laws consistent with WTO obligations. In addition, the dispute settlement procedure contains effective mechanisms aimed at ensuring compliance, including the authorisation of trade sanctions. These are supplemented by compliance mechanisms which do not need a dispute between states to enliven them.

In the case of TRIPS, member states' compliance is monitored by the TRIPS Council, a body established under article IV.5 of the WTO Agreement. This role is facilitated by article 63 of TRIPS, which requires members to notify the Council of '[l]aws, regulations, and final judicial decisions and administrative rulings' pertaining to the subject matter of TRIPS.[117] Article 63 contemplates that the notification procedure may eventually make way for a 'common register containing these laws and regulations' created in conjunction with the World Intellectual Property Organisation.[118] The article further allows a member to require another member to provide it with the same information it is required to submit to the TRIPS Council, and where it has reason to believe that a specific instrument or decision may adversely affect its rights, details of that instrument or decision.[119] As such,

protection to areas of technology which were not patentable as at the date of TRIPS (14 April 1994) (art 65.4). Accordingly, India was required to implement the provisions concerning national treatment by 1 January 1996, the main body of TRIPS by 1 January 2000, and the final changes to its patent law by 1 January 2005. The transitional provisions did not apply to arts 70.8 and 70.9 of TRIPS, which required states which did not allow patents on agricultural and pharmaceutical products to accept and file applications for patents in those areas, and allow exclusive marketing rights, in advance of their being available for consideration for grant once the applicable transition period ended. This obligation formed the basis of the 'mailbox' dispute discussed above.

116 See, e.g., TRIPS, art 1.

117 Art 63.1 of TRIPS summarises this subject matter as 'the availability, scope, acquisition, enforcement and prevention of abuse of intellectual property rights'.

118 Ibid., art 63.2.

119 Ibid.

member states are themselves required to submit their laws for scrutiny, both by the TRIPS Council and other member states. In addition to ensuring an efficient collection of material on which a complaint may be made, the monitoring provisions also have a disciplinary effect on states whereby they internalise the compliance functions of the WTO.

The procedural and enforcement context of the WTO's claim over the patent law of its member states is crucial and I will return to it in Chapter 4. However, it is ancillary to the content of the patent law requirements themselves. It is those requirements against which any question of compliance, dispute and enforcement must be measured. In this context, it should be emphasised that the requirements of TRIPS are peculiar among WTO agreements for their specificity. As such, they provide a good example to test the nature and limits of the WTO's influence over the content of the law of its member states – which I have characterised as a sovereign claim over that law.

The key provision in TRIPS concerning patent law is article 27, which defines patentable subject matter broadly as 'any inventions, whether products or processes, in all fields of technology, provided that they are new, involve an inventive step and are capable of industrial application' and 'without discrimination as to the place of invention, the field of technology and whether products are imported or locally produced.'[120] For India, which had excluded patents on medicinal, chemical and agricultural products, and favoured local producers, this article required significant changes to its existing law. The breadth of the article also means that, despite the exclusions permissible under the remainder of article 27, the starting position is effectively a presumption of patentability.[121] Any departure from this presumption must be justified by recourse to one of the specific exclusions in article 27.2 or 27.3,[122] or subject to a specific restriction of rights

120 TRIPS, art 27.1.

121 Daniel Gervais, *The TRIPS Agreement: Drafting History and Analysis*, 3rd ed., London: Sweet and Maxwell: 2008, p. 337.

122 Gervais argues that the presumption of patentability means that such exceptions are perhaps to be 'interpreted in a restrictive fashion and be the subject

under article 30 a compulsory licence under article 31 or a revocation under article 32.[123]

In addition to specifying the scope of patentable subject matter, TRIPS also specifies a variety of features that the patent law of WTO member states must contain. Member states must provide that the patent holder has the exclusive right to use a patented process or to make, use, sell or import patented products or products made via a patented process.[124] States must also require that patent holders make full disclosure of the patented invention,[125] provide for a minimum term of protection of 20 years,[126] and even provide that the burden of proof switches to the defendant where it is alleged that the defendant has used a patented process if it is shown that they have produced a product identical to that made by the patented process.[127] TRIPS also specifies the remedies available for infringement of intellectual property rights, including injunctions,[128] damages,[129] and disposal of infringing goods.[130] For now, it is enough to note that many of the requirements of TRIPS are sufficiently specific to constitute a substantial claim on the patent law of WTO member states. In Chapter 4,

of future negotiations towards [their] elimination.': Ibid., p. 337 (n 492). I would agree that the structure points to a presumption of patentability but would not share Gervais's view that the exceptions necessarily need to be read restrictively or eliminated.

123 For analysis of art 30, see *Canada – Patent Protection of Pharmaceutical Products*, Report of the Panel (WT/DS114/R), 17 March 2000. See also Fiona Macmillan, *The World Trade Organization and Human Rights*, Oxford, Hart.: forthcoming, Ch. 3. Articles 31 and 32 are further discussed below in Chapter 4.

124 TRIPS, art 28.

125 Ibid., art 29.

126 Ibid., art 33. Blakeney notes that 'the developing countries' had failed at the TRIPS negotiations to have the duration of a patent as a matter to be fixed by national legislation: see Michael Blakeney, *Trade Related Aspects of Intellectual Property Rights: A Concise Guide to the TRIPS Agreement*, London: Sweet and Maxwell, 1996, p. 88.

127 TRIPS, art 34.

128 Ibid., art 44.

129 Ibid., art 45.

130 Ibid., art 46.

I will return to the requirements of TRIPS and argue attention to their varying specificity is crucial in understanding the boundaries between the claims of the WTO and of the Indian state to determine the content of Indian patent law.

3.2 The autopositioned sovereignty of local and indigenous communities

The claims by local and indigenous communities in India to sovereignty over traditional knowledge are obviously more varied and diffuse than that which can be attributed to the WTO. The goal here is to focus on examples as illustrative of a certain type of claim and a certain type of relation between the local and the national. The first example I will use is the claim advocated by prominent Indian social and environmental activist Vandana Shiva and her colleagues at Navdanya (formerly the Research Foundation for Science, Technology and Ecology (RFSTE)). Their work is particularly useful because Shiva's organisation was one of the first to advocate community control of traditional knowledge, a stance which has become very influential. The second example comes in the form of the claims made by and in connection with the Campaign for Community Control over Biodiversity which has included direct petitions by village communities themselves. Both these claims have been initiated through the work of non-government organisations (NGOs) working at the community level. This might appear, at first glance, to cause problems for a theory of sovereign autopositioning – in which the claim to occupy the sovereign position can be made and defended only by the purported sovereign itself. However, despite the role of NGOs in initiating and, in some cases framing, the claims in question, the claims are explicitly grounded in the authority of the community – not in the authority of the NGOs.[131]

131 It should also be noted that NGOs do not speak with one voice on this issue, and that many prominent advocates of traditional knowledge protection, such as Dr Suman Sahai of Gene Campaign, view national laws as their best hope: interview with Suman Sahai, New Delhi, 19 February 2007 (notes on file with author).

It is thus appropriate to consider these claims in terms of their being the local communities' own.

3.2.1 A context for the claims

Before considering the terms in which these claims are made, it is useful to consider the framework within which local and indigenous communities make their claims to sovereignty. These claims occur within a fairly saturated international and national legal and policy environment. At the international level, the Declaration of the Rights of Indigenous Peoples (2007), provides that indigenous peoples shall have the right to 'maintain, control, protect and develop' their traditional knowledge, including through the means of intellectual property.[132] For the international community's attempt to provide some detail as to how such a right might be implemented, one could look to the work of the Intergovernmental Committee on Intellectual Property and Genetic Resources, Traditional Knowledge and Folklore at the World Intellectual Property Organisation (IGC). The IGC was formed in 2000 and is now in its twenty-first session.[133] The detail, however, has proved elusive. In general terms, the various sets of draft articles have contained terms which demonstrate an oscillation between the attempt to vest authority and control over traditional knowledge in local and indigenous communities, and the attempt to maintain the rights of national governments over natural resources and intellectual property law.[134] However, the key

132 Declaration on the Rights of Indigenous Peoples (2007), art 31.

133 WIPO's interest in traditional knowledge predated the establishment of the IGC. In 1998–99, for example, it conducted a fact-finding mission in 28 countries in which traditional knowledge was a significant issue: World Intellectual Property Organisation, *Intellectual Property Needs and Expectations of Traditional Knowledge Holders: WIPO Report on Fact-Finding Missions on Intellectual Property and Traditional Knowledge (1998–1999)*, Geneva: WIPO, 2001, at: http://www.wipo.int/tk/en/tk/ffm/report/final/index.html (last accessed 6 December 2011).

134 For the latest incarnation of the draft articles see: IGC, 'The Protection of Traditional Knowledge: Draft Articles', Annex to Document WIPO/GRTKF/IC/21/4, 18 January 2012, at http://www.wipo.int/tk/en/igc/ (last accessed 20 April 2012).

operative concept in the draft articles is that exploitation of traditional knowledge should only occur with the prior informed consent of traditional knowledge holders and that commercial benefits derived from that exploitation should be shared equitably with them.[135] That concept is embedded in the Convention on Biological Diversity (1992) and its recently adopted Nagoya Protocol under which it is applied to traditional knowledge connected to biological resources.[136]

The principles of prior informed consent and equitable benefit sharing also form the basis of India's key legislation on traditional knowledge relating to biological diversity, the Biological Diversity Act 2002. The scheme established by this Act is one against which the recent claims to local community sovereignty over traditional knowledge have been set. As such, it is important to consider its provisions in some detail. As I argued in the Introduction, while the principles of prior informed consent and equitable benefit sharing have the potential to create a fairer system of exploitation of traditional knowledge than would exist if that knowledge was able to be freely exploited, it does have the effect of commodifying the knowledge. As a result, such laws can work to undermine the role played by traditional knowledge in sustaining the cultural system in which it has been developed, and that system's role in sustaining the knowledge. Combined with a broader intellectual property system in which community practices inconsistent with private rights are allowed, if at all, as limited exceptions

135 Ibid., art 3.

136 Convention on Biological Diversity (1992), art 8(j); Nagoya Protocol on Access to Genetic Resources and the Fair and Equitable Sharing of Benefits Arising from their Utilization to the Convention on Biological Diversity (2010), art 7. Article 8(j) of the Convention goes beyond mere prior informed consent and equitable benefit sharing and includes an obligation to 'respect, preserve and maintain knowledge, innovations and practices of indigenous and local communities embodying traditional lifestyles relevant for the conservation and sustainable use of biological diversity'. (A similar statement can be found in the preamble to the Declaration on the Rights of Indigenous Peoples (2007).) However, these broader concerns with the ways of life in which traditional knowledge is held and developed does not find its way into the Protocol.

to those private rights,[137] the commodification of traditional knowledge under Indian national law and its inconsistency with traditional ways of life is one important reason why claims over traditional knowledge have come to be framed in terms of sovereignty. Beyond the broad implications of commodification, however, lies specific concerns about the quality of the rights granted to local communities under the Biological Diversity Act 2002, to which I will now turn.

The Biological Diversity Act 2002 seeks to ensure that local communities are protected against the misappropriation of 'knowledge associated' with biological resources from 'creators and holders of knowledge and information relating to the use of such biological resources, innovations and practices associated with such use'.[138] It does this by creating a system of prior informed consent and equitable sharing of both commercial and research benefits. And so, in the process of granting approvals for access and use of biological resources and associated knowledge, the National Biodiversity Authority (NBA) (a body established by the Act) is required to secure 'equitable sharing of benefits ... in accordance with mutually agreed terms and conditions between the [applicant], local bodies concerned and the benefit claimers.'[139] This provision appears to place traditional knowledge holders in the position of being able to control all questions of access to traditional knowledge by their capacity to withhold consent. Despite this appearance, however, the provisions of the Act fall short of actually requiring prior informed consent.

Under the Act and its rules, foreigners and non-resident Indian nationals (individuals and corporations) seeking to use a biological resource and traditional knowledge must set out (among other

137 See, e.g., Protection of Plant Varieties and Farmers' Rights Act 2001 (India), ss 16(1)(d), 41.

138 Biological Diversity Act 2002 (India), s 2. As such, the Act applies only to traditional knowledge which is associated with biological resources (as does the CBD and Nagoya Protocol). While this is not the only form of traditional knowledge, it is a highly significant form and is the one which relates most closely to patent law.

139 Biological Diversity Act 2002 (India), s 21.

things), the scientific name of the resource and its traditional use, its geographic location, a description of the traditional knowledge associated with it and whether there is an identified individual or community which holds the traditional knowledge.[140] However, there is nothing in the Act or the Rules which actually requires the applicant to obtain the prior informed consent of traditional knowledge holders. Rather, applicants must obtain the consent of the NBA.[141] Indian nationals are not required to seek approval for the use of biological resources, but must give notice of their intentions to the relevant State Biodiversity Board (SBB), which may prohibit or restrict the intended access and use.[142] The Act also requires consent from the NBA before the results of research into biological resources are transferred or any application is made for intellectual property rights for any invention based on such resources and research.[143] As such, the Indian state has established a centralised scheme governing the exploitation of biological resources and traditional knowledge. In making its decision, the NBA or relevant SBB must consult with a committee formed at the local level (the constitution of which I will describe shortly), but is not bound to follow the wishes of that committee.

Moreover, despite the emphasis on sharing benefits with local communities, it is contemplated that there will be circumstances where identifying the appropriate beneficiaries may be difficult, in which case no sharing would be necessary. The Act provides that intellectual property rights may be granted to benefit claimers 'where benefit claimers are identified'.[144] And while in cases where the resources or knowledge are acquired from a specific group or individual, the NBA may determine that payments be made directly to that group or individual, otherwise, they are to be distributed out of payments made to the National

140 Biological Diversity Rules 2004 (India), r 14.

141 Biological Diversity Act 2002 (India), s 3.

142 Ibid., ss 7, 24.

143 Ibid., s 4.

144 See Ibid., s 21(a) (my emphasis). Elsewhere in s 21 the existence of benefit claimers is assumed.

Biodiversity Fund.[145] In all cases, it is the NBA which holds the ultimate power to determine the terms of access and whether or not benefits will be shared with traditional knowledge holders.[146] As such, it is clear that despite the rhetoric of prior informed consent and the accompanying assumption that such consent could be declined, the Act does not place traditional knowledge holders in a position to control the use and exploitation of traditional knowledge. Rather, in the last instance it falls as something to be controlled by the state. This is consistent with the CBD's strong assertions of national sovereignty over natural resources.[147]

This centralisation is moderated somewhat by the involvement within the scheme for committees operating at the local level. It is in this particular context that the Act has become a touchstone around which claims to sovereignty over traditional knowledge by local communities have been made. The Act gives effect to some of the demands made by local communities while denying others. It provides that a Biodiversity Management Committee (BMC) is to be constituted in all 'local bodies', a term which includes all forms of local self-government provided for under the Constitution or any national or state Act (including 'panchayats', the village councils of which more will be said shortly).[148] The role of these committees is to facilitate the preservation, sustainable use and documentation of biological diversity and related knowledge at the local level.[149] This participation can be read in two ways. On the one hand, it could be argued that the provisions enable local people to be heard on matters concerning their traditional knowledge and even for their customary law to be taken into account since, in many cases, the village panchayat is likely to be representative of traditional knowledge-holding communities. Indeed, as we will see shortly, claims to sovereignty by and for traditional knowledge holders often draw explicitly on the village panchayat as the representative or carrier of this

145 Ibid., s 21.
146 Ibid.
147 Convention on Biological Diversity 1992, arts 3 and 15.
148 Biological Diversity Act 2002 (India), s 41, s 2.
149 Ibid., s 41(1).

sovereignty. On the other hand, it could be argued that the establishment of BMCs provides a mode by which local communities can be brought within the system but managed such that their involvement is marginal and subordinate.

Tellingly, in terms of access to resources, no substantive powers are conferred on the BMCs. It is sufficient only that they be consulted.[150] In the end, it is the NBA or SBB to which applications for, or notifications of, access must be made and which decide whether access should be granted, restricted or prohibited.[151] While in individual cases it may be that the national or state bodies would defer to the wishes of the relevant BMC, they remain free to make determinations contrary to those wishes. Another role designated to BMCs involves establishing community-level registers of traditional knowledge.[152] The purpose of such registers is to prevent knowledge being lost as traditional practices dwindle. It also provides a readily available bank of information which could be used to prevent traditional knowledge becoming patented, by making it easier to prove its status as 'prior art'. However, it also has the capacity to function as a database of knowledge rendered in a form ripe for commercial exploitation and as such plays a role in a process in which, once more, the knowledge of local communities is wrested from its traditional context and turned into a tradeable commodity.

150 Ibid., s 41(2).

151 Under the Act, foreigners must apply to and obtain consent from the NBA before obtaining and using the resource: ibid., ss 3, 4, 6. Locals must notify and can use the resource unless, following the notification, the relevant SBB decides to prohibit or restrict it: ibid., ss 7, 24.

152 Ibid., s 41(1). Indeed, under the Biological Diversity Rules 2004 (India), r 22(6), preparing the registers is noted as the BMC's 'main function'. The issue of documenting traditional knowledge came up frequently in WIPO's fact-finding mission on traditional knowledge, and specifically in the case of India and Sri Lanka, where '[most] stakeholders stated a need for TK documentation ... but emphasized that the increasing reluctance of certain TK holders to divulge their knowledge and their opposition to documentation of TK ... due to inappropriate management of IPRs during the documentation process': World Intellectual Property Organisation, *Intellectual Property Needs and Expectations*, p. 102.

3.2.2 The sovereign claims made by traditional knowledge holders

It is against the backdrop sketched above that we can begin to understand the nature of the claims by local and indigenous communities to sovereignty over their traditional knowledge. Our first example comes from the RFSTE, now known as Navdanya, which, under the leadership of Vandana Shiva, works closely with local communities in a range of political and environmental projects. Writing in the period between India's accession to the CBD and the enactment of the Biological Diversity Act 2002, Shiva and her co-authors noted that under the CBD, biological diversity is 'treated as the sovereign property of the country of origin.'[153] However, according to Shiva *et al.*:

> under the new political climate of decentralisation through the 73rd Amendment to the Constitution as well as liberalisation, it becomes necessary to define biodiversity property rights through the sovereign rights of local communities and traditional practitioners, working in partnership with states to regulate external access to these resources, while being free of state interference in their internal use and management.[154]

The immediate concern of these authors was the imminent reforms required by TRIPS – referred to in the quote above obliquely as 'liberalisation'. For them, it was necessary first to protect the rights of local communities and traditional knowledge holders before enabling patenting of medicinal and agricultural products in the Patents Act 1970. They argued that 'sovereign biodiversity rights, embodying both biological and intellectual heritage' must be recognised as existing prior to, and take priority over, intellectual property rights, otherwise the latter become an 'infringement

153 Vandana Shiva, Afsar Jafri, Gitanjali Bedi and Radha Holla-Bhar, *The Enclosure and Recovery of the Commons: Biodiversity, Indigenous Knowledge and Intellectual Property Rights*, New Delhi: Research Foundation for Science, Technology and Ecology, 1997, p. 158.

154 Ibid., p. 159; see also p. 7.

and violation of sovereignty.'[155] Their reference to the 73rd amendment to the Constitution is to the reforms in the early 1990s in which the local government structures known as gram sabhas (village communities) and gram panchayats (village councils) were recognised in the Indian Constitution. I will touch on these later in this section and then in more detail in Chapter 5.

The claims made in the terms provided by Shiva and her colleagues clearly depend on the community being able to claim authority independently and on its own account. Although, as we will see in Chapter 5, the authority claimed exists in a close relation with that of the state, it is not derived from the state's authority. Their proposals for the law relating to traditional knowledge are 'essentially based in the idea of sovereignty of the community.'[156] For example, Shiva and Jalees have advocated the creation of Community Biodiversity Registers which would, among other things, provide 'the community with a means to assert rightful sovereign control over what is their own.'[157] By contrast to the scheme under the Biological Diversity Act 2002, in which communities are enjoined to create local registers as a way of documenting knowledge but cede ultimate control over it to national or state biodiversity boards, Community Biodiversity Registers would be 'owned by the community', giving them 'the right to set the ethics and laws for biodiversity governance and management, including siting disputes (even … international disputes) at the community level.'[158] In making such a claim, it is clear that Shiva and her colleagues are asserting that the community has the right to determine law, not merely that they should have substantive rights recognised in national law. This is the case

155 Ibid., p. 159.

156 Vandana Shiva and Kunwar Jalees, *Seeds of Suicide: The Ecological and Human Costs of Seed Monopolies and Globalisation of Agriculture*, 4th ed., New Delhi: Navdanya, 2006, p. 274. According to Shiva and Jalees, the 'concept of Community Intellectual Rights and Community Biodiversity Registers was initiated by RFSTE/Navdanya and other groups in the '80s and has since been developed in diverse ways by various groups, NGOs and communities to express diverse priorities': p. 274 (fn).

157 Ibid., p. 275.

158 Ibid.

even as they also assert that national law should give effect to these rights.[159] Indeed, the claim that national law should recognise local community sovereignty does not mean that it is derived from the state's authority. Just as the WTO's sovereign claim operates by making demands on various national legislators, it can be argued that the claims of traditional knowledge holders are no less sovereign for the fact that they seek recognition and enforcement by national legislation.

Further, like the WTO, the sovereignty of traditional knowledge holders in Shiva's terms includes the exclusive power to determine disputes. For example, in 1999 the RFSTE prepared draft letters on behalf of local communities to W.R. Grace and Co. and RiceTec Inc., purporting to declare invalid various patents on the basis of community law (which would, in the terms asserted, prohibit patenting of traditional knowledge) and to claim exclusive competence to hear any dispute.[160] The letter to W.R. Grace, for example, gives 'notice of the cancellation' of eight United States patents 'based on the piracy of our indigenous

159 Ibid.; see also Shiva, Jafri, Bedi and Holla-Bhar, *Enclosure and Recovery of the Commons*, pp. 155–62.

160 Research Foundation for Science, Technology and Ecology, 'Notices Served to Biopirates', at: http://www.ratical.org/co-globalize/BPandWTO.html (last accessed 6 December 2011). Note, Shiva's organisation has also relied on US and European law to join with other activists in opposing specific patents based on traditional knowledge. Adopting the language of 'piracy' used by intellectual property holders against potential infringers, Shiva has argued that the acquisition of private property rights over traditional knowledge constitutes 'biopiracy' by rich corporations of the knowledge and biological resources of local communities: Vandana Shiva, *Biopiracy: Plunder of Nature and Knowledge*, New Delhi: Research Foundation for Science, Technology and Ecology, 1997, pp. 7–17. One mode of action taken to effect these campaigns has been to challenge the grant of specific patents according to the laws of the issuing state. Since patentable inventions must be novel and include an inventive step in relation to what was previously known (see article 53 of the European Patent Convention (2000)), Shiva and others have been able to demonstrate that certain traditional knowledge formed part of the 'prior art' and as such anticipated the relevant patent. Patents for basmati rice, and products of neem and turmeric have been successfully challenged on this basis: see, e.g., *Thermo Trilogy Corporation's Application*, Case No, T 0416/01, EPO Technical Board of Appeal, 8 March 2005.

knowledge.'[161] In these letters, it is asserted that the 'jaiv panchayat, the local community [structure], is the highest competent authority in matters relating to the utilisation of biodiversity, including dispute resolution arising from misuse and abuse of our knowledge systems and resources.'[162] Adopting the institutional language of the WTO, the letter further demands that the corporation present itself to 'the Dispute Settlement Panel of our Jaiv Panchayat.'[163] As such, the community claims a jurisdictional competence in which the laws of the community and its decisions would take precedence, unmediated through any national or international law or decision-making body. While the practical capacity of the community to compel attendance by the corporations or enforce any judgment may be minimal, the form of the claim gives some clue to its radical nature and the conceptual challenge it poses to the sovereign claim of the state.

The second example comes from a wider campaign issued in the name of traditional knowledge holders themselves (though again with assistance from NGOs), who have asserted community sovereignty over traditional knowledge and biological diversity. In December 2004 the 'Campaign for Community Control over Biodiversity'[164] held a rally in Delhi and issued a 'Memorandum to the Government of India' on behalf of over 200 village communities which protested against the Rules issued under the Biological Diversity Act.[165] The Memorandum stated that the

161 Research Foundation for Science, Technology and Ecology, 'Notices'.

162 Ibid. Much more will be said in Chapter 4 on the political form of the 'panchayat' (or village council) in India. It should be noted that the phrase 'jaiv panchayat', as used in these letters, does not refer strictly to a particular form of village council which exists under Indian law but rather is defined by Shiva and her colleagues as 'living democracy'. In their other work cited in this chapter, however, Shiva and her colleagues rely on the usual form of the panchayat as the locus of sovereignty over community resources.

163 Ibid.

164 A campaign linked to environmental group Kalpavriksh: http://www.kalpavriksh.org/biodiversity/campaign-for-comminity-control-over-biodiversity (last accessed 6 December 2011) (although the list of endorsees of the memorandum includes many other groups).

165 'Community Control over Biodiversity: Memorandum to the Government of India', 8 December 2004, submitted by 200 Gram Panchayats and gram sabhas

Act and the Rules 'do not adequately recognise communities' sovereignty over their resources and knowledge.'[166] Contrary to the Minister's statement in Parliament that local groups had been consulted and had their views taken into account,[167] the Memorandum claims that the 'starting point of the discussion and legislation on conservation and control of biological resources and knowledge has not been initiated at the local level' but rather that the Act and the Rules are 'a response to international treaty obligations under the Convention on Biological Diversity.'[168] Moreover, the Memorandum states, submissions made to the Minister during the public consultation period 'were completely ignored.'[169]

One specific failure of the Act and its Rules, according to the Memorandum, is that community consent is not a precondition of access to biological resources.[170] Rather, as we saw above, local communities, through BMCs, are given only the right to be consulted about access and to give advice.[171] According to the Memorandum, it is this, the failure to 'facilitate community decision making and control' over 'resources and knowledge' which means that the Rules 'are not a step towards community sovereignty.'[172] In April 2007, the Campaign for Community

of Chhattisgarh, Madhya Pradesh, Andhra Pradesh, Karnataka, Tamil Nadu, and Uttaranchal, along with Kalpavriksh, Gene Campaign, People's Alliance for Livelihood Rights, Deccan Development Society, Centre For World Solidarity, Green Foundation, Delhi Forum and Beej Bachao Andolan, on behalf of the Campaign on Community Control over Biodiversity, at: http://www.ddsindia.com/www/Biodiversity rules rally report_link MoEF.htm (last accessed 6 December 2011). On the rally, see 'Biodiversity Act, Rules opposed' in *The Hindu*, 8 December 2004, at: http://www.hindu.com/2004/12/08/stories/2004120815390300.htm (last accessed 6 December 2011).

166 Community Memorandum.

167 Parliament of India, 'Consideration of the Biological Diversity Bill, 2001' Lok Sabha Debates, 2 December 2002, at: http://164.100.47.132/LssNew/psearch/Result13.aspx?dbsl=4790 (last accessed 6 December 2011).

168 Community Memorandum.

169 Ibid.

170 Ibid.

171 Ibid. See Biological Diversity Rules 2004 (India), r 17 (and on advice, r 7).

172 Community Memorandum.

Control over Biodiversity wrote to the Prime Minister of India, complaining that 'no action' had been taken in response to the Memorandum. The letter referred to over 3000 resolutions which had been issued to the Prime Minister from village panchayats in which they resolved not to participate in the system set out under the Act by refusing to constitute BMCs. Again, the clear emphasis in the letter was that the Act and its Rules have failed to recognise adequately the rights of local communities to control the nature and terms of access to biological resources and traditional knowledge. This was reflected in the draft resolution prepared by the Campaign which was used as a template for those issued by local communities. It stated that '[c]ontrol over all aspects of local biodiversity and related knowledge must be with the local communities' and that 'all relevant government institutions must recognise existing social formations and customary groups that are the real biodiversity managers.'[173]

Like the claims made through Shiva and her colleagues, the claims made by traditional knowledge holders through the Campaign for Community Control over Biodiversity take the form of an autopositioned sovereign claim to determine law. While they are more focused in that they respond directly to the Biological Diversity Act 2002 and in particular, advocate changes to the Rules made under it, they nevertheless proceed from the basis that the community is the body which holds the rights to determine the law that applies to traditional knowledge. This can be seen not simply through the use of the term 'sovereignty' in the Memorandum, but also in the fact that the claim that '[c]ontrol over all aspects of local biodiversity and related knowledge must be with the local communities' is combined with a demand that the primacy of 'existing social formations and customary groups' with respect to biological diversity and associated

173 Campaign for Community Control over Biodiversity, 'Resolution Regarding the Biological Diversity Rules 2004', kindly provided to the author by Kanchi Kohli of Kalpavriksh, copy on file; see also Campaign for Community Control over Biodiversity, 'Letter to the Prime Minister of India', 27 April 2007, at: www.ddsindia.com/www/Campaign letter to the PM.pdf (last accessed 6 December 2011).

knowledge be recognised. As such, the demand for recognition of local communities' sovereignty is, once again, not simply a matter concerning certain substantive rights, but seeks to place the community as the starting point for the formation of law relating to traditional knowledge. In making the claim in these terms, the Campaign asserts that the community has the authority to declare itself sovereign over the law relating to traditional knowledge. This authority can only come from the community itself.

In both examples, the specific form of community in which sovereignty over traditional knowledge is claimed to rest is the village-level community known as the gram sabha, represented by the village council, the gram panchayat.[174] Gram sabha literally refers to all the members of a village community (sometimes restricted to those of a certain age). The term 'panchayat' derives from the Sanskrit term 'Panchayatan', meaning a group of five (including a spiritual man) appointed or elected to govern

174 See Shiva and Jalees, *Seeds of Suicide*, p. 275; Shiva, Jafri, Bedi and Holla-Bhar, *Enclosure and Recovery of the Commons*, pp. 126–7. The analysis here and in Chapter 5 focuses on the panchayat as the particular institutional form of the community in which its political authority is vested. It should be noted, however, that the panchayat is not accepted as the only institutional form relevant to community autonomy, particularly in tribal or adivasi areas. In such settings other forms of local authority derived from tribal law are asserted as prime. Nonetheless, in the case of tribal institutions, a similar dynamic between the state and the local community to that which exists in the case of panchayats is evident – a dynamic between locally asserted institutions and norms and the provision under the Indian Constitution for such groups (called 'Scheduled Tribes' and 'Scheduled Areas'). One example of legislation dealing specifically with the community-based rights tribal peoples is the Scheduled Tribes and Other Traditional Forest Dwellers (Recognition of Forest Rights) Act 2006 (India). The Panchayats (Extension to the Scheduled Areas) Act 1996 (India), which I will discuss in some detail in Chapter 5, provides a bridge between the provisions applicable to 'ordinary' rural villages and those applicable in tribal areas. As such, while in the remainder of this book I will not discuss many of the specific provisions applicable only to tribal people, I would suggest that the debates over the role of panchayats is in many cases applicable to them, and in cases where it is not directly applicable, a useful analogy can still be drawn there concerning the relation between local and national sovereignty.

the village.[175] Over time, the inclusion of a designated spiritual man ended and the term panchayat came to refer to 'a group of any five selected persons of the village to decide village disputes.'[176] For Shiva and her colleagues, the 'village community or gram sabha represents the basic unit of the self-governing system' and is 'an autonomous, self-reliant entity.'[177] The panchayat as an institution of community authority is also relied on in the work of the Campaign for Community Control over Biodiversity.[178] The Memorandum grounds authority in the gram sabha and panchayat and indeed was written in the name of, and submitted by, over 200 gram panchayats and gram sabhas. Similarly, the resolutions which were sent to the Prime Minister through the Campaign in 2007 were passed by over 3000 gram panchayats, each asserting the empowerment of gram sabhas as the form of community in which control over biodiversity and traditional knowledge should be vested.[179] As such, in the terms advanced in this book, the gram sabha and panchayat constitute the site of autopositioned sovereignty, being the locus of a legal authority which is not grounded any higher authority.

Like the claims made for the nation, claims by local communities are made in absolute and ultimate terms and yet rely on the transcendent notion of 'community', which even in the smallest setting, can never be finally and fully determined or present to itself.[180] As such, it can only be spoken for by representatives. The authority of the community is also posited as indivisible since the community itself is regarded as the irreducible element of political life. And yet, particularly as we will see in Chapter 5, it is dependent on a complex relation with the state. The claim of traditional knowledge holders is one to determine law while

175 M. R. Biju, *Resurgent Rural India: Decade after the Constitutionalisation of Panchayati Raj*, Delhi: Authors Press, 2007, p. 11.

176 Ibid.

177 Shiva, Jafri, Bedi and Holla-Bhar, *Enclosure and Recovery of the Commons*, p. vii.

178 See Community Memorandum. Campaign for Community Control over Biodiversity, 'Letter to the Prime Minister'.

179 Campaign for Community Control over Biodiversity, 'Letter to the Prime Minister'.

180 Fitzpatrick, *Modernism*, pp. 116–17.

being grounded in law, and hence it brings within itself the vacuity of law. Finally, it seeks to ground itself in 'community' as if the local community simply 'exists' and can be taken for granted (like Bodin's commonwealth). However, like Bodin's commonwealth, the modern nation and the WTO, the existence of the local community as a juridical entity depends on the very claim to sovereignty which it purportedly grounds.

As we saw in Chapter 1, the existence of such tensions exposes the self-grounded nature of the sovereign claim of the state and thus makes any instantiation of sovereignty open to question. Just as the state cannot guarantee its position in the purity of the nation for which it claims to speak, local communities cannot ultimately justify their claim to sovereignty on the basis of some pure, originary or unmediated representation of community. As such, the claims to sovereignty of local communities are similarly open to question. But, that does not mean that such communities lack sovereignty. Rather, it means that both sites of sovereignty can be called into question and that the relation between them cannot be determined by a common superior. As such, their position exists and can only be maintained in relation to each other.

Conclusion

The self-grounded nature of autopositioned sovereignty opens the possibility that sovereignty can reside in places other than the state. In this chapter, I have attempted to set out a theoretical framework in defence of 'autopositioned' sovereignty and argued that the form of such a claim can be witnessed in the claims to authority by both the WTO and traditional knowledge holders. Put simply, they are claims to ultimate authority to determine the law of a community. They are not derived from nor subject to any other site of authority but, rather are self-grounded. Returning to Derrida's terminology, each claims the ability to give 'itself its own law'.[181] In the case of the WTO, its constituent documents mark the moment at which the institution became more than the

181 Derrida, *Rogues*, p. 11.

sum of its parts and transcended the authority of any of its member states. Moreover, the ongoing ability of the organs of its dispute settlement procedure to determine the scope and meaning of the requirements of its treaties means that it is not subject to any other authority. In respect of patent law, the WTO's enforcement mechanisms are brought to bear on a number of very specific requirements. While the specificity varies (and, as we will see, tracking the precise variations is crucial to understanding the boundary between the claim of the WTO and of the state), this specificity means that the scope of the claim to determine the detail of member states' patent law is quite extensive. In the case of traditional knowledge holders, the village community or 'gram sabha' is claimed to constitute an autonomous site of authority and to operate as the basic unit of legal and political life. It is said to lack any dependence on the state and to be able to generate and apply its own legal prescriptions for the transmission and use of traditional knowledge.

In invoking the concepts of community and law, the autopositioning of sovereignty is revealed as something more than a simple assertion. It is in the complex dynamic between these three concepts that modern sovereignty comes to be positioned. More precisely, law and community both demand and undermine the claim of an autopositioned sovereign. This claim must be made in absolute terms if the sovereign is to play its part in determining, for the time being, law's content and the boundaries of the community for which it claims to speak. And yet, sovereignty's dependence on law and community mean that an autopositioned sovereign claim can never be as complete as it claims to be, since the responsive dimensions of law and community resist ultimate determination and capture.

Finally, if, as we saw above, a sovereign can rely on no higher authority than itself to justify its own position, then no other entity can be called on to determine rival claims to sovereign authority. This means that the rivalry between national sovereignty and the sovereign claims of the WTO or of local communities in India can only be 're-solved' (in the most provisional sense) by their relation to each other. It cannot be resolved by privileging the nation as the exclusive or originary position of sovereignty. As such, the question of the relation between sovereign positions takes on special significance. But before moving directly to these examples, the question of this relation requires some further elaboration. The relation between sovereign positions plays a constitutive role in what they are. In the next chapter, I will argue that while modern sovereignty is autopositioned, we should not assume that the assertion of sovereignty itself is somehow the prime and originating moment from which all else flows. Rather, I will argue the self-grounded assertion of sovereign position inevitably occurs in a context already saturated by relation. This will further undermine the notion of a pure and exclusive concept of national sovereignty. It will also undermine the notion that the challenges made to national sovereignty, such as those coming from the WTO or local communities, somehow need to out-do the claim of the state by being older or more 'original' in order to have any validity.

Part 2

Relation

Chapter 3

The Constitutive Function of Relation

> 'The very simplicity of "position" implies no more, although no less, than its being discrete, in ... its distinction *from*, in the sense of *with*, other (at least possible) positions.'[1]

Introduction

In Part 1 I put into question the idea that the nation-state is the exclusive occupant of the sovereign position in modernity and tried to show how modern sovereignty is autopositioned. In doing so, I have emphasised how that sovereign autopositioning occurs in relation to community and law. In this Part, I will consider how these autopositioned sovereignties relate to each other. However, this turn to relation should not be seen to indicate a sharp distinction between position and relation; as if position is somehow constitutive of what sovereignty 'is', and relation is something than we can observe positioned sovereigns 'doing'. Rather, the purpose is to investigate the constitutive function of relation itself in how sovereignties come to be positioned.

Intimations of the importance of relation can be observed in the analysis in Chapter 1. In the discussion of indivisibility we

1 Jean-Luc Nancy, *Being Singular Plural*, trs Robert Richardson and Anne O'Byrne, Stanford: Stanford University Press, 2000, p. 12 (original emphasis).

observed how the purported indivisibility of Bodin's sovereignty is exposed by its constitutive relation to its subjects, to law and to God. This dependence on subjects, law and a transcendent concept was also seen to be constitutive of the sovereignty of nation. All of this could be seen to go to a relation of forces within the community of a particular sovereign. But we also briefly observed how nation itself came to be constituted in opposition to that which it was not. It is this mode of relation – a relation between (rather than within) rival sites of authority – on which this chapter will chiefly focus. Of course, as we go it will become apparent that the distinction between inside and outside is quite murky. In Chapter 2, which focused on Derrida's conception of 'autopositioning', we came across the concept of ipseity, described by Derrida as the 'power that *gives itself* its own law, its self-representation, the sovereign and reappropriating gathering of the self in the simultaneity of an assemblage or assembly, being together, or "living together", as we say.'[2] In Chapter 2, I focused on the first part of this statement and on the concept of the 'I can' as revelatory of the way sovereignty is positioned.[3]

In this chapter, I will focus on the second part of Derrida's definition of 'ipseity', the idea that the gathering of the self (autopositioning) occurs 'in the simultaneity of an assemblage or assembly, being together, or "living together"'.[4] That is, I will focus on the constitutive quality of being-together in Derrida's conception of sovereign autopositioning. However, in his work on sovereignty, Derrida himself does not address directly the question of the nature and quality of our being-together.[5] For this reason,

2 Jacques Derrida, *Rogues: Two Essays on Reason*, trs Pascale-Anne Brault and Michael Naas, Stanford: Stanford University Press, 2005, p. 11 (his emphasis).

3 Ibid.; see also Jacques Derrida, *Without Alibi*, tr. Peggy Kamuf, Stanford: Stanford University Press, 2002, p. 275.

4 Derrida, *Rogues*, p. 11.

5 For some reflections on broader themes around this question, see Derrida, *Rogues*, pp. 56–61; Jacques Derrida, 'Faith and Knowledge: The Two Sources of "Religion" at the Limits of Reason Alone', tr. Samuel Weber, in Jacques Derrida, *Acts of Religion*, ed. Gil Anidjar, New York: Routledge, 2002, p. 93 and Jacques Derrida, *The Politics of Friendship*, tr. George Collins, London: Verso, 2005,

in this chapter, I will draw heavily on Jean-Luc Nancy, whose work on community we encountered in Chapter 2. The question of our being-together is at the heart of Nancy's work. By the same token, Nancy's focus on this question means that he doesn't engage as fully as Derrida with the question of sovereign position.[6] For him, the fact of our being-together and the complexity of that relation means that fixed positions are impossible and those which appear quite stable are always in the process of being unravelled. His emphasis is on exposing the impossibility of the Enlightenment notion of the individual as the irreducible starting point of social and political life and of the community as its product.[7] In doing so, his work constitutes a major corrective to conventional Enlightenment philosophy of the subject. But in focusing on the impossibility of assured and originary singularity (and hence on singularity's limits) the inclination of his work tends away from the assertion of position to the point at which it could be argued he neglects it.

As such, it is by reading Derrida and Nancy together that the dynamic between sovereign position and relation is best explored. This chapter will focus on the importance of relation for autopositioning. But in turn autopositioning may provide an answer to the question Nancy himself poses about the implications of his theory on sovereignty. Nancy asks: 'If sovereignty is the grand, political term for defining community (its leader or its essence) that has nothing beyond itself, with no foundation or end but itself, what becomes of sovereignty when it is revealed that it is nothing but a singularly plural spacing?'[8] It may provide an answer because the theory of sovereign autopositioning enables

pp. 80–3; Jacques Derrida, *The Beast and the Sovereign (Volume II)*, tr. Geoffrey Bennington, Chicago: University of Chicago Press, 2011, 258–90.

6 The closest would be in Chapter 2 of Nancy, *Being Singular Plural*, pp. 101–43, entitled: 'War, Right, Sovereignty – Techne'.

7 Jean-Luc Nancy, *The Inoperative Community*, ed. and tr. Peter Connor, Minneapolis: University of Minnesota Press, 1991, pp. 3–35.

8 Nancy, *Being Singular Plural*, p. 36.

one to think through the dynamic of this spacing and how it relates to concrete claims to sovereignty by particular entities.[9]

This chapter will focus on considering the importance of relation primarily in the context of the claim to sovereign completeness conventionally ascribed to the nation-state. The key element of that claim is that nation-states are absolute, sovereign, singular entities which have an existence prior to and independent of their relation to each other and that which they are not. This claim makes possible the view that the existence of nation-states is an empirical fact which precedes the system of international relations and international law. In the first section of this chapter I will set out the conventional view and show that it has support in the work of key early theorists of sovereignty and international law.

I will then note the way in which the claim to self-contained completeness is a feature of the sovereign claims of the World Trade Organisation and of local and indigenous communities. This draws largely on the same terms that we saw enabled their classification as autopositioned claims in Chapter 2. I will argue that because every sovereign claim involves a self-grounded, ultimate claim to determine the identity of the community whose sovereign it 'is', it comes as no surprise that this community (be it 'nation', 'WTO members' or 'local community') is presented as fully bounded and complete in and of itself.

9 One has to be careful here, because this would not necessarily be Nancy's answer (or, perhaps more precisely, it is an answer in different terms to the one Nancy would provide, even if the two are substantially consistent). At times, when Nancy addresses himself directly to the question of sovereignty, he seems to want to move towards its complete dissolution and abandonment: see ibid., pp. 138, 142–3. But the figure of sovereignty he argues should be abandoned is the conventional one which is similarly under attack in this book. At other times, Nancy draws heavily on Bataille's conception of sovereignty as nothing (which takes him very close to the usage here – where sovereignty lacks a solid foundation): see ibid., pp. 35–6 and Nancy, *Inoperative Community*, pp. 16–20. Further, my usage of sovereignty is very close to Nancy's conception of singularity, so where Nancy would use those terms in opposition (singularity opposed to conventional sovereignty), I would use them together (sovereignty recast in terms of Nancy's conception of singularity).

I will then subject this claim to a thorough critique, but this critique is directed not towards showing that the claim to absoluteness itself is wrong. We saw in Chapter 1 that the claim to absoluteness is an integral feature of the sovereign claim, but one which could never be realised in the terms claimed. Sovereign claims must be made in absolute terms if they are to do the work required of them (i.e. to be able to cut through the vacuity and changefulness of community and law to render both in determinate form for the time being). But I also argued that it was impossible precisely because of this vacuity and changefulness. In the second section of this chapter, Nancy's work will be used to show how the dynamic of relation similarly reveals sovereign absoluteness to be imperative and impossible. Just as the vacuity of community and law make a sovereign's claim to complete power of determination both impossible and imperative, so too does the dynamic of relation require the sovereign assertion of position even if relation's restlessness makes such an assertion impossible to realise enduringly.

In the third section of this chapter I will build on this analysis to show that the constitution of nation-state sovereignty occurred in the relation between states and in the process of distinguishing the state from that which was other to it. I will show how this is revealed by the very theorists often used to support the conventional view and also in the historical event most commonly called on to show how the purportedly autarchic state emerged: the Peace of Westphalia. Throughout, the story will be one of mutual constitution, or, to use Nancy's term: 'co-appearance' – in which the sovereign position of any entity is dependent on its relation to others. I will also argue that because this relation is always in operation, sovereign autoposition must constantly be reasserted.

1 The Absolute Sovereign and its Closed Community?

1.1 Nation-states as pure empirical facts?

In conventional treatments of the subject, sovereign statehood is taken to have two aspects. One faces inwards. This is the internal or domestic aspect of sovereign authority. It refers to the power of a sovereign ruler over the population and territory of a given space on the earth. The second faces outwards. This is the external aspect of sovereignty. It refers to the capacity of a sovereign to represent its population and territory in interactions with other sovereigns. In the classical view of international law, internal sovereignty is a precondition, both philosophically and practically, of external sovereignty. And so, international law comes to be regarded as deriving from the pre-existence of states each with sovereigns having achieved the requisite level of domestic authority. In this section, I will first set out an example of this conventional view and then show how support for it can be found in the work of luminaries such as Bodin, Vitoria, Grotius, Pufendorf, Vattel and Rousseau.[10]

The example of a conventional view of classical international law used here is that provided by Robert Jackson.[11] For Jackson, the 'starting point of international relations undoubtedly is empirical statehood.'[12] He writes that in Machiavelli, Bodin and Hobbes, one can see a political theory based on the state being 'an independent reality in the world.'[13] Jackson's concern with empiricism would make this independence a double one. The early modern states were not only independent, it would seem, from each other or any superior power, but also from political theory. Both then and now, it would follow that the existence and authority of states cannot be put into question. In support of his conception of early modern states as empirical facts, Jackson observes that the 'earliest modern states such as France and England or rather Francis I and Henry VIII were palpable political realities internally and in their neighbourhoods' adding that only by

10 I will begin with Bodin, rather than Vitoria (who preceded him), because of how central Bodin's work is to this book (see Chapter 1) and also because Bodin stands somewhat apart in this company since he does not expressly engage with the relations between states.

11 Robert Jackson, *Quasi-states: Sovereignty, International Relations and the Third World*, Cambridge: Cambridge University Press, 1990.

12 Ibid., p. 51.

13 Ibid.

pretence could one have 'den[ied] their existence'.[14] And yet, while the concern with 'facts' would make it appear that we need not be concerned with legitimacy, we find that legitimacy follows in any event. Drawing on an 'empirical view of morality' in which 'morality arises out of the facts of human existence', he finds by virtue of 'a small step', legitimacy soon follows the bare fact of sovereign statehood.[15] For Jackson, the fact that humans 'can collide' in 'the pursuit of their desires ... lays the groundwork of common morality and law which seeks to regulate the use of power and to reduce collisions and therefore harm.'[16] Jackson finds that '[c]lassical international legitimacy and law operate the same way' that is, on the basis of 'the reality of multiple sovereign powers each possessed of pride and capable of doing or suffering harm.'[17] On this view, the reality of sovereign powers precedes the law that exists to regulate their behaviour; '[c]lassical international law is therefore the child and not the parent of states.'[18]

There is a certain philosophical pedigree to the notion that states are entities of their own creation, and that international law is derived from them. Bodin's treatise on sovereignty chiefly concerns the relationship between the sovereign and its subjects. In attempting to ground sovereignty in a 'commonwealth', Bodin finds a place for sovereignty cast in terms of it being a complete and singular jurisdiction, dependent on no higher authority than

14 Ibid.
15 Ibid., p. 52.
16 Ibid.
17 Ibid.
18 Ibid., p. 53. Jackson contrasts this with the situation after World War Two, where countries in the Third World were granted sovereignty by operation of international law and could not have, in his view, qualified on the basis of their own power. While this may seem to complicate the idea that international law is derived from state sovereignty, for Jackson it reveals two different kinds of sovereignty. The sovereignty of established states is termed 'positive' sovereignty and flows from the presence of effective domestic authority. The authority of states created by international law is known as negative sovereignty (merely a formal sovereignty concerned with non-interference) and the states themselves are termed 'quasi-states'. As such, true or complete sovereignty remains something which, for Jackson, would precede international law.

that of itself and of God; a place where the sovereign alone has the power to 'give law to all' and 'not to receive law from anyone but God.'[19] Vitoria describes an independent commonwealth (one in which the right to wage war resides) as 'one which is complete in itself' and 'self sufficient' in that it 'is not part of another commonwealth, but has its own laws, its own independent policy, and its own magistrates.'[20] In a similar vein, Grotius defines the state as 'a *compleat* Body of free Persons, associated together to enjoy peaceably their Rights, and for their common Benefit.'[21] Pufendorf writes that a king to whom authority has been conferred by the body politic 'owes his Dignity and his Empire to no Foreign Power, so he need not wait for the Consent and Approbation of other Princes or States, in order to [assume] the Actions or the Character proper to his office.'[22] Vattel, echoing Vitoria, finds the condition of statehood arises where a political entity is 'really sovereign and independent' in that 'it must govern itself by its own authority and laws' and 'without dependence on any foreign power.'[23] This lack of dependence is also a feature of Rousseau's ideal sovereign state. He writes that a well constituted state, one fit to legislate for itself, is 'one that can do without other nations and which every other nation can do without.'[24] A similar sense of self-contained completeness can be found in the sovereign claims of the WTO and traditional knowledge holders. I will

19 Jean Bodin, *On Sovereignty: Four Chapters from the Six Books of the Commonwealth*, ed. and tr. Julian Franklin, Cambridge: Cambridge University Press, 1992, p. 59 (see also p. 49).

20 Francisco de Vitoria, *Political Writings*, eds Anthony Pagden and Jeremy Lawrence, Cambridge: Cambridge University Press, 1991, p. 301.

21 Hugo Grotius, *The Rights of War and Peace*, ed. Richard Tuck, Indianapolis: Liberty Fund, 2004, vol 1, p. 162 (my emphasis).

22 Samuel Pufendorf, *On the Law of Nature and Nations, Eight Books*, tr. Basil Kennet, 3rd ed., London, 1717, p. 489.

23 Emer de Vattel, *The Law of Nations*, ed. Joseph Chitty, Philadelphia: Johnson & Co, 1863, p. 2. See George Cavallar, *The Rights of Strangers: Theories of International Hospitality, the Global Community, and Political Justice since Vitoria*, Aldershot: Ashgate, 2002, p. 310.

24 Jean-Jacques Rousseau, *The Social Contract*, tr. Christopher Betts, Oxford: Oxford University Press, 1994, p. 86. See Peter Fitzpatrick, *Modernism and the Grounds of Law*, Cambridge: Cambridge University Press, 2001, pp. 148–50.

turn to these before making the case, in theoretical terms, that such self-contained completeness is impossible and that the relation between sovereigns is an essential constitutive element in their (auto)positioning.

1.2 The WTO: a perfect community?

In Chapter 2 I argued that the WTO can be seen to make an autopositioned sovereign claim over the law of its member states. I argued that the WTO's constitutive documents illustrate certain key characteristics of the claim, in particular the claim to govern through law. I also relied on the terms of the dispute settlement procedure to show how the WTO arrogates singular, absolute and ultimate authority to determine the meaning of the law of its community.

If sovereignty can be understood as an autopositioned claim to determine the law of a community, the quality of absoluteness which is entailed within that claim encompasses both the identity of the community and its law. In the case of the community of WTO members, it might be thought that the identity of the community is simply and only determined by the question of whether a particular state has agreed to become bound by its agreements. Certainly the WTO presents itself as the product of the perfect consent of its member states.[25] Together, through their consent to the agreements, these member states constitute a community whose terms are, on their face, fully determined by those agreements. This would appear to be a community closed in by the terms of the agreements.

However, such a view presupposes two things which this chapter and those that follow will seek to disprove. The first is that WTO members are themselves closed and complete entities whose existence is a mere fact which precedes their capacity to enter (and the fact of entering) into international agreements. That concerns the question of the absoluteness of nation which will be the focus

25 World Trade Organisation, 'Who's WTO is it anyway?' at: http://www.wto.org/english/thewto_e/whatis_e/tif_e/org1_e.htm (last accessed 6 December 2011).

of the final part of this chapter. The second is that the WTO agreements themselves create a fixed and closed identity for their members in terms of the obligations imposed. As I intimated in Chapter 2 and will discuss in more detail in Chapter 4, entering into the WTO agreements changes what it means to be a sovereign state. Moreover, this meaning changes with every challenge and change to the legal rights and responsibilities of member states under WTO law. If, as I have argued, the WTO claims ultimate authority to determine the meaning of WTO law, then by extension it claims authority to determine what it means to be a member of the WTO. That identity is not determined automatically, by the agreements themselves, without the imposition of a sovereign claim. What demands that claim, as we will see, is the dynamic of relation.

1.3 The fixed and stable local community?

The claims by local and indigenous communities also, by their very nature, imagine the community as a fixed, stable and complete ground. As we saw above, for Shiva and her colleagues the 'village community or gram sabha represents the basic unit of the self-governing system' and is 'an autonomous, self-reliant entity.'[26] The community's identity is, much like that of the nation-state, presumed to be an empirical fact which precedes other forms of belonging which might engulf it or challenges which might threaten it more directly. In India, this sense is aided by the longevity of the village form and of the councils or 'panchayats' which exercise authority in and over them. No history or collective memory recounts a time in India where the village form and village councils were not in existence. Claims to ground authority in that form, such as the claims by traditional knowledge holders, rely in particular on its having pre-dated the nation itself.

26 Vandana Shiva, Afsar Jafri, Gitanjali Bedi and Radha Holla-Bhar, *The Enclosure and Recovery of the Commons: Biodiversity, Indigenous Knowledge and Intellectual Property Rights*, New Delhi: Research Foundation for Science, Technology and Ecology, 1997, p. vii.

Moreover the village is seen as a bulwark against all manner of impositions. As we will see in Chapter 5, this is a sense shared both by British colonialists and Indian nationalists. Nonetheless, the village form and the village council exist in a complicated relationship to the state, which has at various times attempted to undermine and at others to elevate the significance of local authority structures. Their longevity is testament not only to their endurance and stability but also their ability to adapt. They are affected, indeed constituted, by their relation to other forms of community and authority. This will be demonstrated in theoretical terms below and pursued in context in Chapter 5.

2 The Impossibility of Absolute Sovereign Position

In this section I will set out a theoretical exposition and defence of the argument that the sovereign's claimed quality of absoluteness is compromised and yet demanded by the constitutive function of relation. First, I will argue that the inescapability of relation makes it impossible for any entity to be absolute unto itself. This means that it is impossible for the existence and character of any entity (be it nation-state, international organisation or local community) to precede its relation to other entities. Second, I will consider in more detail Nancy's conception of singularity and how it applies to collective entities. Drawing on this analysis, I will show how the impossibility of a singular entity preceding its relation reveals how singular entities (and therefore sovereignties) co-appear – that is, that the existence of any singular entity (including a collective entity), is always and already dependent on its relation to other entities. This analysis will show that no single entity or form can be, in Sieyès's terms, the 'origin of everything.'[27] It will also show why any position must constantly be reasserted.

27 Emmanuel Sieyès, *Political Writings*, ed. and tr. Michael Sonenscher, Indianapolis: Hackett Publishing Company, 2003, pp. 136–7.

2.1 The logic of the absolute

As Nancy writes, an absolute being would be an entity 'perfectly detached, distinct and closed'; a 'being without relation'.[28] Such a conception of absoluteness, he writes, can be found in notions of the 'Individual' and the 'State', among others.[29] But for Nancy, this kind of absoluteness is impossible. For, not only would the purportedly absolute entity need to be separated from other entities, it would also be necessary for this entity to fully control the circumstances of that separation. This presupposes not only a boundary between it and another entity, but an enclosure of that very boundary itself, such that it was not in contact (and thus not in communication) with another entity.[30] As Nancy writes, the

> absolute must be the absolute of its own absoluteness, or not be at all. In other words: to be absolutely alone, it is not enough that I be so; I must also be alone in being alone – and this of course is contradictory. The logic of the absolute violates the absolute.[31]

The very notion of being alone involves a separation from something. Hence separation is constitutive of the alone-ness which the absolute entity claims as its own and is thus dependent on a relation between the entity that is alone and what it is separated from. Indeed, the notion of a boundary, without which a purportedly absolute entity could not exist, presupposes two sides. That is, it presupposes relation. But this cannot be the relation of more than one absolute. It cannot be, for example, that the relation of nation-states is the relation of a number of absolute entities. The quality of absoluteness would itself deny the very possibility of relation. As Nancy writes, 'one cannot make a world with simple atoms.'[32] And since we are, quite simply, with each other in the

28 Nancy, *Inoperative Community*, p. 4.
29 Ibid.
30 Ibid.
31 Ibid.
32 Ibid., p. 3.

world, relation is inescapable; it is absoluteness which must yield.

For Nancy, the impossibility of absoluteness means that 'a single being is a contradiction in terms. Such a being, which would be its own foundation, origin and intimacy, would be incapable of *Being*...'[33] since all '[e]xistence is with: otherwise nothing exists.'[34] If the absolute detachment of the individual or the state can be shown to be impossible, what does this mean for the possibility of singularity? If we are all enmeshed in an inescapable relation, how is any position or separation possible at all? And since sovereignty is fundamentally a question of the possibility of separation and especially of singularity, what consequences flow from the impossibility of absolute singularity? As we saw in Chapter 1, even if indivisibility (an intense form of singularity) is an impossible characteristic of sovereignty, it is nonetheless an essential one. As Derrida writes, '[s]overeignty is undivided, unshared, or it is not', even as he asks '[w]hat happens when this trait [sovereignty] divides? When it must, when it cannot not divide?'[35]

Sovereignty thus poses the question of the possibility of singularity; and the limits of singularity would in turn constitute the limits of sovereignty. While the logic of the absolute shows that an absolutely singular sovereign is impossible, the inescapability of relation would also show the necessity of some form of singularity – a singularity which is less than absolute. Just as one cannot be alone being alone, neither can relation exist without some notion of singularity. And so, Nancy's emphasis on relation (more specifically, the emphasis on the 'with' of being),[36] does not

33 Nancy, *Being Singular Plural*, p. 12 (original emphasis).

34 Ibid., p. 4 (original emphasis).

35 Derrida, *Without Alibi*, p. xix; Jacques Derrida, *The Beast and the Sovereign (Volume I)*, tr. Geoffrey Bennington, Chicago: University of Chicago Press, 2009, pp. 76–7.

36 In this book, I concentrate on the constitutive function of relation. As such, I use the term 'relation' in a way which is very close to Nancy's conception of 'the with'. However, Nancy distinguishes the concept of 'with' as 'being at once both more and less than "relation" or "bond," especially if such relation

dissolve all notions of distinctness or singularity. If singular beings are not different from one another; that is, if they cannot maintain a position distinct from that of others, then there is nothing to 'relate'. There is just an undifferentiated mass. As such, just as relation is necessary to constitute the singular, so too singular assertion is necessary for the possibility of relation. Consequently, Nancy's emphasis on the impossibility of absolute singularity does not mean that there is no such thing as singularity. And like sovereignty, what makes singularity impossible (an inescapable relation which cannot be finally determined or contained) is what makes it imperative. In the next section, I will examine in more detail Nancy's conception of singularity and will follow that with further reflections on how singularity comes into existence in (or, more precisely, co-appears with) community.

2.2 Singularity

As noted above, the limits of singularity are the limits of sovereignty. For that reason, Nancy's rigorous testing of these limits is very useful in understanding modern sovereignty. However, it is first necessary to clarify the use of terminology. In Chapter 2, we encountered Nancy's conception of community as something which exists because of the inescapable relation of singular beings. Community was seen not to be the product or work of those singularities and nor was it an embodiment of an essence common to them. Rather, it was something which was always oriented towards openness and change. To use Nancy's term (or at least that of his translator) community is inoperative.[37] This made it impossible for community to exist as a solid ground upon which a sovereign claim could be based – and yet its very openness and vacuity created an imperative for sovereign assertion.

or bond presupposes the preexistence of the terms upon which it relies': Nancy, *Being Singular Plural*, p. 34. Nonetheless, a focus on the constitutive function of relation is precisely one that does not presuppose its terms and so the use here is consistent with Nancy's work.

37 See Chapter 2, note 18.

In this chapter, my focus is not the relation between singular beings within a community for which a sovereign claims to speak, but the relation between sovereign positions themselves. When we come to consider the relation between sovereign positions, we are also considering the relation between different 'communities' as instantiated things. In this later context, the community is a form of singularity. This creates potential confusion when using Nancy's terminology, because for him, community is always that which is set against singularity. The way through this potential confusion is to conceive of a community for which the sovereign claims to speak as being a singular collective entity. That entity is cohered by the sovereign claim and as such, carries a determinate form for the time being such that it is able to relate to others. This claim must constantly be reasserted as the sovereign responds to the forces both within and outside (as provisional as these concepts must be[38]) that community. But in the instant of the sovereign's determination, it can be said that the community exists as a singular collective entity. As such, a community for which a sovereign speaks is both an inoperative community which can never be fully and enduringly determined by sovereign determination and, at the same time, a singularity (by virtue of the sovereign claim) which relates to other singularities (other sovereignties) in a larger (inoperative) community. In order to better understand this dynamic, it is necessary to consider in some detail Nancy's conception of singularity.

I will draw out three key points which assist in understanding Nancy's conception of singularity and the implications it has for a theory of sovereignty. First, singularity is something which must be distinguished from the notion of the individual. Second, singularity is always formed in and through the process of communication. Without communication, there can be no singularity. Third, the limit of singularity is constituted through an exposure to (its) finitude. Again, as we will see, this can only happen in the context of relation to other entities and as such, even at its limit singularity, and therefore sovereignty, is dependent on relation.

38 Nancy, *Being Singular Plural*, p. 13: 'The outside is inside.'

First, Nancy's conception of singularity is distinguished from the individual. This is not just the human individual, but also collective entities which purportedly have an individual character. He writes that 'behind the theme of the individual, but beyond it, lurks the question of singularity.'[39] For Nancy, the concept of singularity avoids the essentialising aspects of individualism and enables one to think of the self not as a unified, complete entity, but as something through which multiple subjectivities are in play. Nancy writes that '[a]s for singular differences, they are not only "individual", but infraindividual. It is never the case that I have met Pierre or Marie per se, but I have met him or her in such and such a "form," in such and such a "state," in such and such a "mood," and so on.'[40] This particular example operates to draw one's mind away from modernity's atomistic human individual and towards a more fluid conception of singularity. But the human individual is not the only form against which the concept of singularity is set.[41] Nancy's conception of singularity is also set against the notion of an absolute, complete and contained collective entity – most notably the notion of the state.[42] Nancy refers to 'the impossibility either of an individuality, in the precise sense of the term, or of a pure collective totality.'[43] As such, while the individuality of a collective entity may be impossible for Nancy, a collective entity can, nonetheless, be a singularity.

A second characteristic of Nancy's conception of singularity is that it is formed in and through the process of communication. Nancy describes the communication between singularities as an exposure to one another which occurs through the skin, the heart, or the 'speaking mouth'.[44] Once again we see the motif of human traits, but as we saw above the human is not the only possible

39 Nancy, *Inoperative Community*, p. 6.
40 Nancy, *Being Singular Plural*, p. 8.
41 As Nancy writes, the self is 'not necessarily, or exclusively, an individual': Nancy, *Inoperative Community*, p. xxxvii.
42 Ibid., p. 4. (Note, here he is referring to the 'individual or the *total* State' (my emphasis).)
43 Ibid., p. 6.
44 Ibid., pp. 28, 30–1.

form of singularity. These bodily characteristics are images only, used to evoke a distinction between inside and outside – but not exhaustive of these things. If body parts are exemplary of the distinction between inside and outside, it is only because they reveal that even when determinations of inside and outside are thought to be most natural and fixed, they are actually constructed and mutable.[45] What Nancy's images of bodily characteristics do is to focus attention on the fact that a distinction between inside and outside is necessary for communication to occur. The possibility of inside and outside, of borders and spacing, is what distinguishes communication (and community) from communion. As Nancy writes, communication is 'the constitutive fact of an exposition to an outside that defines singularity.'[46] This applies to collective entities as much as it does to any other form of singularity. In the marking out of borders, the designation of what is inside and what is outside, collective entities (operating through representatives of one kind or another) are necessarily in communication with other entities. Hence such collective entities, or the sovereignties that seek to represent them, cannot be completely self-generating.

The third quality concerns the way in which singularity reaches its limit (and its truth is revealed) through an exposure to finitude. He writes that 'the *singular being*, which is not the individual, is the finite being.'[47] For the human being, finitude is connected to death. My finitude, my mortality, is what marks me as singular. As such, my singularity is revealed only in my death, in what 'precisely is most proper to [me] and most inalienably [my] own'.[48] And yet, this thing which is most my own is not something I can experience. As Nancy writes, 'the *I* cannot say that it

45 See Nancy's reflections on his own heart transplant – a process which provoked a very intimate consideration of what 'he' is and what is 'his'; of what is inside and what is outside: Jean-Luc Nancy, 'L'antrus', tr. Susan Janson, *New Centennial Review* 3(2), 2002, 1.

46 Nancy, *Inoperative Community*, p. 29.

47 Ibid., p. 27 (original emphasis).

48 Ibid., p. 14.

is dead'.[49] Finitude is thus the existence of a limit which can be approached but never experienced. The truth of my finitude (and thus my singularity) is something that is revealed only to others. Similarly, it is only through the death of another that finitude as such (and consequently a sense of my own finitude) is revealed to me. As such, my experience of finitude (even, perhaps especially, my own) is foreign to me. Therefore, what singularity reveals is an irreducible alterity both within and between what we generally call individuals. As Nancy writes, 'I experience the other's alterity, or I experience alterity in the other together with the alteration that "in me" sets my singularity outside me and infinitely delimits it.'[50] And if the truth of our singularity is revealed only to and through others, then it does not exist as such except by communication with others; that is *in* community. At the same time, this irreducible alterity marks a spacing; a spacing which means that community *as communion* is impossible.[51] But this alterity also means that community is possible, indeed imperative, as spacing itself. Again, we find that the limit of singularity is something that can only exist in the context of relation to other entities.

If the finitude of a human being (and hence its singularity) is revealed in his or her death, something else would be need to be the measure of the finitude of a collective entity. That something else is the sovereign claim. As Nancy writes, sovereignty, in its conventional sense, 'is the power of execution or the power of finishing as such, absolutely so and without further subordination to something else (to another end).'[52] As such, what the sovereign claims (in seeking to determine and speak for a collective entity) is a complete and absolute power of finishing or execution. This is how the concept of finitude is related to the singularity of

49 Ibid. (original emphasis).
50 Ibid., p. 33.
51 Ibid., p. 15.
52 Nancy, *Being Singular Plural*, p. 120. I note here that Nancy is using sovereignty 'in the conventional sense' to distinguish this usage from the one he draws from Bataille: see above note 9.

the collective entity for which the sovereign claims to speak. However, it does not mean that the finitude of the mortal being is somehow fully replicated in the sovereign claim. Indeed, only death is capable of the finitude which the sovereign claims to determine.[53] Nor does it follow from the sovereign's claim to power over life and death (whether from the death penalty[54] or to wage war[55]) – although this is clearly part of it. Rather, it is in the failure of the sovereign to achieve the power of finishing it claims, that the limit of its singularity is revealed. The sovereign's claim to an absolute power of determination marks the collective entity as a finite, singular, being only in the instant of this determination.[56] It cannot be enduringly set. For Nancy, 'the sovereign extremity signifies that there is nothing to "attain"; there is no "accomplishment" or "achievement"; there is no "finishing".'[57] Instead, the marking out of a sovereign position is not a beginning nor an end in itself but a spacing from other positions[58] – always contingent on the position of other singularities and always subject to change. Connecting this sentiment to the question of politics, Nancy writes that politics 'never leads to ends. It leads to stages of transient equilibria.'[59] The singularity of a collective

53 And even that, as we have seen, is something that is experienced only by the living and as such, remains unfinished: 'The finishing of finite existence is an unfinishing [*infinition*], which everywhere overflows the death that contains it.' Nancy, *Being Singular Plural*, p. 139.

54 See Peter Fitzpatrick, 'Making Difference: Modernity and the Political Formations of Death' in Austin Sarat and Charles J. Ogletree Jr. (eds), *The Road to Abolition: The Future of Capital Punishment in the United States*, New York: New York University Press, 2009, pp. 319–47. See also, Bodin, *On Sovereignty*, p. 56.

55 As Nancy might himself argue: see Nancy, *Being Singular Plural*, p. 121.

56 Nancy describes singularity as 'indivisible in each instant [*au coup par coup*], within the event of its singularization.' Ibid., p. 32.

57 Ibid., p. 139.

58 Ibid.

59 Jean-Luc Nancy, 'Démocratie Finie et Infinie' in La Fabrique (ed.), *Démocratie dans quel état?*, Paris: La Fabrique editions, 2009, p. 93. Thanks to Gilbert Leung for providing an unofficial translation of this text. In the original French, the quote reads: 'La politique n'aboutit jamais à des fins. Elle conduit à des paliers d'équilibres transitoires.' See also, Jacques Derrida, 'Remarks on Deconstruction and Pragmatism' in Simon Critchley, Jacques Derrida, Ernesto Laclau and

entity is dependent, therefore, on its relation to other collective entities – not just on the sovereign. But this relation also goes towards each singularity's unworking and necessitates the reassertion of position. In the next section, I will consider in more detail the way in which this relation goes to constitute singularity not by preceding it, but by co-appearing with it.

2.3 The co-appearance of singularity and community

As we just saw, what makes the collective entity singular is not just the assertion of a sovereign, but also its spacing from other entities. Singularities (and hence sovereign positions) are constituted in and through their relation to one another; that is, constituted in community (here the community of singular collective entities). But community does not anticipate these singularities or their relation. As we saw in Chapter 1, for Nancy, community exists simply because of the fact that we are inescapably with each other in the world. Community is that which is constituted by the relation of singular entities and is nothing other than those relations (it is not their cause or their product). It has no fixed essence, content or set determinate form.[60] In conceiving of community as nothing other than the relations between singular entities, Nancy emphasises its vacuity: the necessary possibility of its being other than what it currently 'is'.[61] But this emphasis on vacuity does not mean that communities lack any form or substance at all (or, that such form or substance are wholly left to an autopositioned sovereign to determine out of thin air). Certainly any community will have a certain density of substance or

Richard Rorty, *Deconstruction and Pragmatism*, London: Routledge, 1996, pp. 83–4.

60 Nancy, *Inoperative Community*, pp. 12–15.

61 A quality we observed as a necessary characteristic of law in Chapter 1: see Peter Fitzpatrick, 'What are the Gods to Us Now?: Secular Theology and the Modernity of Law', *Theoretical Inquiries in Law* 8, 2007, 161, 185.

content which we might regard as being characteristic of it, if only for the time being. As Nancy writes:

> *We* can never simply be 'the we,' understood as a unique subject, or understood as an indistinct 'we' that is like a diffuse generality. 'We' always expresses a plurality, expresses our being divided and entangled: 'one' is not 'with' in some general sort of way, but each time according to determined modes that are themselves multiple and simultaneous (people, culture, language, lineage, network, group, couple, band, and so on).[62]

As such, in the formation of *a* community, these modes provide something of a raw material from which a sovereign could draw when making a claim to cohere and determine the content and character of that community. Like community itself, these modes are at once open to appropriation and resistant to capture.

But if community is nothing other than the relation between singular entities, then it cannot precede those singularities nor envelop them. That would require community to somehow embody a characteristic, fixed and invariable, common to the singularities it would constitute and hold within it. Put another way, we could say that singularities relate *in* community, but they are not contained *within* community. For Nancy, this distinction is one between communion and community. A communion would be the immanent realisation of an essence common to its members – a totalitarian ideal.[63] But the ever-changing nature of our relations with each other would make a fixed common essence impossible to realise. And given this impossibility, an obsession with 'communal fusion' could, for Nancy, only have disastrous consequences – as attempts at totalitarianism would show.[64] By contrast to this conception of communion as a pure, immanent

62 Nancy, *Being Singular Plural*, p. 65 (original emphasis).

63 Nancy, *Inoperative Community*, pp. 12–13.

64 For Nancy, 'Immanence, communal fusion, contains no other logic than that of the suicide of the community that is governed by it.' Ibid., p. 12.

fusion, community simply denotes spacing.[65] It is in the spacing of singularities that they come to appear. For Nancy, 'singular beings are themselves constituted by sharing, they are distributed and placed, or rather *spaced*, by the sharing that makes them *others*.'[66] Hence Nancy's identification of the singular as 'what is distinguished in the distinction'.[67]

This spacing or distinction can only happen because of the fact that these singularities are 'with' each other in the world. As such, the *with* does not contain each singularity but rather provides a space within which it can *be*. Hence the *with* (or relation) is originary.[68] If for Derrida, ipseity is a force which makes position possible,[69] for Nancy, such positioning can only occur in a space made possible by the *with* of being. For Nancy, '"with" is the pre-position of the position [of the self] in general.'[70] Nancy refers to this as a 'time-space of "self-referentiality" in general,' where each singularity can, in its turn and on its own account (if not invariantly) designate itself as an 'I'.[71] Crucial in all of this is that it is the dynamic of relation, rather than community or singularity, which is originary.[72] It is through the relation between singularities that both singularity and community appear. More precisely, singularities co-appear and in their co-appearance community exists. As we saw above, singularities only exist in their distinction from one another. At the moment this distinction occurs (and singularity appears), community exists, since these singularities are, inescapably, with each other in the world; not before (as if community somehow provides a contained space within which singularities can come into existence and relate) and not subsequent (as if the existence of community is somehow the work, project or product of these singularities).[73]

65 Nancy, *Being Singular Plural*, pp. 33, 60, 65. See also ibid., p. 25.
66 Nancy, *Inoperative Community*, p. 25 (original emphasis).
67 Nancy, *Being Singular Plural*, p. 33.
68 Ibid., p. 83.
69 Derrida, *Rogues*, pp. 11–12.
70 Nancy, *Being Singular Plural*, p. 40.
71 Ibid., pp. 65–6.
72 Ibid., p. 16: 'the origin is a distancing'.
73 Nancy, *Inoperative Community*, pp. 14–15.

The notion that neither community nor singularity precedes the other is one aspect of the notion of co-appearance. The other is the continuing dynamic it sets in motion. Not only is relation originary, but it creates a dynamic in which position must constantly be re-asserted.[74] It is this restless dynamic which makes an enduringly fixed and contained singularity impossible. But, continuing the argument so far, what makes claims to singularity impossible is also what makes them imperative. The claim of the self to what it is, is a constant process, a movement, or a coming to.[75] Its self-referential ipseity cannot be permanently fixed, for its position depends on its relation to other constantly changing entities. Since a sovereign cannot rely for its position on a ground outside of itself and yet is constantly exposed to that with which it relates, it must follow that position and relation happen together. And so, any sovereign autopositioning is part of a constant dynamic of position and relation. It is not simply a case of appropriation, but to use Derrida's term again, also a *reappropriation*, a perpetual gathering in of the self in the context of the forces which would influence its content.[76] It is in this continuing dynamic that we can make sense of what Nancy means by co-appearance. Co-appearance cannot be understood in strict temporal terms; it cannot mean that all things appear together at the same time. If that were the case the theory of co-appearance would be disproved by the fact that some things come into existence before others. Rather, what co-appearance denotes is that as soon as a new position is asserted, two things happen. First, the new position is asserted in relation to what currently exists. Second, singularities that existed before this new assertion have to re-position themselves in relation to what has just been asserted. As such, a conception of the co-appearance of singularities and community allows an analysis of positions which is not fixated on

74 See Jacques Derrida, 'Remarks on Deconstruction', pp. 83–4; see also Jacques Derrida, 'Force of Law: The Mystical Foundation of Authority', tr. Mary Quaintance, in Jacques Derrida, *Acts of Religion*, ed. Gil Anidjar, New York: Routledge, 2002, pp. 272–5.

75 Nancy, *Being Singular Plural*, pp. 95–6.

76 Derrida, *Rogues*, p. 11.

pure origins or on showing that some forms of community or sovereignty are more authentic because they precede others. As we will see in Chapters 4 and 5, this creates a freedom necessary to reconceptualise the nature of, and interaction between, the authority of the WTO, the Indian state and local communities in India.

3 The Constitutive Function of Relation in the Creation of Nation-States

As we saw in Chapter 1, the failure of the nation-state to resolve or provide a distinctive embodiment of the irresolutions in the concept of sovereignty showed that it could not be the exclusive and originary sovereign position from which all other authority flows. Nancy's work goes further to show that no position is originary, further supporting the argument in Chapter 1. More specifically, it undermines the notion that any entity could be the self-sufficient origin and foundation of its own sovereign position. This means that the idea that nation-states are empirical facts which precede their relations with each other (international law) and with other forms of power is wrong. As such, the kind of autarchic absolute position of state sovereignty to which Bodin, Vitoria, Grotius, Pufendorf, Vattel and Rousseau (as I presented them above) appeared to subscribe is impossible. In the next section, I will return to these theorists and show how this impossibility is actually reflected in their work. I will then relate this insight to the event which is commonly seen as the marker of the origin of modern sovereignty: the Peace of Westphalia and show that it too actually reveals that the sovereignty of the state was created by the relation between states themselves and also what was (and remains) other to them.

3.1 Theory

Earlier in this chapter I set out a series of quotes from Bodin, Vitoria, Grotius, Pufendorf, Vattel and Rousseau in which it appeared that these theorists posited that the state was an absolute, complete and self-sufficient entity. Rousseau, as we saw, went furthest, arguing that a state fit to legislate for itself is one which 'can do without other nations and which every other nation can do without.'[77] With some help from Nancy, we have since seen that such isolated singularity is impossible. However, the purpose of that exercise was not to expose the work of these theorists as inadequate. Rather, it was to expose the errors in the conventional view of international relations and law which is drawn from them – foremost being the view exemplified by Jackson that classical international law is the 'child of states'.[78] In this section I will seek to build on that critique to show that, as Fitzpatrick argues, 'international society or community is a necessary condition for the existence of the individual or singular nation.'[79] Moreover, we will see that close attention to the work of the theorists relied on for the conventional view actually supports this contrary argument that the relation between states is constitutive of what they are (and thus of their sovereign singularity). As such, their work can be read in a way which is consistent with Nancy's exposition of singularity and community. Indeed, in the oscillation between the purported autarchy of states and their constitution in relation, these theorists demonstrate the operation of the dynamic of position and relation in which sovereignty comes continually to be autopositioned.

In his oscillation between autarchy and relation in the constitution of sovereign states, Rousseau again goes the furthest. Having set out complete and autarchic independence as the marker of a well constituted state, Rousseau then proceeds to find that in fact, very few states have this characteristic. Indeed only Corsica and the even more unlikely example of Poland are given as states so well isolated as to have this quality.[80] As Fitzpatrick has observed, Rousseau's ambivalence on the possibility of complete autarchy goes beyond the difficulty he had in finding examples.[81] In stark

77 Rousseau, *Social Contract*, p. 86.
78 See above note 18.
79 Fitzpatrick, *Modernism*, p. 150.
80 Rousseau, *Social Contract*, p. 86. See also Fitzpatrick, *Modernism*, p. 148.
81 Fitzpatrick, *Modernism*, pp. 148–9.

contrast to his advice to Corsica to maintain its state of isolation as best it can (even this reveals some concern about the possibility of it actually doing so), Rousseau writes that '[s]ince the size of the political body is entirely relative, it is forced to enter steadily into comparison in order to know itself; it depends on everything that surrounds it, and must take an interest in everything that happens outside'.[82] And while the explicit nature of Rousseau's ambivalence on the necessity of relation could be seen to set him apart from the other theorists quoted above, such ambivalence can be found in each of them.

Despite his undoubted importance in the development of a theory of sovereign statehood, Bodin is not generally regarded as a theorist of the early law of nations. His main focus was on the functions of government within a state. As such, the significance of the relation between states to Bodin's theory of sovereignty is revealed not so much by his express statements, but by his methodology. His methodology for coming to terms with the meaning of sovereignty not only reveals the importance of relation, but also prefigures one of the key modes by which international law gains its content – an observation of comparative political practice.[83] For having developed this methodology, Franklin places Bodin at the forefront of a revolution in the study of jurisprudence which occurred in the latter part of the sixteenth century.[84] For Franklin, prior to this point, late middle ages scholarship on law had focused on Roman law and even novel legal developments were 'obscured and hidden' by scholars seeking to place and interpret them within the 'universal' Justinian code.[85] Bodin, by contrast, disregarded the 'absurdity of attempting to establish principles of universal jurisprudence from the Roman

82 Quoted in Paul de Man, *Allegories of Reading: Figural Language in Rousseau, Nietzsche, Rilke, and Proust*, New Haven: Yale University Press, 1979, p. 256 (from Rousseau's *Ecrits sur l'Abbé de Saint Pierre*). See Fitzpatrick, *Modernism*, p. 149.

83 See Article 38.1 of the Statute of the International Court of Justice (1945).

84 Julian Franklin, *Jean Bodin and the Sixteenth-Century Revolution in the Methodology of Law and History*, New York: Columbia University Press, 1963, ch. IV.

85 Ibid., p. 1.

decrees', since not only were they simply 'the legislation of one particular state,' but were themselves 'subject to change within a brief period' and 'supplanted by an infinite multitude of edicts and statutes.'[86] For Bodin, the only way to embark on the study of a universal legal science (and to determine how best to govern a state) was 'to bring together and compare the legal framework of all states, or of the more famous states, and from them compile the best kind.'[87] A similar technique would be employed by Grotius in deciphering a law of nations by virtue of comparative analysis of the common conventions of 'all, or at least, the most civilised, Nations.'[88]

Bodin's comparative research included study of laws found in Biblical texts, in ancient Greece, Rome and Egypt, in contemporary Spain, England, Turkey, Poland, Scandanavia and the cities of Italy, Germany, as well as a more limited survey of eastern Europe, Muscovy, North Africa and America.[89] Undertaking this study led Bodin to conclude that:

> every people, or certainly the better part of peoples, have a public law, a private law, legislation by princes, edicts of magistrates, laws of sovereignty, various customs and institutions, and, where law does not exist or even custom, at least the principle of equity.[90]

Bodin's concern, of course, was not simply to consider the laws of different states, but in focusing on the meaning and content of

86 Jean Bodin, *Method for the Easy Comprehension of History*, tr. Beatrice Reynolds, New York: Columbia University Press, 1945, p. 2. Bodin credited Plato for developing this kind of approach.

87 Ibid.

88 Grotius, *Rights of War*, vol 1, p. 159. See also Franklin, *Jean Bodin*, p. 73. Grotius also distinguished between natural law and the law of nations: See Grotius, *Rights of War*, vol 1, p. 94.

89 Franklin, *Jean Bodin*, pp. 71–2.

90 Bodin, quoted in ibid., p. 70. In Latin, the text reads: '*Habent autem omnes populi, aut certe quidem populorum bona pars, jus publicum, jus privatum, leges principum, edicta magistratuum, jura majestatis, conseutudines quasdam & institua, & ubi*

sovereignty, he used comparative method to determine what it meant to be a sovereign state. And so, to take an example we encountered in Chapter 1, the unequivocal location in them of the right to wage war meant that the 'genuine monarchs of France, Spain, England, Scotland, Ethiopia, Turkey, Persia, and Moscovy'[91] possessed absolute sovereign power, by contrast to the 'kingdoms of Poland, Denmark and Sweden' where this right shifted between the prince and the nobility.[92] The right to wage war is not the sole measure of sovereignty or of the character of a state, however, but one of a number of factors through which Bodin constructed his view of sovereignty through the comparison of different legal systems. As Franklin argues, Bodin's 'definitions and ... precepts' were not arrived at in 'complete abstraction' but, 'for the most part, [were] constructed step by step through a genuine comparison of laws.'[93] If sovereign statehood was merely a question of empirical fact, it would be sufficient to take one example in order to describe its essential features. Therefore, foreshadowing Rousseau's observation that a body politic can know itself only by comparison, Bodin's method shows that we cannot understand what a state is except by the comparison of various forms of political organisation. Such comparative method cannot operate unless one presupposes the possibility of relation between the things being compared. The characteristics of the state are not an empirical fact from which Bodin's analysis proceeds. Rather, the characteristics of the state only emerge in the process of undertaking the comparative method. As such, the state is not the starting point. The starting point is relation.

For the other theorists noted above, from Vitoria to Vattel, their concern with relation is even more central to their conception of sovereignty. This is because they expressly address the question

lex desit, aut ipsa consuetudo, aequitatem': Jean Bodin, 'Texts from Bodin's *Distributio*' in A. London Fell, *Origins of Legislative Sovereignty and the Legislative State: Volume Three: Bodin's Humanistic Legal System and Rejection of "Medieval Political Theology"*, Boston: Oelgeschlager, Gunn & Hain, 1987, p. 375.

91 Bodin, *On Sovereignty*, p. 115.

92 Ibid., pp. 61, 63.

93 Franklin, *Jean Bodin*, p. 73.

of the law of nations. In each case their primary concern was with the limits of state power in the context of the rights enjoyed by states and the obligations owed between them. It was common ground among all of them that there was no earthly authority superior to the entities they designated as sovereign. But each found that law nonetheless applied. The very possibility of such a law is contingent on the entities being in some kind of relation – for them a relation contained by a divine power. Two sources of law (to use the contemporary expression) were crucial. The first was natural law, which brought with it a concern with natural society. The second was state practice, which focused on the actual relations between states. It is obvious, then, that in addressing the question of the limits of state power the chief concern of these theorists was relation between states. What does need to be emphasised (for present purposes) is that in addressing the question of the limits of state power, these theorists were addressing the question of what it meant to be a sovereign state – which in their time (and as they developed their work) fully encompassed the meaning of sovereignty itself. That is, they were not simply considering what the relationship was between pre-existing political entities – rather, they were analysing and shaping the meaning of what these political entities were by investigating their relations with each other.

The problem which animates Vitoria's analysis of the sovereign state as a '"perfect" community' and 'complete in itself', is the question of the point at which a principality, within a European empire, could be regarded as sufficiently independent such that it could declare war.[94] For Vitoria, the rights and characteristics of these communities were to be determined by virtue of what they could do *vis-à-vis* each other under precepts of natural law. Like Bodin, Vitoria also draws on comparative examples of political practice[95] – this exercise once again revelatory of the fact that the meaning over what is sovereign can only be determined by

94 Vitoria, *Political Writings*, p. 301.

95 The kingdoms of Castile and Aragon are given as examples of sovereign communities complete in themselves: ibid.

reference to a relation between bodies holding similar powers. Indeed, anticipating much that would follow, Vitoria finds that this relation generated its own law – customary law.[96] As such, the content of the right to wage war[97] (along with its effect on the meaning of sovereignty) is susceptible to further development in the course of the relation between (European) states.[98]

For Grotius and Pufendorf, both with a heavy dependence on natural law, the idea of a society of nations was integral to their conception of sovereignty.[99] It is true that they each had a very different conception of the character of that society and the obligations that membership entailed. Grotius, keen to find justifications for Holland's violent wresting of control of trade in the East Indies from Spain and Portugal, argued for an expansive right for states to wage war in their interests.[100] His defence of state rights to wage war might seem to make him an unlikely source for the significance of relation in constituting state sovereignty. Tuck, for example, writes that 'natural society, for Grotius, was very unlike civil society in an essential respect, it wholly lacked a genuine community of interests and resources.'[101] However, just because Grotius's society of nations was not a particularly friendly place, we should not conclude that it was without relation. Of course,

96 Ibid., p. 302.

97 In this, Bodin's range of reference was broader since it extended beyond the right to wage war. Not only did Vitoria focus on the right to wage war as the marker of sovereignty within Europe, but as Anghie notes, his work on the limits of sovereignty in the encounter of Europe with the new world was also 'developed primarily in terms of the sovereign's right to wage war.' Antony Anghie, *Imperialism, Sovereignty and the Making of International Law*, Cambridge: Cambridge University Press, 2005, p. 23.

98 Vitoria, *Political Writings*, p. 302.

99 Cf Nancy, *Inoperative Community*, p. 9, where community is distinguished from society (society being 'a simple association and division of forces and needs'). However, the character of international society would appear to fit better with Nancy's understanding of community, not society.

100 Hugo Grotius, *The Free Sea*, tr. Richard Hakluyt, ed. David Armitage, Indianapolis: Liberty Fund, 2004.

101 Richard Tuck, *The Rights of War and Peace: Political Thought and the International Order from Grotius to Kant*, Oxford: Oxford University Press, 1999, p. 88.

a society without relation is impossible. And at a basic level, one can observe that for Grotius, the right of states to wage war derived precisely from a *mutual* right of self-preservation in them – it was necessary and could only be enjoyed by virtue of the fact that every similar entity possessed it.[102] But his concern with society went deeper. For Grotius, the state from which civil societies emerged (and which still governed the relations between them) was not a state of nothingness. With the gift of speech unique to them, humans have, for Grotius, 'an exquisite Desire of Society.'[103] And so, civil societies developed 'not with the intention of abolishing the society which links all men as a whole, but rather in order to fortify that universal society by a more dependable means of protection'.[104]

Pufendorf's natural society was eminently more sociable than that of Grotius and he sought to distinguish his theory from that of the Dutchman and also that of Hobbes. For Pufendorf, states not only had a mutual right of self-preservation, but also a duty of mutual aid.[105] He writes that 'whatsoever we can part with to another, without any Damage to ourselves, this is our Duty to give, though to a Stranger.'[106] In making this argument, he would have been influenced by the context in which he wrote. As Tuck argues, Pufendorf was 'a citizen of a state which stood in an extremely complex relationship to other states, and whose sovereignty (as a member of the German empire, even after the Treaty of Westphalia) seemed very different from the model used by

102 Grotius, *Rights of War*, vol 1, p. 189.

103 Ibid., p. 84. See also Tuck, *The Rights of War*, p. 97.

104 Hugo Grotius, *Commentary on the Law of Prize and Booty*, ed. Martine Julia van Ittersum, Indianapolis: Liberty Fund, 2006, p. 35. See Tuck, *The Rights of War*, p. 87.

105 Book 3 of Pudendorf's treatise was entitled 'Of the Common Duties of Humanity'. See Pufendorf, *Law of Nature and Nations*, p. 23: 'For such a power by which we may oblige others, and not unjure ourselves, unless it be on due Occasion, put into Action and Effect, appears to be *Vain*, and only turns to the Reproach of him that has it.'

106 Ibid., p. 24. For Pufendorf, the question of mutually was strict, such that if you did not take or require a liberty from your neighbour, you were under no obligation to provide the same to them: ibid., p. 33.

Grotius or Hobbes.'[107] Such states, writes Tuck, 'felt themselves most at risk of the kind of militarist and imperialist expansion in which the Dutch and English gloried.'[108] Pufendorf's emphasis on the natural sociability of states, and his addition of more positive content to that sociability than one observes in Grotius, serves to emphasise the importance of relation in the constitution of what it means to be a sovereign state. But in some ways, the work of Grotius provides a more telling example of the argument pursued here because his state is resolutely more self-possessed and self-interested, and yet despite all of that still comes to be constituted in its relation to others.

Vattel provides another example of how the attempt to posit a self-possessed sovereign is undone by the constitutive force of relation. The Vattel we encountered in the first part of this chapter, while still reliant on natural law to set the scene, as it were, focused more on state practice as generative of a 'positive' law of nations through which the general precepts of natural law would be determined and applied in particular circumstances.[109] For Vattel, in the absence of a common superior, every sovereign state is the 'sole arbitress of her own actions'[110] and has 'a right to determine, according to the dictates of her own conscience, what her duties require of her'[111] and 'what is proper or improper for her to do.'[112] At times, Vattel draws a pessimistic conclusion that this freedom allows states to dominate others. He writes that 'the will and inclination to oppress may be almost always supposed, where there is a power of oppressing with impunity.'[113] Vattel's emphasis on state freedom, his rejection of the idea of a 'universal commonwealth' and his elevation of state practice as *the* source of international law mean that he is most remembered for 'bringing the theory of the law of nations into line with state practice' and

107 Tuck, *The Rights of War*, p. 145.
108 Ibid., p. 142.
109 Cavallar, *Rights of Strangers*, pp. 307–8.
110 Vattel, *Law of Nations*, p. 137.
111 Ibid., p. 381.
112 Ibid.: Preliminary, para. 16.
113 Ibid., p. 308.

marks a shift towards '"classical" nineteenth century European international law'.[114] As we saw in the first part of this chapter, it is this classical international law which Jackson remarks as being the child, and not the parent, of states.[115] But as Cavallar shows, this view of Vattel is one-sided.[116] While he did not subscribe to a universal commonwealth, Vattel's conception of international law is one in which a certain regard and reciprocity between states is central.

Most significantly, the freedom Vattel ascribes to states is not something which each state had alone, but something which it had by virtue of the freedom being shared mutually by all states. This meant, for Vattel, that the existence and the scope of authority of sovereign states is determined according to 'the political balance, or the equilibrium of power, by which is understood such a disposition of things, as that no one potentate be absolutely to predominate, and prescribe laws to the others.'[117] And a now more optimistic Vattel would go further to find that Europe, at least, was not 'a confused heap of detached pieces, each of which thought herself very little concerned with the fate of others, and seldom regarded things which did not immediately concern her.'[118] Rather, increased attention to occurrences in foreign countries, diplomatic activities and perpetual negotiations made 'of modern Europe a kind of republic, of which the members – each independent, but all linked together by the ties of a common interest – unite for the maintenance of order and liberty.'[119] It was for this reason that, for Vattel, the state of nature within which nations found themselves did not necessitate the creation of a

114 Cavallar, *Rights of Strangers*, pp. 306–19. See also Peter Fitzpatrick, 'Latin Roots: Imperialism and the Formation of Modern Law' in Peter Fitzpatrick, *Law as Resistance: Modernism, Imperialism, Legalism*, Aldershot: Ashgate, 2008, 275–91, p. 280.

115 See above note 18 and accompanying text.

116 Cavallar, *Rights of Strangers*, pp. 309–18.

117 Vattel, *Law of Nations*, p. 311.

118 Ibid.

119 Ibid.

Leviathan above them.[120] As such, not only does the relation between states (understood as a simple balance of power system) go to determine the scope of their sovereign authority, but the very condition of their relation and its attendant norms creates the conditions by which they are not to be made subject to any higher authority.

It should be noted, however, that the relation between states is not the only relation relevant to the constitution of the modern sovereign state. There is also the relation between sovereign states and that which was posed as other to them. Here, the work of Vitoria is of prime significance, but Grotius will be seen to play a supporting role. The discovery and conquest of the Americas put in view the question of the limits of (European) sovereign power like no event within Europe could do. Vitoria's work is important in this respect because he took the encounter not as an opportunity to cast the New World as a place without law, and thus without limits, but as a place where universal laws, and limits, applied. And yet, determining the basis for such laws presented great difficulty since, as Anghie argues, it posed 'the problem of creating a system of law to account for relations between societies which [Vitoria] understood to belong to two very different cultural orders, each with its own ideas of propriety and governance.'[121] And so, according to Anghie:

> Vitoria [did] not interpret the problem of Spanish-Indian relations as a problem of creating order among sovereign states. Vitoria's analysis does not proceed on the basis that both the Indians and the Spaniards are sovereign, that sovereigns possess certain powers and that the interaction between the two parties is therefore regulated by the rules managing and limiting the exercise of such powers which he, the jurist, identifies, examines and applies. Rather, Vitoria's work addresses a prior set of questions. Who is sovereign?

120 Cavallar, *Rights of Strangers*, pp. 312–13. See also Tuck, *The Rights of War*, pp. 140–2.

121 Anghie, *Imperialism*, p. 16.

> What are the powers of a sovereign? Are the Indians sovereign? What are the rights and duties of the Indians and the Spaniards? How are the respective rights and duties of the Spanish and the Indians to be decided?[122]

Vitoria's answer to these questions was complex. The fact that the Indians were not Christian did not prevent them from 'being true masters' – as Vitoria finds by way of numerous biblical references to unbelievers who were also 'kings', and by Peter and Paul's instructions to Christians to obey their rulers (who were at the time unbelievers).[123] Moreover, the argument that the Indians could not hold rights of dominion because they lacked reason is similarly rejected by Vitoria. He writes that the 'barbarians' are 'not in point of fact madmen, but have judgment[124] like other men. This is self evident because they have some order (*ordo*) in their affairs: they have properly organized cities, proper marriages, magistrates and overlords (*domini*), laws, industries, and commerce, all of which require the use of reason.'[125] Finding that the Indians had both reason and dominium, Vitoria rejected the notion that either the Emperor, Charles I, or the Pope, was 'master of the whole world' and could therefore legitimately claim possession of Indian lands and authority over their inhabitants.[126] Nor was discovery enough to grant title, since the lands were not without an owner.[127] All of which would appear to place the Indians on an equivalent footing and undermine not only the title claimed by the Spanish but the brutal measures used to put that claim into effect. Such regard for the rights of the Indians was certainly unusual and accounts for one of the ways Vitoria is remembered, 'as espousing the interests of indigenous

122 Ibid., p. 15.
123 Vitoria, *Political Writings*, p. 244.
124 Another version of the text substitutes 'judgment' for 'use of reason': see ibid., at p. 250 (note 34).
125 Ibid., p. 250.
126 Ibid., pp. 252–64.
127 Ibid., pp. 264–5.

populations against a predatory colonization' and, as such, 'as a remote parent of international law.'[128]

But Vitoria's work prompts another way in which he is remembered – as someone who developed a more 'refined justification of imperial acquisition.'[129] On this score, Vitoria is able to find just grounds for colonial acquisition in a *ius gentium* that gave the Spanish a right to trade, travel and dwell in the lands of the New World and the right to preach Christian gospel and convert the Indians even against their will. Local resistance to the exercise of these rights would justify a war, and that war could generate and perfect title to the lands themselves.[130] The reciprocity which might be thought to flow from the Indians possessing universal reason evaporates as soon as we consider, as Schmitt did, the question of whether the Indians would have enjoyed a right of proselytising their religions in Europe.[131] And so, while they had universal reason and dominium over their lands, the Indians were not sovereign in the same way as the Spanish. They were 'encompassed in the sameness of a universal humanity yet set apart from it as different.'[132] Vitoria manages to conceive of this dichotomy through a complex combination of secularism and theology and through this elevated the *ius gentium* as both a universal law and as something which could be determined from within Europe.[133] As Fitzpatrick shows, a similar, if less nuanced, dichotomy appears in Grotius's work, where the 'Christian and civilised character' of international law is set firmly against the 'heathen and the barbarian, even if Grotius would extend international law in part so as to include such peoples.'[134] What makes this encounter relevant to the present concern with the constitution of sovereignty by virtue of relation, is the way in which the content and character of European sovereignty is shaped in and

128 Fitzpatrick, 'Latin Roots', p. 279.
129 Ibid.
130 Vitoria, *Political Writings*, pp. 281–6; Fitzpatrick, 'Latin Roots', pp. 285–7.
131 See Carl Schmitt, *The* Nomos *of the Earth*, tr. G. Ulmen, New York: Telos Press, 2003, ch. 2; See also Fitzpatrick, 'Latin Roots'.
132 Fitzpatrick, 'Latin Roots', p. 286.
133 Ibid. pp. 284–91.
134 Ibid., p. 280.

through early imperialism. It enables us to see how European sovereignty was positioned as supreme through the elevation of its law as universal. As such, its position was formed in the process of the formation of an international law.

The analysis above shows that each of these theorists oscillated between an assertion of absolute sovereign self-sufficiency and a concern with the constitution of sovereignties in their relation to one another and, in the case of Vitoria and Grotius, to a 'savage' other. The conclusion to be drawn from this is not that they were misguided when referring to sovereign self-sufficiency and correct when recognising (or reflecting) the significance of relation. Rather, it is that the oscillation itself reflects the dynamic of position and relation which this chapter has sought to show is the operative dynamic of modern sovereignty. The references to the self-assured autarchic state quoted at the beginning of the chapter reflect the imperative of positioning; and specifically an autopositioning by states not determined or guaranteed by any authority outside of themselves. All sovereign claims must have, as we saw in Chapter 1, the quality of absoluteness. Without this quality *in their claim*, sovereigns would not be able to do the work modernity requires of them (most particularly the work of determining the boundaries of communities and the content of their law). But as I showed in my analysis of Nancy's work, such a claim is impossible to realise in practice given that no entity can isolate itself from the forces within which it exists and to which it relates. Hence why the theorists from Vitoria to Vattel combined their statements of absolute autarchic sovereignty with an awareness of relation in the constitution of the sovereign state. This shows that neither position nor relation can tell the full story; a conclusion supported by Nancy's work which finds that singularity cannot exist purely as position nor be dissolved in relation.

But it is not just in the work of the early theorists of international law that one can observe the constitutive function of relation. It is also evident in the history of international law itself.[135] In the next section, I will develop this theme further by examining

135 Not that I would subscribe to a strict dichotomy between a theory and a history of international law.

that iconic, supposedly formative, 'event' in international law, the Peace of Westphalia. To be clear, this event is not exemplary for my purposes. If my argument about the ongoing nature of sovereign autopositioning is correct, then the entire history of international law would serve as an example. In Chapters 4 and 5, I will examine in detail the question of the WTO's influence over Indian patent law, and the relation between the Indian state and local communities over 'traditional knowledge' and show them to be examples of this dynamic. But since the Peace of Westphalia is so commonly taken as exemplifying the elevation of self-sufficient sovereign statehood, it seems a good place to test the argument advanced in this chapter. I will argue that contrary to the standard view, the Peace of Westphalia reveals the inescapability of relation and the role it plays in constituting singular sovereignties.

3.2 Practice: Westphalia

The Peace of Westphalia looms so large in the imagination of international lawyers as the key moment in the formation of the modern nation-state that it provides a useful site of analysis to show the way in which the sovereignty of the modern state is constituted in relation, even at the moment of its apparent autonomous self-creation.[136] It is the event which is generally taken to be the decisive break which inaugurated or consecrated the idea of the sovereign state in European political life and through which Europe made the transition from the medieval to the modern. Relating this to the conventional view of state sovereignty as an empirical fact which precedes its relation to other states, Westphalia would mark a point at which the atomistic state emerges self-sufficient and complete unto itself. And this is the

136 The Peace of Westphalia is the name given to the treaties of Münster and Osnabrück (1648) which brought an end to the Thirty Years War. The versions used here are from C. Parry (ed.), *The Consolidated Treaty Series; Treaty of Münster* (1648) *and Treaty of Osnabrück* (1648), vol. 1, New York: Oceana Publications, 1969. Subsequent references will be to the treaties directly.

conventional view of Westphalia.[137] Following the arguments advanced by Stephen Krasner[138] and more recently Stephane Beaulac,[139] that this conventional view of Westphalia as a decisive break is wrong, I will make the further point that Westphalia demonstrates the way in which singularities (in this case sovereign states) come to be positioned or constituted in relation.

For many commentators on international relations and law, Westphalia is the moment at which the sovereign nation-state as the principal actor in European political life emerges. Even for many who do not see Westphalia as inaugurating the sovereign state, it still resonates as a consolidation or 'consecration' of the sovereign state.[140] However, as Krasner argues, the 'widely held view among international relations theorists and international lawyers which sees Westphalia as a major, perhaps a decisive, break marking the transition from the medieval to the modern world' – a world now divided into sovereign states – 'is wrong'.[141] Features of government which are taken to be characteristic of

137 For a survey of the conventional view, see Stephen Krasner, 'Westphalia and All That' in Judith Goldstein and Robert O. Keohane (eds), *Ideas and Foreign Policy: Beliefs, Institutions and Political Change*, Ithica: Cornell University Press, 1993, pp. 238–40. For a recent, nuanced defence of the conventional view, see Daniel Philpott, *Revolutions in Sovereignty: How Ideas Shaped Modern International Relations*, Princeton: Princeton University Press, 2001, chs 5 and 6. For a critique of Philpott's attachment to a stable concept of sovereignty and its consequent influence on his view of Westphalia, see Richard Joyce, 'Westphalia: Event, Memory, Myth' in Fleur Johns, Richard Joyce and Sundhya Pahuja (eds), *Events: The Force of International Law*, Abingdon: Routledge, 2011, pp. 55–68.

138 Krasner, 'Westphalia and All That'.

139 Stephane Beaulac, 'The Westphalian Model in Defining International Law: Challenging the Myth', *Australian Journal of Legal History* 8, 2004, 181.

140 See Phillpot, *Revolutions in Sovereignty*, p. 77; Gianfranco Poggi, *The Development of the Modern State: A Sociological Introduction*, London: Hutchinson, 1987, p. 89; Leo Gross, 'The Peace of Westphalia: 1648–1948', *American Journal of International Law* 42, 1948, 20; James Crawford, *The Creation of States in International Law*, 2nd ed., Oxford: Clarendon Press, 2006, p. 10. See also Krasner, 'Westphalia and All That', p. 239.

141 Krasner, 'Westphalia and All That', pp. 235, 238; Beaulac, 'The Westphalian Model', p. 211.

modern sovereignty – most notably something approximating exclusive control over a territorial space – can be observed hundreds of years before Westphalia, especially in England, France and Italian city-states.[142] And the authority of the Holy Roman Empire, while weakened by Westphalia, nonetheless remained a vital force at least until the early nineteenth century.[143] This is not to say that everything about the treaties is inconsistent with the conventional view; as Philpott shows, counter-examples can be found.[144] But even Philpott admits that there is a disjuncture between the historical record and the conventional view, disagreeing only as to its extent.[145]

The aspect of the treaties themselves which is most often cited in support of the argument that Westphalia inaugurated or confirmed a system of sovereign states, concerns the ability of princes within the Holy Roman Empire to conduct foreign relations. The article of the Treaty of Münster which bestowed on the princes the right to conclude treaties provided that 'it shall be free perpetually to each of the States of the Empire, to make Alliances with Strangers for their Preservation and Safety.'[146] However, this was only one small part of the overall settlement. As Krasner argues, the chief goals of the treaties were to institute a more stable resolution of religious differences than had been achieved in Augsburg in 1555 (problems with which had ultimately led to the Thirty-Years War), and to satisfy the territorial ambitions of France and Sweden (which had won) while at the same time undermining the authority of the Holy Roman (Habsburg) Empire (which had lost).[147]

142 Krasner, 'Westphalia and All That', pp. 253–4; Beaulac, 'The Westphalian Model', pp. 194–5.

143 Until another (but shorter-lived) emperor, Napeoleon, brought an end to the Holy Roman empire from 1803–1806: see Krasner, 'Westphalia and All That', p. 251.

144 Philpott, *Revolutions in Sovereignty*, chs 5 and 6.

145 Ibid., p. 73.

146 Treaty of Münster (1648), art 65.

147 Krasner, 'Westphalia and All That', pp. 240–1; Beaulac, 'The Westphalian Model', pp. 201–3.

The French claims were satisfied by a transfer of certain territories (including the bishoprics of Metz, Toul and Verdun), which was explicitly stated to be a transfer of 'all Jurisdiction and Sovereignty'.[148] However, the transfer to France of Austria's rights in certain parts of Alsace was not so neat. Austria's rights in Alsace had been subject to a superior claim by the Holy Roman Empire on which various local bishoprics and mayories depended. The transfer to France of Austria's rights did not affect those imperial rights (and the local rights derived from them). The relevant article thus contains complicated reservations reflecting the existing medieval arrangements.[149] By virtue of those reservations, the French king, while in receipt of certain rights in relation to the Alsatian territories, could not 'pretend any Royal Superiority over them'.[150] The settlement of Sweden's claims were based even more on medieval and imperial institutional forms than those of France.[151] Sweden was granted rights in territories on the south shore of the Baltic. However, these rights were not absolute and the territories did not become part of a singular Swedish Crown. Instead, they were transferred in 'perpetual and immediate Fief of the Empire'.[152] These grants of fiefdoms gave the ruler of Sweden the right to sit in the Imperial Diet as representative of the regions covered by the grants. As such, not only did the settlement keep in place the medieval form of the fief, it also cast the Swedish Crown in multiple roles – sovereign over certain territories, a subject of the Empire in others. As Krasner argues, the 'statesmen at Osnabruck and Munster had available to them a variety of institutional forms, and they saw no problem in cobbling together arrangements that now appear anomalous.'[153]

The goal of weakening the authority of the Holy Roman Empire was achieved by France and Sweden's insistence that the

148 Treaty of Münster (1648), art 76.
149 Ibid., art 92. See Beaulac, The Westphalian Model, p. 202.
150 Treaty of Münster (1648), art 92.
151 Krasner, 'Westphalia and All That', p. 241; Beaulac, 'The Westphalian Model', pp. 201–3.
152 Treaty of Osnabrück (1648), art 10.
153 Krasner, 'Westphalia and All That', p. 242.

German princes within the Holy Roman Empire be included in the negotiations, leading to the autonomy subsequently negotiated by them.[154] As such, it was a strategic decision by the victors, not respect for the authority of the princes, which set the scene for this aspect of the treaties. Moreover, the autonomy won by the princes in the negotiations was heavily qualified. The very same provision which granted a right to conduct foreign relations also stated that no treaty could result in an alliance 'against the Emperor, and the Empire, nor against the Public Peace'.[155] Other 'marks' of sovereignty (as Bodin might have described them) remained located in the Empire, albeit with extensive rights of consultation conferred on the states. Again, the same article gives the princes and states of the Empire the

> Right of Suffrage in all Deliberations touching the Affairs of the Empire; but above all, when the Business in hand shall be the making or interpreting of Laws, the declaring of Wars, imposing of Taxes [and] levying or quartering of Soldiers.[156]

The bestowal of a mere right of suffrage shows that the so-called sovereign princes did not themselves have ultimate authority over law, war and tax – three things most commonly associated with state sovereignty. In fact, as the territorial settlements reveal, what remained after Westphalia was a complex relationship of principalities and empires, with territories subject to various forms of government and rulers in different places holding very different forms of power – especially in the German states and central Europe.[157] As such, rather than marking a decisive break, Westphalia demonstrated how the modern states system emerged gradually out of complex political and religious relations.

154 Ibid., pp. 240–1.
155 Treaty of Münster (1648), art 65.
156 Ibid.
157 This complex situation, as we saw above, informed Pufendorf's theory of international society (see text accompanying note 107 above).

Indeed, to the extent that Westphalia did inaugurate or consolidate the idea of sovereign statehood, it did so in a way which emphasised the significance of relation in the constitution of the singular. It shows that the sovereignty of states was constituted in the relation between states (a relation of singularities) and also in the distinction of the state from other forms of social and political organisation. First, and most obviously, the treaties were agreements between various political powers. As such, to the extent that Westphalia was constitutive of sovereign statehood, this occurred in the context of agreements between entities which were not already sovereign and complete in and of themselves. Moreover, this occurred in the context of distinguishing statehood from other forms of power: imperial, religious and local (even if it did, at the same time, leave much of these powers intact). Second, the demarcation of the scope of authority of the various bodies involved (even if we arbitrarily limit this to the ones which most closely resemble the classical idea of modern sovereignty) was determined in the course of negotiations. The sovereignty of states was not purely self-positioned, nor did it come out of nothingness, nor out of fidelity to an abstract principle of state sovereignty. Rather, the extent of authority varied according to the material concerns and power of the parties – hence the varied political forms which the treaties covered – drawing on a wide range of ideas about government.[158] As such, the extent of the power of each of the entities (and hence the extent of and meaning of their singular sovereign authority) resulted from the negotiations (i.e. the relations) between them.

Another key observation which can be drawn from Westphalia is the way in which a certain positive content is embedded in what it means to be a sovereign state. It would be one thing if, somehow, the entities involved agreed to establish themselves (and recognise in others) a purely formal notion of state sovereignty. But Westphalia went further than this and actually embedded positive obligations into the emerging sovereign states. As we saw above, the main issue to which the treaties were directed was

158 See Krasner, 'Westphalia and All That', pp. 261–4.

not how to establish a system of nation-states, but how to cope with religious difference[159] and specifically the question of what to do when a ruler's religion differed from that of a certain proportion of their population. The solution, a limited guarantee of tolerance of religious minorities within states,[160] was not simply an obligation which applied to states, but was constitutive of what it meant to be a state in the post-Westphalian system. Indeed, it was the corollary of freedom from the papacy (i.e., the freedom of rulers from imperial religious domination was conditional on them foregoing any right to require the conversion of their subjects). As such, the moment in which the idea of a complete and absolute sovereign state is meant to have emerged, one finds not only that its formal condition is determined by its relation to other entities, but that a substantive content already applies to it.

The existence of substantive content to the meaning of sovereign statehood is a result of the process by which the terms of relation between states constitute what they are. And it has ever been the case. As we saw above, Vitoria's elevation of European sovereignty occurred in the distinction (complex as his was) between civilised nations and their colonial other. This distinction reached its most extreme form in the period of nineteenth-century colonisation and continued into the period of decolonisation, with standards of 'civilisation' remaining the marker of a positive content of sovereignty. However, as a consequence of the way this measure was drawn, progressively fewer states or peoples were found to qualify.[161] A more recent manifestation of this can also be observed in the standards of human rights, democracy, the rule of law and facilitation of free markets (particularly the free movement of capital) prescribed as, to take one conspicuous recent example, the 'single sustainable model

159 Of course, this concerned the differences with the Christian religion between Protestants and Catholics – not religious difference in the broader sense.

160 Treaty of Münster (1648), arts 28 and 49; Treaty of Osnabrück (1648), arts 5, 11.

161 See Fitzpatrick, *Modernism*, p. 157.

for national success.'[162] At each moment, the self or autopositioning of states occurs in the context of a relation between states, and between states and other forms of political organisation, which is not devoid of content. That is not to say that the content created in this relation fully determines the kind of sovereign positioning that can take place. Rather, it is to say that in the act of positioning and re-positioning the sovereign state must necessarily be attuned and responsive to this content.

Conclusion

Considering sovereign autopositioning through the lens of Nancy's work enables a fuller recognition of the importance of relation in the process by which sovereignties are autopositioned and how they remain exposed and must respond to the changeful effects of relation if they are to maintain their position. I have sought to show that contrary to conventional readings of the development of the nation-state and of international law, the idea of the state as an empirical fact which precedes its relation to other states is wrong. I have shown this not only with help from Nancy, but from the very theorists of sovereignty and international law commonly called on to support the conventional view. I have also sought to show how the Peace of Westphalia, that most iconic of events through which the self-sufficiency of sovereign statehood is meant to have emerged, actually reveals the dependence of sovereign states on their relation to each other.

Emphasising the significance of relation goes not only to correct a deficiency that exists if we focus purely on position. As Nancy's work helps us appreciate, autopositioned sovereign claims are always made in the context of relation to other sovereign claims, spaced and distinguished from each other.

162 See George W. Bush, *The National Security Strategy of the United States of America*, Washington: Office of the President of the United States, 2002, preface; see also George W. Bush, *The National Security Strategy of the United States of America*, Washington: Office of the President of the United States, 2006, paras. I, II, VI.

This spacing and distinction occurs by communication – by contact. As such, it is extremely important in considering the question of boundaries. This is for two reasons. First, it enables us to see how in the constant positioning and re-positioning which occurs in relation, the boundaries of sovereign claims are never met without challenge. Given the absolute nature of a sovereign claim, the absence of any resistance would mean the absence of any boundary. And without a limit or boundary, it would dissipate entirely. So a sovereign claim, given its orientation towards the infinite, must find its limit through transgression. It must extend beyond or exceed what could possibly be its effective scope. Accordingly, the sovereign claim must always be challenged, and must always provoke challenges. This means that the resolution in the world of the effective scope of a particular sovereign claim always proceeds by way of contact, contest and conflict between entities with overlapping or competing sovereign claims. In this way, the effective scope and boundary of a sovereign claim is always played out in the relation between entities each of which makes a sovereign claim.

Second, the constitutive function of relation shows how the questions of the scope and boundary of a sovereign claim are essentially connected – such that attempting to delineate the boundary between sovereign claims is indeed how one determines their scope and content in any particular situation. As we saw in Chapter 2, the theory of sovereign autopositioning reveals that any sovereign has, at any one time, as much sovereignty as it has. There is no fixed and settled content to any sovereign claim. Nor, since they are based on the vacuous foundation of community and law, are there solid and immovable grounds for them. Focusing on the relation between sovereign positions further highlights the dynamic nature of modern sovereignty. As competing claims relate to one another, the boundary between them shifts. As the boundary shifts, what it means to be sovereign in that context shifts with it. Indeed, the question of what is inside and outside a sovereign claim, and where the boundary between one claim and another lies, is in fact the question of what it means, in any particular context, to be sovereign. This is not something which can be drawn at a high level of abstraction by demarcating physical borders or neat jurisdictional divides between, for example, the international, national and local. The boundary between sovereign claims can only be determined (for the time being) in practice, in the very detail of the law and its application in the world. As such, the remaining chapters will look to the detail of the law over which a contest between rival sovereign positions at the international, national and local levels is played out. Addressing this detail in light of the theoretical analysis offered so far will illustrate that the constant positioning and re-positioning of sovereignty is the operative dynamic informing the relationship between the claims to authority made by and for the WTO, the Indian state and local communities in India.

In Chapter 4, I will argue that the case of patent law in India provides a glimpse of the way in which the sovereignty of both the WTO and the Indian state is constituted by their relation to each other. Moreover, the boundaries between their respective claims will be shown to lie in the detail of treaty obligations and domestic legislation. In Chapter 5 I will examine the close and complex relation between sovereign claims by local and indigenous groups in India and the state itself, focusing on constitutional protections for such groups and local authority structures. We will see that these structures have a life both within and outside the framework of the state and indeed, as the analysis proceeds, that the Indian state relies for its own sovereignty on the kinds of claims made against it by these local communities.

Chapter 4

The Relation of Sovereigns at the National and International Levels

India and the WTO

> 'The nation in its very "sovereign" particularity constituently depends on the sphere of the international, which cannot then simply be a supine emanation.'[1]

So far I have argued that sovereignty in modernity is 'autopositioned' and relies essentially on self-assertion. I have argued that this is a feature of the sovereignty of the state but also of the claims to sovereignty made or acted out by the World Trade Organisation and local and indigenous communities in India. In Chapter 3, I added the complication that such autoposition necessarily occurs in relation; and that relation is a constitutive element of the autopositioned sovereign claim. In this chapter and the one which follows, I will instantiate these claims by focusing more closely on the relationship between India and the WTO in respect of patent law, and between India and its local communities over traditional knowledge.

Paying attention to the role of relation in the positioning of sovereignties is important to the question of considering the interaction between the WTO, the Indian state and local communities in India for three reasons. First, as Chapter 3 showed, the constitutive function of relation further exposes the fallacy of the idea

1 Peter Fitzpatrick, *Modernism and the Grounds of Law*, Cambridge: Cambridge University Press, 2001, p. 200.

of the pure origin of the sovereign nation-state. This distancing from the myth of a pure origin serves not only to debunk the solidity of the nation-state's claim to exclusive sovereignty, but also emphasises the continuing need to assert position in the face of new challenges. As Nancy's concept of co-appearance puts in focus, the presence of new challenges to existing sovereign positions provokes the need to reassert that sovereign position in light of each challenge. As such, the challenge itself becomes constitutive of the content and boundary of the sovereign claim.

The second reason for paying close attention to the relation between sovereign positions is that it avoids the temptation lurking within a conception of 'autopositioning' to replace the fallacy of the exclusive sovereign state with a new fallacy of a multiplicity of supposedly pure and self-possessed sovereignties. A simple account of sovereign autopositioning would stop at the point of the self-grounded assertion on which the sovereign relies. But that would presuppose that atomistic entities are able to create themselves out of nothing and then somehow impose themselves on the world. As I argued in Chapter 3, this is impossible.

Third, in exposing the limits of singularity, a focus on the constitutive function of relation helps us to understand the limits of sovereignty. In doing so, it enables us to think in a more complex way about debates in which the sovereignty of the state appears to be in decline, since it forces us to rethink the notion that there was a fixed starting point from which to measure this apparent decline. If the content of what it means to be sovereign (and therefore, a sovereign state) is constantly subject to the dynamic relationship and shifting boundaries between rival claims to authority, then it no longer makes sense to speak in terms of the rise and fall of 'sovereignty'. Instead, we should focus our attention more closely on the nature and effect of competing claims to determine law and the responsibilities which flow from them.

Relating these insights to the concern of this chapter, we will observe that the WTO operates as a rival site of authority in light of which the content and scope of the sovereign authority of states is and must be re-cast. We will see that, just as the terms of the Peace of Westphalia shaped the content, meaning and scope of sovereign authority in medieval continental Europe, the terms of membership of the WTO are (for WTO members)[2] a significant factor in constituting what it means to be a sovereign state in a globalised economy. Similarly, the continuing challenges of local and indigenous communities force states to adapt and reassert their sovereign position in relation to those challenges. This is particularly evident in states like India which have colonial histories and active claims to authority being made by local and indigenous communities. As such, the clash of European sovereignty with an indigenous other did not just shape sovereignty in Vitoria's time, but continues to do so today.

In this chapter I will focus on the relationship between the WTO and the Indian state over patent law. I will argue that the relation between these sites of legal authority reveals how each depends on the sovereignty of the other. In the first two sections I will show how the sovereignties of India and the WTO are constitutively dependent on each other. I will then examine this relation in light of the content of TRIPS and the Indian Patents Act 1970. I will argue that the boundary between these sites of sovereignty exists in the level of the detail of this content and present the content of Indian patent law as the result of the interaction between these sovereign positions – neither of which has ultimate determining power.

1 The Constitutive Dependence of India's Sovereignty on the WTO

As I intimated in the Introduction, India's active participation in a variety of international fora (including within various rounds of WTO negotiations) serves to complicate the notion that India's relationship to international economic institutions involves a simple reduction of its sovereignty. Instead, we find that the same institutions and processes which are meant to deny India's sovereignty (such as the WTO in particular, or treaty-making in general) are the same institutions and processes which the state uses

2 And for non-members, it could be argued that it is also a significant factor – defining what it is that they are not part of – the benefits from which they are excluded and the freedoms which their exclusion might yet offer them.

to contest such purported impositions. This phenomenon puts some additional context on the dry observation by the Permanent Court of International Justice in the *Wimbledon Case* that entering into treaty obligations is as much an exercise as it is a denial of state sovereignty. Indeed, in line with the argument that sovereign positions are constituted in relation to one another, the sovereignty of the Indian state depends essentially on its membership of the WTO, alongside other modes of international engagement.

The significance of institutions like the WTO in constituting the sovereignty of states can be shown by the example of India's efforts (along with certain other countries) to alter the effect of the TRIPS regime at the Fourth WTO Ministerial Conference in Doha and before the TRIPS Council, and through its reliance in these fora and in the development of its domestic law on the Convention on Biological Diversity (1992) (CBD).

In the years immediately following the formation of the WTO, issues of public health in developing countries became closely linked to the patent requirements in TRIPS and the conduct of multi-national corporations seeking to enforce them. High profile cases of pharmaceutical companies pursuing patent rights on treatments for HIV, particularly in South Africa, forced attention onto the issue.[3] It then became a key focus of the Fourth Ministerial Conference in Doha in 2001. India was a key part of a group of developing countries which lobbied hard for a Ministerial Declaration stating that TRIPS did not restrict their capacity to take measures to protect public health. India's position and that of other developing countries was ultimately reflected in the 'Declaration on the TRIPS Agreement and Public Health'.[4] It states that:

> the TRIPS Agreement does not and should not prevent members from taking measures to protect public health …

3 Carlos Correa, 'Implications of the Doha Declaration on the TRIPS Agreement and Public Health', 2002, World Health Organisation: WHO/EDM/PAR/2002.3, pp. 1–2.

4 World Trade Organisation, 'Declaration on the TRIPS Agreement and Public Health', Ministerial Conference, 14 November 2001, WT/MIN(01)/DEC/2, at: http://www.wto.org/English/thewto_e/minist_e/min01_e/mindecl_trips_e.htm (last accessed 6 December 2011) (Doha TRIPS Declaration).

> and can and should be interpreted and implemented in a manner supportive of WTO members' right to protect public health and, in particular, to promote access to medicines for all.[5]

It is important to note that this declaration does not alter the terms of TRIPS and as such does not reduce any of the obligations it contains with respect to patenting medicines. Nonetheless, it may make broad interpretations of the flexibility within TRIPS, particularly regarding compulsory licensing, easier to defend if a complaint comes before the WTO dispute settlement procedure. As we will see below, India's Patents Act 1970 contains broad compulsory licensing provisions.[6] Even to the extent of using the same diseases as examples of potential public health crises (HIV/ AIDS, tuberculosis and malaria), these provisions draw directly on the language of the Doha TRIPS Declaration. As such, India's exercise of its standing as a sovereign state at the Fourth WTO Ministerial Conference enabled it not only to make submissions which may impact on the interpretation of TRIPS, but provided a basis upon which it may defend particular measures in its domestic law.

In addition to its submissions at Doha, India has also actively participated in the review of article 27.3(b) by the TRIPS Council, which commenced in 1999. Article 27.3(b) determines the extent to which inventions relating to biological resources may be excluded from patentability. India's participation in the review helps to highlight the importance of institutions like the WTO in constituting its sovereignty. First, India relies on its status as a sovereign state and member of the WTO to participate in the review of article 27.3(b). Were it not a 'sovereign state' it would not be able to play this role. As Commerce and Industry Minister Kamal Nath argued during debates on the patent law reforms in 2005, membership of the WTO enables 'India to have a leadership role in taking on the unilateralism in global trade which is

5 Ibid., para 4.
6 Patents Act 1970 (India), ss 84–92A.

taking place.'[7] In doing so, India relies on its status as a signatory to another international agreement, the CBD, to bolster its arguments and in particular relies strongly on that treaty's emphasis on national sovereignty over biological resources.[8] These submissions argue that TRIPS facilitates 'biopiracy' by allowing the patenting of inventions based on traditional knowledge and advocate amendments to TRIPS to provide for a system of prior informed consent and equitable benefit sharing whose content mirrors that of India's Biological Diversity Act 2002.[9]

7 Parliament of India, 'Combined Discussion on the Statutory Resolution Regarding Disapproval of Patents (Amendment) Ordinance, 2004 (No. 7 of 2004) and passing of the Patents (Amendment) Bill, 2005' Lok Sabha Debates, 22 March 2005, at: http://164.100.47.132/LssNew/psearch/result14.aspx?dbsl=1866 (last accessed 6 December 2011).

8 Convention on Biological Diversity (1992), arts 3 and 15.

9 The following is a selection of the submissions made by India (with other states) to the Council for Trade-Related Aspects of Intellectual Property Rights, World Trade Organisation. A complete record of these submissions is available at: http://www.wto.org/english/tratop_e/trips_e/art27_3b_e.htm (last accessed 6 December 2011): Brazil, China, Colombia, Ecuador, India, Indonesia, Peru, Thailand, the ACP Group, and the African Group, 'Draft Decision To Enhance Mutual Supportiveness Between the TRIPS Agreement and the Convention on Biological Diversity' (TN/C/W/59) 19 April 2011; Brazil, China, Colombia, Cuba, Dominican Republic, Ecuador, India, Indonesia, Pakistan, Paraguay, Peru, South Africa, Tanzania, Thailand, Venezuela, LDC Group and ACP Group, 'Doha Work Programme – Relationship Between the TRIPS Agreement and the Convention on Biological Diversity' (WT/GC/W/590), 28 May 2008; Brazil, China, Colombia, Cuba, India, Pakistan, Peru, Thailand and Tanzania, 'Doha Work Programme – The Outstanding Implementation Issue on the Relationship Between the TRIPS Agreement and the Convention on Biological Diversity' (WT/GC/W/564/Rev.2) 5 July 2006; Brazil and India, 'The Relationship between the TRIPS Agreement and the Convention on Biological Diversity (CBD) and the Protection of Traditional Knowledge: Technical Observations on Issues raised in a Communication by the United States' (IP/C/W/434), 18 March 2005; Bolivia, Brazil, Cuba, Ecuador, India, Pakistan, Peru, Thailand and Venezuela, 'The Relationship Between the TRIPS Agreement and the Convention on Biological Diversity (CBD) and the Protection of Traditional Knowledge: Elements of the Obligation to Disclose Evidence of Prior Informed Consent under the Relevant National Regime' (IP/C/W/438), 10 December 2004; Bolivia, Brazil, Cuba, Ecuador, India, Pakistan, Peru, Thailand and Venezuela, 'The Relationship Between the TRIPS Agreement and the

Indeed, the Biological Diversity Act 2002 provides a good example of a reflexive relationship between authority exercised at the national and international levels. Negotiating and agreeing to the terms of the CBD provided the Indian government with an opportunity to project its domestic authority on the international stage. In enacting the Biological Diversity Act 2002, the Indian government expressly intended to give effect to the CBD within Indian domestic law. And so its international obligations performed a justificatory role for its domestic legislative agenda.

In turn, India has projected this domestic reflection of its international obligations back onto the international stage through its agitation for changes to TRIPS that would require other states to enact laws in compliance with the CBD and which are similar to its own Biological Diversity Act.[10] This would mean that those states would need to enact laws preventing patenting of biological resources or traditional knowledge (from India or elsewhere) unless access and benefit sharing procedures were complied with. As such, India seeks to influence the law of other states by lobbying for changes to TRIPS, and in doing so seeks to rely on the very same treaty which has been said to have undermined its own sovereignty. Accordingly, the same mechanisms which are said to deny India's sovereignty (international organisations and the undertaking of treaty obligations, especially at the WTO), are the very same mechanisms which India uses to press its interests on the international stage and which its government uses to project its authority domestically. In short, they are mechanisms which go towards constituting India's sovereignty at the international and domestic levels.

Convention on Biological Diversity and the Protection of Traditional Knowledge', (IP/C/W/403), 24 June 2003; Permanent Mission of Brazil on behalf of the delegations of Brazil, China, Cuba, Dominican Republic, Ecuador, India, Pakistan, Thailand, Venezuela, Zambia and Zimbabwe, 'The Relationship Between the TRIPS Agreement and the Convention on Biological Diversity and the Protection of Traditional Knowledge', (IP/C/W/356), 24 June 2002 (this submission contains the charge the TRIPS facilitates 'biopiracy').

10 Ibid.

2 The Constitutive Dependence of the WTO on Member-State Sovereignty

We saw in the Introduction that the authority of the WTO is formally constituted by the consent of its member states. In that sense, it is uncontroversial to argue that through the process of negotiation, conclusion and amendment of its agreements, the WTO depends constitutively on the relation between it and its member states and their relation with each other.

A more complicated aspect of the WTO's dependence on its member states concerns the implementation of its requirements in domestic law, both in terms of general compliance with WTO agreements and in terms of compliance with specific rulings made under its dispute settlement procedure. The WTO relies on the authority and ability of its member states to implement and enforce laws which meet the standards comprised in the WTO agreements. It also relies on states to bring actions against each other to enliven the jurisdiction of its dispute settlement procedures such that decisions on the meaning of WTO law can be made. Where such decisions find non-compliance with WTO standards, the WTO relies on the losing party to implement changes to its domestic law. As we will see, despite the extensive sanctions available under WTO law, the question of implementation reveals a significant limitation in the scope of its sovereign claim over the domestic law of its member states. Not only that, but the nature of this limitation reveals the boundary between these sites of authority to be messy and contested.

The enforcement mechanisms under the WTO's dispute settlement procedure are extensive.[11] The Dispute Settlement Body (DSB) is granted power to 'keep under surveillance the implementation of adopted recommendations or rulings.'[12] In addition

11 The WTO's dispute settlement procedures are set out in the Understanding on Rules and Procedures Governing the Settlement of Disputes (commonly referred to as the Dispute Settlement Understanding or DSU), annex 2 to the Marrakesh Agreement Establishing the World Trade Organisation (WTO Agreement).

12 DSU, art 21.6.

to requiring losing parties to notify the DSB of their intentions regarding implementation within 30 days of the adoption of the report,[13] the DSB may also be notified of failures to comply at any time by any member. If the losing party does not implement appropriate measures within a reasonable time, the focus then shifts to compensation or the suspension of concessions. In this situation, the winning party may require the losing party to enter into negotiations 'with a view to developing mutually acceptable compensation.'[14] If this cannot be achieved, the winning party may request authorisation from the DSB to suspend the application of concessions or other obligations under the WTO agreements in respect of that party. On request, the DSB will grant authorisation to suspend concessions or other obligations unless it decides by consensus not to do so.[15] If the losing party objects to the measure requested or considers that the relevant procedures have not been complied with, this issue may be referred to arbitration by the original Panel or another arbitrator, whose decision will be final.[16]

Most significantly, the range of measures available to the winning party are not restricted to the subject matter of the dispute, although some attempt to keep the breach and remedy within the same sector or agreement is required and cross-sector retaliation requires more justification before authorisation from the DSB will be granted. For example, in response to a failure to implement adequate protection of patent rights, a winning party may request authority to suspend equal treatment of the infringing state's nationals within its patent system.[17] If this is not likely to be effective, the winning party may request authority to suspend concessions under TRIPS generally (for example in copyright or trade-marks).[18] If this is not likely to be effective, and the situation

13 Ibid., art 21.3.
14 Ibid., art 22.2.
15 Ibid., art 22.6.
16 Ibid.
17 Ibid., art 22.3(a).
18 Ibid., art 22.3(b).

is 'serious enough' the winning party may request authority to suspend concessions in any other WTO agreement, such as those concerning tariffs or quotas in other sectors of trade.[19] Given the range and importance of the interests which may be affected by a suspension of concessions, it is clear that the WTO has effective means of enforcing its decisions even though it lacks the power to implement changes to member states' domestic law directly.

The extent of the WTO's ability to directly influence the implementation of a decision is set out in article 19 of the DSU. Under that article, where a Panel or the Appellate Body concludes that a state is not in compliance with a WTO agreement, it shall recommend measures to achieve compliance and may suggest appropriate methods of implementation.[20] In practice, suggestions as to the method of implementation are rarely made, particularly at the Panel level.[21] Depending on the specificity of the issue at hand, there may be significant scope for the losing party to choose its preferred method of implementing the recommendation.[22] This can potentially lead to a new dispute about whether measures taken by a losing party in response to a Panel or Appellate Body recommendation actually place that party in compliance with its obligations. Where this occurs, the new dispute is to be decided under the same dispute settlement procedures, if possible using the original Panel.[23]

19 Ibid., see art 22.3(c).

20 Ibid., art 19.1.

21 Mitsuo Matsushita, Thomas Schoenbaum and Petros Mavroidis, *The World Trade Organisation*, Oxford: Oxford University Press, 2004, p. 80.

22 Ibid., 82.

23 DSU, art 21.5. The gap between the decision of the DSB and its implementation by the losing state is exacerbated by the drafting error in the DSU, known as the 'sequencing error'. The DSU provides different and concurrent timeframes for the determination of a dispute about compliance measures (90 days from the referral of the compliance dispute to the Panel) (art 21.5) and a request for enforcement measures (30 days from the expiry of the 'reasonable time' given for compliance) (art 22.6). This means that a winning party can request authorisation of enforcement measures while at the same time a dispute can be ongoing about whether measures taken by the losing party place it in compliance with the WTO agreements. This issue came to a head in the

The scope open to the losing party to choose its method of implementing the recommendation is a significant indication of the limits of the WTO's sovereign claim. It demonstrates the nature of the relation between the WTO and its member states as being one between rival sovereign positions in the absence of a common superior authority. The WTO claims authority over the content of domestic law by the text of its treaties, but the state itself must interpret them in the first instance and decide what it needs to do in order to comply. This decision can only be contested at the WTO, which can deliver an authoritative decision on whether the state is in compliance, and if it is not, make a recommendation that it amend its law to comply. At this point, however, it is again up to the state in question to change its law to comply with the decision, and once more it needs to decide what it should do to comply. Matsushita, Schoenbaum and Mavroidis argue that 'the tendency has been for the losing party to take minimal steps and declare itself in full compliance.'[24] And while the quality of its compliance can again be the subject of a dispute at the WTO and a decision by the Panel or Appellate Body, it is yet again up to the state in question to change its law to comply with this later decision, and once more it needs to decide what it should do to comply. In theory, this could lead to an endless cycle of dispute, decision, recommendation and reform of

EC – Bananas III case, when the EC and Ecuador requested the establishment of a panel under article 21.5 to determine the question of compliance, after the US had sought suspension of concessions under article 22: see David Palmeter and Petros Mavroidis, *Dispute Settlement in the World Trade Organisation: Practice and Procedure*, Cambridge: Cambridge University Press, 2004, pp. 280–4. In that case, the problem was avoided by the respective decisions being delivered within days of each other. Since then, the problem has generally been avoided by agreement between the parties to suspend the question of enforcement measures (and the 30 day period) pending determination of a compliance dispute: Rüdiger Wolfrum, Peter-Tobias Stoll and Karen Kaiser (eds), *WTO: Institutions and Dispute Settlement*, Leiden: Martinus Nijhoff, 2006, pp. 517–8. However, even if, as has been proposed, the drafting error is rectified, it will still not overcome the fact that the final step of implementing measures into domestic law is always left to the domestic institutions of the losing party.

24 Matsushita, Schoenbaum and Mavroidis, *World Trade Organisation*, p. 30.

domestic law, in which the last stage always remains contested. As such, a member state such as India can use whatever scope exists for interpretation at the first and last implementation stages. Accordingly, the content of Indian patent law can be seen as the result of the dynamic relation between the WTO's requirements reflected in TRIPS and any relevant Panel or Appellate Body decisions, and the Indian state's ability to interpret TRIPS or these decisions to give effect to local concerns. It is to the detail of this content that I now turn.

3 Indian Patent Law as the Product of Competing Sovereignties

Concentrating on the relation between the WTO and the Indian state helps put in focus the way in which each depends on the other to constitute its authority in a general sense. But keeping things at such a broad level of generality does little to elucidate the more contentious elements of the relationship between the WTO and its member states. These have to do with the content of the law which the WTO requires its member states to enact.

I have argued above that viewing the WTO's patent law requirements as simply constituting a denial of India's sovereignty imposition fails to appreciate the nature of the relationship between these sites of authority. By displacing the state as the sole locus of sovereignty and as the sole source of legal authority in modernity, the theory of sovereign autopositioning allows us to look at competing claims to determine law in a new way. In the case of Indian patent law and the WTO, it allows us to see that the boundary between the authority of the WTO and the state is not marked out in a neat division between the domestic and the international, where that division itself is marked by formal notions of consent. Instead, the boundary between these sites of authority exists in the detail of the content of the law over which the competing claims are made. In what follows, I will argue that the competing claims by the Indian state and the WTO over Indian patent law intersect and overlap, but not entirely. In the absence of a higher authority to determine any dispute between them, the boundary between these claims can only be provisionally determined by the relation between them. And since that relation is dynamic, the boundary is constantly shifting. As each sovereign claim meets its point of resistance in the claim of its rival, the scope of each is made and continually remade. Examining the terms of TRIPS in detail, we will see that the WTO's claim is strongest when the terms of TRIPS are precise, and weakest where the terms are ambiguous and are yet to be interpreted by the WTO's dispute settlement bodies. We will also see that Indian patent law contains elements which could be seen to take advantage of these ambiguities and as such, illustrate the extent of India's control over its patent law.

3.1 The scope of the WTO's claim over Indian patent law

As I suggested in Chapter 2, the requirements of TRIPS are sufficiently specific to constitute a substantial claim on the patent law of its member states. This is the case despite the impression given by articles 1 and 8, that there is significant scope for states to choose how to implement the requirements. After stating that members must comply with TRIPS, article 1 provides that '[m]embers shall be free to determine the appropriate method of implementing the provisions of this Agreement within their own legal systems.'[25] However, the extent of the freedom provided by this article depends on the specificity of the substantive requirements which states are required to implement.

Like article 1, article 8 also appears at first to provide for a wide scope of legislative freedom, but on closer inspection may do little more than aid interpretation of other provisions. It contains a general statement that member states are free to 'adopt measures necessary to protect public health and nutrition and to promote the public interest in sectors of vital importance to their socio-economic and technological development.'[26] It is also permissible for members to adopt measures to prevent the abuse of

25 TRIPS, art 1.
26 Ibid., art 8.1.

intellectual property rights.[27] Both parts of article 8 would at first appear to provide substantial legislative freedom to ensure the public interest is served in areas such as access to medicines and access to seed for agriculture, which have provoked so much opposition to TRIPS in India and elsewhere. However in both cases this freedom is tempered by the substantial proviso that such measures must be 'consistent with the provisions of this Agreement'.[28] To avoid the obvious circularity, it is likely that, in respect of patent law, 'consistent with the provisions of this Agreement' really means consistent with the substantive provisions of TRIPS.[29] Given the proviso, it is questionable whether article 8 adds anything to what would be the ordinary legislative freedom of a member state. It would be impossible to argue that without this article, TRIPS would somehow, by implication, curtail the freedom of nation-state legislatures to adopt measures relating to public health and the public interest where such measures were, in any event, consistent with TRIPS. Nonetheless, combined with the Doha TRIPS Declaration, which affirms states' ability to interpret TRIPS in a manner conducive to protecting public health,[30] this article may assist in bolstering an argument that a particular public health measure is consistent with TRIPS.

Articles 1 and 8, together with the Doha TRIPS Declaration, may provide some background support to states wishing to push the boundaries of the interpretation of TRIPS in their domestic law. But the real extent of a member state's legislative freedom in respect of patent law is not conditioned by these general statements, but by the precision with which the requirements of (and exceptions within) the patent system under TRIPS are drafted,

27 Ibid., art 8.2.
28 Ibid., arts 8.1 and 8.2.
29 The approach of the panel in the Canadian Pharmaceuticals case would suggest that the impact of art 8 will be marginal: *Canada – Patent Protection of Pharmaceutical Products*, Report of the Panel (WT/DS114/R), 17 March 2000, para. 7.26; see Fiona Macmillan, *The World Trade Organization and Human Rights*, Oxford, Hart: forthcoming, ch. 3.
30 World Trade Organisation, 'Doha TRIPS Declaration'.

in addition to the institutional framework, described above and in Chapter 2, which monitors compliance and enforces decisions arising from disputes between states. As we will see, some of the requirements of TRIPS are very specific, while others leave more room for interpretation. Thus a tension exists between the claims of the WTO specified in the text of TRIPS and the ability of states to interpret TRIPS in a manner to suit local concerns. This point of tension is the boundary between the sovereign claims of the WTO and the Indian state to determine the content of patent law in India.

The minimum standards of patent protection required of TRIPS members are set out in section 5 of TRIPS. The key provision is article 27, which sets out what constitutes patentable subject matter. This is a significant step from the position under the Paris Convention, which left the content of what constitutes a patent to be determined by domestic law.[31] Under article 27.1, as we saw in Chapter 2, member states are required to ensure that patents are, subject to specified exclusions, 'available for any inventions, whether products or processes, in all fields of technology, provided that they are new, involve an inventive step and are capable of industrial application' and 'without discrimination as to the place of invention, the field of technology and whether products are imported or locally produced.'[32] Two key points emerge from this article. The first is the breadth of the requirement that patents be available without discrimination as to type or place of invention. For India, which had excluded patents on medicinal, chemical and agricultural products, and favoured local producers, this article required significant changes to be made to its existing law. As we saw in Chapter 2, article 27 effectively creates a presumption of patentability, departure from which must be justified by one of the specific exclusions.[33]

The second point is that the key criteria of patentability in Western patent law systems: 'novelty', 'inventive step' (defined to

31 Paris Convention for the Protection of Industrial Property (1883), art 1(4).

32 TRIPS art 27.1.

33 Daniel Gervais, *The TRIPS Agreement: Drafting History and Analysis*, 3rd ed., London: Sweet and Maxwell, 2008, pp. 337, 379–401.

be synonymous with 'non-obviousness', the term used in the United States) and 'capable of industrial application' (defined to be synonymous with 'useful') are enshrined in TRIPS. In Blakeney's terms article 27.1 follows the 'conventional jurisprudence which has been developed in this area.'[34] Gervais simply states that these are the 'three usual criteria.'[35] The 'conventional jurisprudence' is, of course, particular to the legal systems in which these terms have developed. It is instructive to note that Blakeney's guide to TRIPS, which does not overlook the issues affecting developing countries, nevertheless relies exclusively on European, North American and Australian cases in explaining the meaning of its terms.[36] Each of the terms has a long history of interpretation in Western legal systems and a concern has been raised that 'developing countries do not have administrative or judicial history which can provide interpretation for these terms.'[37]

Taken together, the requirement that patents be available in all fields of technology, and the use of Western criteria for patentability, suggest that there is little freedom for member states to fashion divergent patent laws. However, while the particular origin and interpretive history from which the terms in TRIPS emerge is significant, one cannot simply assume that their meaning is fixed. The requirement that patents be available in all fields of technology might be hard to avoid, but the question of what constitutes an inventive step, for example, might create more scope for differing standards. Not only is there divergence within Western systems about the standard of 'inventive step' or 'non-obviousness' necessary to obtain a patent, for example,[38] but the possibility of new interpretations of these terms is not limited by TRIPS, which, as we will see below, does not expressly define them.

34 Michael Blakeney, *Trade Related Aspects of Intellectual Property Rights: A Concise Guide to the TRIPS Agreement*, London: Sweet and Maxwell, 1996, p. 83.

35 Gervais, *TRIPS Agreement*, p. 337.

36 Blakeney, *Trade Related Aspects*.

37 Gervais, *TRIPS Agreement*, p. 338.

38 See Matthew Fisher, *Fundamentals of Patent Law: Interpretation and Scope of Protection*, Oxford, Hart: 2007; Blakeney, *Trade Related Aspects*, pp. 84–5.

Correa notes that 'less technologically advanced countries may prefer to set higher standards of novelty and inventive step in order to preserve and enhance competition without violating minimum international standards.'[39] As I will argue below, the possibility that new interpretations might take root in new contexts provides scope for unpredictable divergences in member states' patent laws despite the prescriptions in TRIPS.

Beyond the broad question of patentability, TRIPS also sets out a number of specific features that the patent law of WTO member states must contain. I noted in Chapter 2 the most specific of these, such as the requirement that states provide a minimum term protection for patents of 20 years.[40] Such specific requirements leave scarce room for divergent approaches and, as such, constitute a substantial claim on the patent law of WTO member states. But other provisions allow more room for divergent approaches. This tension is most readily apparent in the area of exceptions to patentability. The main exceptions are in articles 27.2, 27.3, 30, 31 and 32. Article 27.2 allows countries to exclude from patentability inventions whose commercial exploitation is 'necessary' to prevent in order to 'protect *ordre public* or morality, including to protect human, animal or plant life or health or to avoid serious prejudice to the environment.'[41] Such exclusion cannot be based solely on the basis that a domestic law prohibits such exploitation.[42] Like the terms 'inventive step' and 'novelty',

39 Carlos Correa 'Public Health and Patent Legislation in Developing Countries', *Tulane Journal of Technology and Intellectual Property* 3, 2001, 1, 23. See Janice Mueller, 'The Tiger Awakens: The Tumultuous Transformation of India's Patent System and the Rise of Indian Pharmaceutical Innovation', *University of Pittsburgh Law Review* 68, 2007, 491, 563.

40 TRIPS, art 33. As we saw in Chapter 2, Blakeney notes that 'the developing countries' had failed at the TRIPS negotiations to have the duration of a patent be a matter to be fixed by national legislation: see Blakeney, *Trade Related Aspects*, p. 88.

41 TRIPS, art 27.2. Section 3 of the Patents Act 1970 (India) renders *ordre public* as 'public order'. It would appear likely that it would nonetheless be interpreted in accordance with the conventional sense of *ordre public* as meaning 'public policy', but this cannot be taken for granted.

42 Ibid., art 27.2. See Blakeney, *Trade Related Aspects*, p. 82.

the concept of *ordre public* and morality have a history in Western patent law. But as debates about stem cell research and other aspects of biotechnology show, their meaning is far from settled.[43] The broad terms of article 27.2 clearly leave much to interpretation. Different states may have very different views on what constitutes a threat to human health or serious prejudice to the environment and, at least in theory, be able to frame exceptions to suit local conditions. However, when it comes to defending such measures in response to a complaint under the WTO dispute settlement procedure, a state will be required to show that they are 'objectively justifiable.'[44] Decisions by the Appellate Body have held that determining whether a measure conflicting with a member state's obligation is 'necessary' involves 'weighing and balancing a series of factors' one of which is whether 'a WTO-consistent alternative measure which the member concerned could reasonably be expected to employ is available, or whether a less WTO-inconsistent measure is reasonably available.'[45]

Article 27.3 contains additional permitted exclusions which do not have to be justified on the basis of public policy or morality or serious prejudice to the environment. Under this article, member states may exclude from patentability: (a) medical methods for treating humans or animals; and (b) plants and animals themselves, along with essentially biological processes for their production.[46] However, patents must be available for micro-organisms and for non-biological and microbiological

43 See, e.g., *Diamond v Chakrabarty* (1980) 206 USPQ 193; *OncoMouse/Harvard* [1990] EPOR 4; [1991] EPOR 525; [2003] 10 OJ EPO 473; *Re Wisconsin Alumni Research Foundation's Application*, Case No. G 0002/06, EPO Enlarged Board of Appeal, 25 November 2008.

44 Gervais, *TRIPS Agreement*, p. 346.

45 *Korea – Measures Affecting Imports of Fresh, Chilled and Frozen Beef*, Report of the Appellate Body, (WT/DS161/AB/R; WT/DS169/AB/R), 11 December 2000, para 164; *Dominican Republic – Measures Affecting the Importation and Internal Sale Of Cigarettes*, Report of the Appellate Body, (WT/DS302/AB/R), 25 April 2005, para 70; see ibid., pp. 346–50.

46 TRIPS, art 27.3(b).

processes.[47] Member states must also provide patent protection for plant varieties and species, or alternatively create an 'effective *sui generis* system' for their protection.[48] India has used the flexibility in relation to plant variety protection to enact laws which diverge significantly from the international standard set by the main treaty in the field.[49] Article 27.3(b) also contains a review clause under which its provisions were to be reviewed after 1 January 1999. The review, administered by the TRIPS Council, is ongoing.[50] As I noted in the first section of this chapter, India has made a number of submissions to the TRIPS Council during this review, mostly concerning the ability of states to set the terms of access to biological resources and related traditional knowledge.

Article 30 also allows members to provide 'limited exceptions' to the rights conferred by a patent. However, these limitations must not 'unreasonably conflict with a normal exploitation of a patent' and while the 'legitimate interests of third parties' can be taken into account, the limitations must also not 'unreasonably prejudice the legitimate interests of the patent owner'.[51] This provision clearly requires a determination on what is the 'normal exploitation of a patent' and what interests of patent holders and third parties might be 'legitimate.' Blakeney notes that 'the usual exceptions' would include compulsory licensing in the public interest, manufacture purely for scientific research and good faith use or preparation for use before the application for the patent.[52] However, in the context of public health concerns on the scale which exist in India, the 'legitimate' interests involved might be

47 Ibid., art 27.3(b).

48 TRIPS, art 27.3(b).

49 *Protection of Plant Varieties and Farmers' Rights Act 2001* (India); cf International Union for the Protection of New Varieties of Plants (1961).

50 World Trade Organisation, 'TRIPS Reviews, Article 27.3(b) and Related Issues: Background and Current Situation', at: http://www.wto.org/english/tratop_e/trips_e/art27_3b_background_e.htm (last accessed 6 December 2011).

51 TRIPS, art 30.

52 Blakeney, *Trade Related Aspects*, p. 87.

considered in a way very different to that contemplated by trade negotiators in Washington or Geneva. Despite this potential variation, the determination of what article 30 allows may be left to Panel and Appellate Body decisions under the WTO dispute settlement procedure, should complaints be made about the scope of limitations set under article 30. A narrow interpretation was taken by the Panel in *Canada – Patent Protection of Pharmaceutical Products*, which relied on the history of international instruments on intellectual property in order to determine what was meant by 'legitimate interests.'[53] It held that a 'limited exception' involves only a 'small diminution of the right in question', that the 'normal exploitation of a patent' meant the right to exclude all forms of competition that could detract from the benefits flowing from market exclusivity.[54] This would indicate that the possibility of using this exception to radically reinterpret the balance of 'legitimate' interests in developing countries may be more limited than the text of article 30 promises. On the other hand, the *Canadian Pharmaceuticals* case came before the Doha TRIPS Declaration, which may now prompt a reinterpretation of how public health sits in the balance of 'legitimate interests'.[55]

The provisions with the most scope for countering the broad requirements of patentability in TRIPS are articles 31 and 32, which set out the permitted grounds for compulsory licences and revocation of patents. Significantly though, it must be noted that licences under article 31 and revocations under article 32 can only be made on an individual basis and as such, these provisions do not allow for blanket exceptions to patentability for particular technologies.[56] I will examine these in more detail

53 *Canada – Patent Protection of Pharmaceutical Products*, Report of the Panel (WT/DS114/R), 17 March 2000, para. 7.70–7.72. For a detailed analysis of this case, see Macmillan, *World Trade Organization*, ch. 3.

54 *Canada – Patent Protection of Pharmaceutical Products*, Report of the Panel (WT/DS114/R), 17 March 2000, paras 7.30, 7.70–7.72, 7.55; See Gervais, *TRIPS Agreement*, pp. 382–3.

55 See Dwijen Rangnekar, 'Is Plagiarism the Only Problem with the Mashelkar Report?', *Economic and Political Weekly* 42, 2007, 816, 817.

56 TRIPS, art 31(a).

below when discussing the compulsory licensing and revocation provisions in India's Patents Act 1970.

The claim of the WTO over the patent law of its member states is strongest where the terms of TRIPS are very specific and weakest where the terms are sufficiently vague to allow for divergent interpretations. Somewhere in between are the provisions that draw on terms which have acquired certain meanings in Western intellectual property law but which may be open to divergent interpretations in different contexts over time. Beyond the text of TRIPS itself, it is also important to remember the role of the WTO's dispute settlement procedure. Where states' views on the interpretation of TRIPS conflict, the WTO's dispute settlement procedure may be invoked. Since TRIPS aims at a harmonisation of intellectual property standards, it is likely that the WTO dispute settlement bodies will attempt to reduce ambiguities in the text by offering authoritative interpretations when cases are brought before them. As the India 'mailbox' case showed, a Panel or the Appellate Body will form its own opinion as to the effect of a member state's law (in determining whether it complies with TRIPS).[57] Further, the *Canadian Pharmaceuticals* case would also make it seem likely that a fairly conservative stance will be taken on the interpretation of the balance between the legitimate interests of patent owners and third parties. Whether this will change following the Doha TRIPS Declaration remains to be seen. But crucially, this process is ongoing. There is no overarching authority which can fix the content of patent law under TRIPS or in the domestic law of member states enduringly. Instead, there is a tension between rival sites of authority which cannot be resolved and must simply be played out over time. In what follows, I will examine two areas of Indian patent law which reflect the nature of this dynamic.

57 *India – Patent Protection for Pharmaceutical and Chemical Products*, Report of the Panel (WT/DS50/R), 5 September 1997; *India – Patent Protection for Pharmaceutical and Chemical Products*, Report of the Appellate Body, (WT/DS50/AB/R), 19 December 1997. See discussion of this case in Chapter 2, in the text accompanying notes 107–9.

3.2 The scope of Indian sovereignty over patent law

Once it is acknowledged that the WTO makes a sovereign claim on the patent law of its member states and that the strength and scope of this claim depends on the specificity of the requirements of TRIPS, it is possible to view the content of the patent law in states like India in a new light. It is clear that India cannot provide for a different term of patent protection, unless it is able to effect a change to the terms of TRIPS itself by gathering sufficient support for an amendment. On the other hand, other terms used in the agreement allow more room for interpretation. It should follow that ambiguous terms may take on different meanings, in subtle or substantial ways, when exported into different contexts. This room for interpretation, combined with the fact that the state is the entity which must (even if subject to a WTO recommendation and the possibility of sanctions) implement any TRIPS requirements, means that the greater the degree of ambiguity and the greater the scope for divergent interpretations, the weaker the claim of the WTO becomes and the more scope the state has for addressing local concerns. Crucially, it is the scope for divergent interpretations, not the particular content of the requirements (i.e. whether they affect public health), which reveals the extent of the WTO's sovereign claim on Indian patent law. The two examples set out below show that even as India has been required to adopt patent law which complies with TRIPS, it has also retained the capacity to frame this law in ways which seek to give effect to local concerns.[58] In this way, the content of Indian patent law can be seen as the product of the dynamic between the competing sovereign claims of the WTO and the state, rather than being the product of one of these entities occupying a superior position. The first concerns particular exclusions from the meaning of

58 For a general discussion of the range of policy options open to India in light of TRIPS (written before the TRIPS reforms to India's patent law were implemented), see Jayasharee Watal, 'Implementing the TRIPS Agreement: Policy Options Open to India', *Economic and Political Weekly* 32(39), 1997, 2461–8. The discussion below will focus on particular post-implementation issues.

'invention' which could limit the scope of patentable subject matter. The second concerns the scope of compulsory licences which operate as exceptions to the monopoly rights granted to patent holders.

3.2.1 The definition of 'invention'

Despite its various prescriptions, TRIPS does not define 'invention' nor does it offer a precise way of distinguishing invention from the term typically opposed to it, 'discovery'. As Correa notes, this is not 'a loophole or inadvertent omission of the Agreement' but rather 'just reflects the lack of a unique concept of invention.'[59] Most national patent laws also avoid attempting to define 'invention' itself, but require that a patentable invention meet the key requirements of novelty, inventive step and industrial applicability. They also typically contain more detailed provisions which set out what is not an invention. Indian patent law differs from this convention slightly by attempting a definition of invention which simply incorporates the key patentability requirements.[60] What matters most in this context is the question of what is excluded from the definition. As noted above, TRIPS contains some permitted exclusions from patentability.[61] It also constrains the way in which things can be excluded from the definition of invention by prohibiting an exclusion which would operate to deny patentability within a particular field of technology.[62] It also prevents 'micro-organisms' and 'non-biological and microbiological processes' being excluded from patentability.[63] But with no express definition of invention, states have a reasonable degree of flexibility on the question of where they choose to draw the line between inventions and discoveries, particularly where the

59 Carlos Correa, *Intellectual Property Rights, the WTO and Developing Countries: The TRIPS Agreement and Policy Options*, New York: Zed Books, 2000, p. 51.

60 Patents Act 1970 (India), s 2.

61 TRIPS, arts 27.2 and 27.3.

62 TRIPS, art 27.1.

63 Ibid., art 27.3(b).

subject matter of the alleged invention is (or is based on) natural or living material.

India has not gone as far as some other countries in broadly excluding natural and living materials from patentability.[64] However, its patent law does contain two particular exclusions which demonstrate India's ability to respond to national concerns and adopt an interpretation of the requirements of TRIPS which diverges from the intellectual property laws of the developed states from which the requirements of TRIPS were drawn.

The first is the exclusion of 'traditional knowledge' from the definition of invention. The amending Act in 2002 excluded from patentability any invention 'which, in effect, is traditional knowledge or which is an aggregation of duplication of known properties of traditionally known component or components.'[65] The amendment requires the patent office to reject applications which fail to disclose the 'source or geographical origin of biological material used for the invention' and also where the claims in the application are 'anticipated having regard to the knowledge, oral or otherwise, available within any local or indigenous community in India or elsewhere.'[66]

The provisions preventing patenting of inventions based on traditional knowledge mark an important distinction between Indian patent law and its United States and European counterparts. However, it is arguable that if traditional knowledge is properly read as 'prior art', such inventions would not be patentable under even the most patent-friendly interpretation of TRIPS, due to lack of novelty – as challenges to patents relating to neem, basmati rice and turmeric would suggest.[67] As such, whether these provisions achieve substantial additional protection for traditional knowledge holders or reflect their wishes is contested.

64 Many South American countries, including Brazil and Argentina, have broad exclusions along these lines. See Correa, *Intellectual Property Rights*, p. 54.

65 Patents (Amendment) Act 2002 (India), s 4(p); Patents Act 1970 (India), s 3(p).

66 Patents (Amendment) Act 2002 (India), s 18; Patents Act 1970 (India), ss 25(j)–(k).

67 See R. A. Mashelkar, 'Intellectual Property Rights and the Third World', *Current Science* 81, 2001, 955, 959–62.

However, from the Indian government's perspective, the provisions do make a difference.[68] As such, despite the presumption of patentability in TRIPS, India has used the flexibility within the treaty to protect traditional knowledge outside the system and thus attempt to address a serious local policy concern. This example shows that TRIPS does not fully determine the provisions which may be brought to bear on patent law. While there may not be room for a patent law which is based on principles wholly contrary to the security of private property rights in inventions, not all aspects of Indian patent law are determined by TRIPS.

A second exclusion from the definition of invention which is aimed at preventing 'evergreening' of patents even more acutely demonstrates the way in which India is able to interpret TRIPS in a unique way. 'Evergreening' is a practice where patent owners seek patents on minor variations of existing inventions in order to prolong the effective life of the original patent. Under s 3(d) of the Patents Act 1970, patents are not available for the discovery of new forms, properties or uses of known substances or processes which do not improve the previous invention's efficacy or employ at least one new reactant.[69] The validity of s 3(d) has already been the subject of a case in the Indian courts, brought by Swiss pharmaceutical company Novartis following the refusal of its patent application for 'Glivec', a cancer drug. Novartis' claim was defeated. The High Court in Madras held that TRIPS does not automatically form part of Indian law.[70] As such, it found that the question of whether Indian legislation complies with TRIPS can only be determined through the WTO dispute settlement procedure and not in domestic Indian courts, and so declined to consider whether s 3(d) complied with TRIPS.[71] It would appear unlikely that the Indian Parliament would be quick to amend the provision in the absence of a complaint before the WTO dispute

68 Parliament of India, 'Combined Discussion' (Kamal Nath).

69 Patents Act 1970 (India), s 3(d).

70 *Novartis AG v Union of India* (2007) High Court of Judicature at Madras, Case No 24759 and 24760 of 2006 (judgment delivered 6 August 2007).

71 Ibid.

settlement procedure or other external pressure. As such, it stands as an indication of the scope within which the Indian state is able to exercise its sovereign capacity to determine its patent law. But even if a complaint was brought and a WTO Panel or Appellate Body decision found s 3(d) to fall foul of TRIPS, and the Indian Parliament was required to amend s 3(d) as a result, such a chain of events would still demonstrate the dynamic which I have been endeavouring to uncover. That is, it would show that the content of Indian patent law is the product of the demands of the WTO (which vary in degrees of specificity) and the capacity of the Indian state to frame its own law in relation to those demands. Until the WTO is able to amend Indian law without the Indian Parliament, this dynamic will continue to exist.

This dynamic is one whose potential exists not only at the legislative level, but also in the courts. Other key terms which are used but not defined in TRIPS include 'novelty' and 'inventive step', which are the core elements of a valid patent.[72] While these terms have a history of interpretation in the jurisdictions from which they come, there are marked differences in the way they are applied in each of those jurisdictions and they are not defined in TRIPS. As such, it is open not only for the Indian legislature to define such terms (the definition of 'inventive step' in the Patents Act 1970 is unusual in form, but perhaps not in substance),[73] but also for Indian courts to set different standards on what constitutes novelty and inventive step, than exist elsewhere.

3.2.2 Compulsory licensing and revocation

The provisions of the Patents Act 1970 dealing with compulsory licences also illustrate the dynamic between the demands of

72 TRIPS, art 27.1.

73 A common definition brought in in 2002 was replaced in 2005 with a more unusual one which refers explicitly to an invention needing to demonstrate a 'technical advance' or 'economic significance', but it nonetheless still emphasizes the requirement of non-obviousness which lies at the heart of the common standard of 'inventive step.' See Patents (Amendment) Act 2005 (India), s 2.

TRIPS and the response of the Indian state. Article 31 of TRIPS allows for compulsory licences in a range of situations involving the public interest and in response to anti-competitive conduct by the patent holder.[74] The prescriptive conditions set out for the grant of compulsory licences fit well with the perception that these are to be used only in exceptional circumstances. However, it has been observed that quite extensive use of compulsory licences has occurred, for example, in the United States (as a remedy for anti-competitive conduct) and in the UK and Canada (particularly in the field of pharmaceuticals prior to TRIPS).[75] In the case of post-TRIPS India, there is significant scope on the face of the text to apply them broadly. It is perhaps not only the terms of the text which make this so, but the nature and scale of the potential public interest in granting such licences in India when one considers, for example in the area of medicines, the scale of current and potential health crises. Expectations that the provisions will be deployed in cases of acute public need will also have been heightened by the way in which the Indian government expressly relied on the presence of the provisions in order to answer concerns that the patentability of medicinal and agricultural products would have disastrous effects on millions of impoverished Indians.[76]

Section 92 of the Patents Act 1970 contains a fairly common ground for the issue of compulsory licences. It enables the Indian government to issue a notification that a patent be subject to a compulsory licence in 'circumstances of national emergency or ... extreme urgency or in the case of public non-commercial use'.[77] This can occur at any time after the patent is granted. Apart from the procedure it sets out for allowing licences to be issued without giving the patent owner a right to be heard in the case of a public health crisis relating to AIDS, HIV, tuberculosis, malaria

74 TRIPS, art 31.

75 See F. M. Scherer and Jayasharee Watal, 'Post-Trips Options for Access to Patented Medicines in Developing Nations', *Journal of International Economic Law* 5, 2002, 913, 916–19.

76 Parliament of India, 'Combined Discussion' (Kamal Nath).

77 Patents Act 1970 (India), s 92.

or other epidemics, this provision is unlikely to be controversial unless it becomes widely or frequently used.[78]

Introduced in 2005, s 92A of the Patents Act 1970 allows for the granting of a compulsory licence to enable the manufacture in India of medicines for export to countries which lack their own manufacturing capacity.[79] This provision directly conflicts with article 31(f) of TRIPS, which provides that use of patented technology under compulsory licences be predominantly for the supply of the domestic market. However, following the Doha conference, a framework was put in place providing for a limited waiver of article 3(f) where certain requirements are met.[80] This framework includes requirements that the recipient country inform the WTO that it lacks manufacturing capacity and that the exporting country inform the WTO that it has granted a licence which restricts the manufacture to meeting the needs of the recipient country. Despite criticism that this framework is cumbersome, WTO members agreed on 6 December 2005 to formally incorporate it into TRIPS.[81] It has so far been used in only one case.[82] However, s 92A of the Patents Act does not incorporate

78 Ibid., s 92(3), which specifies that the procedure in s 87 is not to be followed in these circumstances. Note, the same diseases are listed in the Doha TRIPS Declaration: World Trade Organisation, 'Doha TRIPS Declaration', para. 1.

79 Patents Act 1970 (India), s 92A.

80 World Trade Organisation, 'Implementation of Paragraph 6 of the Doha Declaration on the TRIPS Agreement and Public Health', Decision of the General Council, 30 August 2003, WT/L/540 and Corr.1, at: http://www.wto.org/English/tratop_e/trips_e/implem_para6_e.htm (last accessed 6 December 2011).

81 World Trade Organisation, 'Amendment of the TRIPS Agreement', Decision of the General Council, 6 December 2005, WT/L/641, at: http://www.wto.org/english/tratop_e/trips_e/wtl641_e.htm (last accessed 6 December 2011).

82 For the manufacture and importation into Rwanda of a generic version of the anti-retroviral drug 'TriAvir'. See Rwanda, 'Notification under Paragraph 2(A) of the Decision of 30 August 2003 on the Implementation of Paragraph 6 of the Doha Declaration on the TRIPS Agreement and Public Health' (IP/N/9/RWA/1), 19 July 2007; Canada, 'Notification under Paragraph 2(C) of the Decision of 30 August 2003 on the Implementation of Paragraph 6 of the Doha Declaration on the TRIPS Agreement and Public Health' (IP/N/10/CAN/1), 8 October 2007. For a detailed examination of the difficulties and possibilities in the framework, see Frederick M. Abbott and Jerome H.

the procedure specified in the framework. It does not, for example, require that the recipient country inform the WTO of its needs nor does it specify limits on quantity of production.[83] However, it would be open for the Controller of Patents to impose limits on production and as such, whether this section will be challenged may depend both on how it is administered in practice, as well as the danger to a complainant of negative public reaction to any complaint.

The broadest grounds for the issue of compulsory licences are in s 84 of the Patents Act 1970. Once three years have passed since the granting of a patent, a compulsory licence may be granted on the following grounds:

a) that the reasonable requirements of the public have not been met;
b) that the patented invention is not available to the public at a reasonably affordable price; or
c) that the patented invention is not worked in the territory of India.[84]

Once satisfied that any of the grounds above are met, the Controller of Patents may grant a licence on terms that he or she deems fit,[85] although the Act sets out guidance on what considerations must be taken into account when determining such terms, including the investment of the patentee in creating the invention.[86] If the conditions justifying the grant of the compulsory licence persist, the patent itself may be revoked on the application of the Indian government or any interested person.[87]

Reichman, 'The Doha Round's Public Health Legacy: Strategies for the Production and Diffusion of Patented Medicines under the Amended TRIPS Provisions', *Journal of International Economic Law* 10, 2007, 921.

83 See Patents Act 1970 (India), s 92A. See Mueller, 'The Tiger Awakens', p. 604.
84 Patents Act 1970 (India), s 84.
85 Ibid., s 84(4).
86 Ibid., s 90(1)(i).
87 Ibid., s 85 (not sooner than two years after the compulsory licence has been granted).

Revocation may also occur outside the compulsory licensing regime, under s 66 of the Patents Act 1970. That section, which pre-dated and survived the TRIPS reforms, provides that a patent may be revoked (after giving the patentee an opportunity to be heard), where 'the Central Government is of opinion that a patent or the mode in which it is exercised is mischievous to the State or generally prejudicial to the public.'[88] This section is not, on its face, contrary to the requirements of TRIPS; article 32 simply requires that the exercise of powers of revocation be subject to judicial review.[89] And while it is designed to deal with exceptional circumstances, it was relied on in Parliament by Minister Nath to allay concerns that the 2005 reforms would result in dramatic price rises for essential products. Indeed, Nath mentioned it while expressly invoking the sovereignty of the Indian Parliament, reminding his colleagues that '[t]his House, at the end of the day, is supreme ... if there was any upsurge in the prices, if there were apprehensions, then the hon. Members, in discharge of their obligations, would they ever let that happen?'[90]

What is particularly striking about India's compulsory licensing regime is that the provisions which guide its application echo many of the same policies on which the post-independence Patents Act 1970 was based.[91] These include the policies that patents are to be worked in India on a commercial scale; that they are not to be granted merely to enable patentees to enjoy a monopoly on importation; that they are to encourage innovation to the mutual advantage of producers and users and in a manner conducive to social and economic welfare; that they should not impede protection of public health and nutrition and should promote public interest in critical sectors in India; and that the benefits of patented inventions should be made available at reasonably affordable prices.[92] They also reflect the policies pursued

88 Ibid., s 66.

89 TRIPS, art 32. See Watal, 'Implementing the TRIPS Agreement', p. 2462.

90 Parliament of India, 'Combined Discussion' (Kamal Nath).

91 See N. Rajagopala Ayyangar, *Report on the Revision of the Patents Law*, New Delhi: Government of India, 1959.

92 Ibid., s 83.

by India and other developing countries at Doha concerning the capacity of states to protect public health. As the parliamentary debates reveal, similar policies underlie the revocation provisions.[93] However, the provisions are not a direct substitute for the prior exclusion of patentability for medicines and agricultural products. The starting point is that products concerning these policy areas are patentable and only in particular cases will licences be granted (and in those cases, remuneration is to be paid to the patent holder). Accordingly, although the same policies are operative, the scope for their application under the amended Patents Act 1970 is different from that which existed before TRIPS. Precisely how different this scope is will depend on how frequently the provisions are used in practice.

Indeed, one of the interesting aspects of the compulsory licensing and revocation provisions is that it will not be possible even to address the question of compliance with TRIPS until a pattern of use becomes evident. Given the scale of poverty in India and the need for medicines, the 'reasonable requirements of the public' could be enormous. As such, the Indian context would cause the provisions to mean something very different there than similar terms mean in the context of the United Kingdom, for example.[94] Moreover, the determination in India of a 'reasonably affordable price' could mean something very different than in developed states. In addition, if used extensively, licences issued for failing to work a patent domestically may also contravene the requirement in article 27 of TRIPS that patents be available 'whether products are imported or locally produced.'[95] In 2000 the United States initiated a complaint against Brazil in respect of a domestic working requirement, but withdrew the complaint, apparently amidst public pressure.[96] On the other hand, if the provisions are used sparingly, they are unlikely to become the

93 Parliament of India, 'Combined Discussion' (Kamal Nath).

94 United Kingdom patent law allows for compulsory licences of patents where there is unmet public demand caused by a refusal to licence on reasonable terms: see Patents Act 1977 (UK), ss 48 and 48A.

95 TRIPS, art. 27.1.

96 Mueller, 'The Tiger Awakens', p. 595.

subject of a complaint. One can imagine that their use will be carefully monitored by pharmaceutical companies and the United States and European Union and that the possibility of a complaint at the WTO would be a factor contributing to the way the Indian government decides to apply the provisions. It is clear that a broad use of the provisions would conflict with a narrow reading of TRIPS. On the other hand, a moderate use of the provisions may be entirely compatible with a more flexible reading of TRIPS, particularly one influenced by the Doha TRIPS Declaration. While the scope of their application is yet to be tested, the breadth of the compulsory licensing provisions and their presentation by the Indian government as a response to the strict requirements within TRIPS concerning patenting of medicines provides another example of how India's patent law is the product of the relation between the claims of the WTO and the Indian state to determine India's patent law.

Conclusion

The claims to authority of the WTO and the Indian state rely on each other. India's sovereignty would not be realised if it were unable to engage in relations with other states. Hence it needs entities like the WTO through which it can exercise its sovereignty on the international stage. In addition, the exercise of such rights enables the incumbent government to project its authority in the domestic sphere. At the same time, the WTO draws its authority from the formal agreement of sovereign nation-states, which together form the community whose interests the WTO claims to represent and whose law it claims authority to determine. It also relies on states to enliven its dispute settlement jurisdiction and to implement its decisions.

Rather than examining sovereignty solely from the perspective of the state, I have shown that the WTO makes a sovereign claim over the patent law of India. This claim is not absolute in scope, but it is absolute in nature. To the extent of the authority it claims via its constituent treaties, its Ministerial Conference Declarations and decisions of its General Council and dispute settlement bodies, the WTO is not answerable to any other entity. In relation to patent law, the limits of its claim relate to the precision of the terms of TRIPS. Where the terms are imprecise, the capacity of the Indian state to determine the law in accordance with local concerns is able to be exercised most fully. Given that the boundary between these claims exists in the area of textual interpretation, it follows that this boundary is not clear. India's broad compulsory licensing provisions in the Patents Act 1970, and the prospect that they might be challenged and found not to be compliant with TRIPS provides an example of how this dynamic relation will continue to shape India's patent law. Neither entity is able to dominate the field entirely.

The explanation of the relationship of the WTO and India in relation to patent law as being one between sovereign claims avoids the circularity which plagues the usual attempts to measure the WTO's effect on national sovereignty. It does so because it avoids the trap of thinking about sovereignty as the exclusive preserve of nation-states and that a state's sovereignty exists (or at one time existed) outside of its relation with other states and international organisations. In my view, this means we should focus less on tracking the rise or fall of the sovereignty of the state, as if the state is the only entity capable of such a position – and focus more on the variety of human organisations and institutions that can and do make sovereign claims to determine law for various forms of community. Once it is accepted that entities other than the state make sovereign claims, the focus can shift to the process by which these claims interact. One possible criticism of the argument presented here is that by giving the claims of the WTO the status of 'sovereignty' it normalises the power of the WTO and overlooks the power relations which go to create the content of this claim. However, such criticism implicitly privileges the sovereignty of the nation-state. The approach advocated here does not privilege the claim of any entity. In doing so, it enables a closer examination of the content of such claims than arguments obscured by an attachment to the false notion that all authority flows from the state. If one accepts that the WTO and the Indian state each make effective claims to determine the content of patent law within India, then proper regard can be had for the responsibility of each entity for the law that results.

Chapter 5

The Relation of Sovereigns at the National and Local Levels

Traditional Knowledge and Local Community Autonomy in India

> '[T]hat which challenges nation in its alterity is also and always constitutive of it'.[1]

In Chapter 2 I set out the terms in which sovereignty over traditional knowledge is claimed by and for local and indigenous communities. As we saw in that chapter, the relevant site in which this sovereignty is said to reside is alternatively the village itself (the 'gram sabha') and the village council (the 'panchayat'). In this chapter, I will consider more closely the relationship between that site of authority and the sovereignty of the state.[2] The first and

1 Peter Fitzpatrick, *Modernism and the Grounds of Law*, Cambridge: Cambridge University Press, 2001, p. 146.

2 The focus in this chapter is on the relation between local communities and the Indian state. The reference by Vandana Shiva and her colleagues to the Convention on Biological Diversity (1992) and their opposition to the World Trade Organisation demonstrates that, to some extent, the authority claimed by local communities is also constituted in their relation with international forms of authority: see Vandana Shiva, Afsar Jafri, Gitanjali Bedi and Radha Holla-Bhar, *The Enclosure and Recovery of the Commons: Biodiversity, Indigenous Knowledge and Intellectual Property Rights*, New Delhi: Research Foundation for Science, Technology and Ecology, 1997, p. 158–9; Research Foundation for Science, Technology and Ecology, 'Notices Served to Biopirates', at: http://www.ratical.org/co-globalize/BPandWTO.html (last accessed 6 December 2011): see above Chapter 2, text accompanying notes 158–63. However, the constitutive force of this relation is comparatively insignificant when contrasted with that which

most obvious point to mention is that these forms of local community are recognised by the Indian Constitution and by legislation providing for local community autonomy. The tension between these positions emerges because the scope of authority claimed by local communities exceeds that which is provided under the laws of the state. In a way similar to the relationship between the World Trade Organisation and India, it is the detail of the law which provides the point of contestation and reveals a situation in which neither the state nor local communities have ultimate determining power over that law. I will argue that the relation between these claims and the provisions of the Indian Constitution and legislation which provide for local community autonomy, reveal that each site of authority depends essentially on its relation to the other and, more particularly, on the other as sovereign.

Since 1993, the gram sabha has been recognised as a form of local government in India's Constitution.[3] It is these constitutional provisions to which Shiva and her colleagues refer when

flows from the intense relation between local communities and the Indian state, and it is not explored here.

3 It should be noted at the outset that while the Indian Constitution now prescribes certain mandatory features for panchayats, much remains within the power of state legislatures to determine and hence there is great variety between those states. In many cases, the level of autonomy legislated for local communities at the state level falls short of that envisaged by the Constitutional reforms. This is especially true of the requirements under the Panchayats (Extension to the Scheduled Areas) Act 1996 (India), which have not been fully acted on in any of the states in which Scheduled Areas exist. There are also difficulties at the local level in terms of implementing certain features of the national scheme, such as the quotas for participation of women and disadvantaged groups in cases where discrimination and disadvantage are socially entrenched at the local level. For example, despite quotas and the like, local elites and social pressure (often violent) can prevent the fulsome participation of marginalised groups. These practical difficulties are crucial in the operation of the gram sabhas and the continuing development of local government across India. However, they touch on some of the most complex social, religious and economic problems in rural India and it is outside the scope of this book to consider them in any detail. My focus will be on how India's national law recognises community autonomy, specifically in respect of local resources, what it requires state legislatures to enact, and how this relates to the claims by and for traditional knowledge holders.

they argue (as noted in Chapter 2) that the recognition of community sovereignty over resources is necessary under the 'new political climate of decentralisation through the 73rd Amendment to the Constitution.'[4] Even before these amendments, the constitution made oblique provision for village councils in a local government structure by leaving such questions to the states.[5] There was also an attempt under British rule to incorporate village councils into the colonial administrative apparatus.[6] Given its long history of incorporation into the state, and in particular the express provisions in the Indian Constitution, it could be argued that the gram sabha is a body which derives its authority from the state. One might conclude that Shiva's organisation and the Campaign for Community Control over Biological Diversity contradict themselves by seeking to use national law to challenge the authority of the state.

However, what we are faced with here is only an apparent contradiction. The close and complex relation between the authority of local communities and the state in India in debates over traditional knowledge provides an excellent example of the way in which autopositioned sovereignties rely not only on their own authority but also draw on the authority of entities with which they are in relation. This is something we have already observed in the case of the WTO. We have seen that the WTO relies on the formal undertakings of nation-states to ground its authority and yet at the same time exists as an independent entity which claims the ability to determine its identity and the scope of its own authority (most notably through its dispute settlement procedures). No other entity exists which can make a superior claim. Similarly, communities claiming sovereignty over traditional knowledge and resources maintain a grounding of authority which exists in the community itself and is not wholly derived from the state even as they rely on the state to some extent. Once we move beyond the notion that all authority originates in and derives from the

4 Shiva, Jafri, Bedi and Holla-Bhar, *Enclosure and Recovery of the Commons*, p. 159.

5 Constitution of India, art 40.

6 M. R. Biju, *Resurgent Rural India: Decade after the Constitutionalisation of Panchayati Raj*, Delhi: Authors Press, 2007, pp. 14–18.

state, it is possible to view the state as recognising prior forms of authority which have existed (and would continue to exist) independently of the particular provision made for them in national law. Such a view is clearly evident in the claims made by local communities, but it is also evident in the actions of the Indian state itself. In making laws which give effect to a form of local community autonomy, the Indian state has sought to draw on the ancient tradition of these forms, hoping to make the national laws effective by engaging the traditional practices of local people. While the authority of local communities draws to some degree on the authority of the state (via the constitutional and legislative provisions providing for community autonomy), those very provisions rely on there being a substance and life to traditional forms of community governance which is not derived from the state. What can be seen, then, is a relation between two sites of autopositioned sovereignty, where each relies not just on their own authority but also on their relation with each other.

In this chapter I will first provide an overview of the current framework under the Indian Constitution and related legislation for the recognition and participation in government of gram sabhas and panchayats. While these forms operate in rural areas across India, I will concentrate on the law as it applies to the parts of India designated as 'Scheduled Areas' under the Panchayats (Extension to the Scheduled Areas) Act 1996. This Act provides the fullest recognition of local communities' rights over local resources that currently exists under Indian national law.[7] Scheduled Areas are those areas which have the highest proportion of tribal peoples and are designated as such under the Constitution. However, this law is also of relevance to scheduled tribes who are not within Scheduled Areas, since it provides a model which activists and commentators argue should apply more broadly, both to tribal peoples outside Scheduled Areas

7 With the possible exception of the Scheduled Tribes and Other Traditional Forest Dwellers (Recognition of Forest Rights) Act 2006 (India).

and also non-tribal rural communities.[8] I will then show how the claims to sovereignty outlined in Chapter 2 draw on these reforms to ground, in part, the authority of the local community over traditional knowledge.

After setting out this overview, I will argue that the attempt by the Indian state to institutionalise the gram sabha and panchayat into the national legal framework does not exhaust the substance or potential of the claims to sovereignty by local communities over traditional knowledge. Simply because forms of village government are incorporated into the Indian state does not mean that their authority is wholly derived from the state. Rather, we will see that local forms of government on which the sovereign claims of local communities are based have a life and energy of their own which exists outside (but necessarily in relation to) the state.

I The Constitutive Dependence of Local Community Sovereignty on National Sovereignty

Despite the importance placed on the autonomy of rural villages by Gandhi in the period leading up to independence (to which I will return below), the first drafts of India's Constitution did not include provision for them. The chairman of the constitution drafting committee, B. R. Ambedkar, viewed villages as 'a sink of localism' and a 'den of narrow mindedness', as 'caste-ridden' and

8 Shiva, Jafri, Bedi and Holla-Bhar, *Enclosure and Recovery of the Commons*, pp. 126–7, 139. In Madya Pradesh, legislation containing many of the features of the Panchayats (Extension to Scheduled Areas) Act 1996 (India) applies even for non-tribals (and this despite the fact that it is yet to be implemented fully in the Scheduled Areas): see Biju, *Resurgent Rural India*, p. 71. S. S. Meenakshisundaram argues that the provisions in the Extension Act concerning the constitution and role of the gram sabha should form the basis of a constitutional amendment applicable to all villages in India: S. S. Meenakshisundaram, 'Rural Development for Panchayati Raj' in L. C. Jain (ed.) *Decentralisation and Local Governance: Essays for George Mathew*, Hyderabad: Orient Longman, 2005, p. 430.

having 'little prospects of success as institutions of self-government.'[9] He is reported to have been 'glad that the Draft Constitution has discarded the village and adopted the individual as its unit.'[10] As we will see below, the project of Indian nation-building in many ways set itself against the local and particular forms of authority which existed prior to and during British colonisation. But this project also relied on the Indian nation's singular ability to embrace and hold within itself a diversity of which the village panchayats were an important part. As such, the Indian nation did not define itself by stark opposition to the local and particular, but by its ability to embrace and transcend those elements. Indian nationhood (and its sovereignty) thus depends on a close relation between the local and the national – a relation whose dynamic must constantly be in play and cannot be resolved without either entity losing something vital to its being.

With the insistence of Gandhi and others, a provision covering panchayats was eventually included in the Constitution. This provision required the states to 'take steps to organise village panchayats and endow them with such powers and authority as may be necessary for them to function as units of self-government.'[11] In order to set out proposals to give effect to this provision, the Balvantray Mehta Committee was established in 1957.[12] Following its report, a three-tier system of 'panchayati raj' (local government)

9 For the first two quotes, see Shiva Rao (ed.), *The Framing of India's Constitution*, New Delhi: The Indian Institute of Public Administration, 1968, p. 330 (note 3), where these views are also reported to have 'evoked strong resentment and protests from a number of members.' For the second two quotes, see Biju, *Resurgent Rural India*, p. 19.

10 See Rao (ed.), *India's Constitution*, p. 330. See also D. Bandyopadhyay, 'Rajiv Gandhi and the Third Tier of Governance' in L. C. Jain (ed.), *Decentralisation and Local Governance*, p. 81.

11 Constitution of India, art 40.

12 Government of India, 'Report of the Team for the Study of Community Projects and National Extension Service' (Chairperson: Balvantray Mehta), Committee on Plan Projects, National Development Council, New Delhi: Government of India, 1957, vol. 1, pp. 5–23; See Hoshiar Singh, 'Constitutional Base for Panchayati Raj in India: The 73rd Amendment Act', *Asian Survey* 34, 1994, 818–27, 818-19.

was introduced, with the 'gram panchayat' at the village level, the 'panchayat samiti' at an intermediate level and the 'zilla panchayat' at the district level. Each higher body was meant to be representative of the ones below it.[13] It was also intended that the three tiers would provide a link between the local people and the national and state governments.[14]

From 1959 to 1961 the states gradually implemented this system, with some states vesting more power in the village and others more in the intermediate bodies.[15] In practice, the village councils 'were made subordinate units of the government to implement its programs at the lowest level, and not the agencies of self-government, or gram swaraj as Gandhi had advocated.'[16] Over the following decade, this led to the decreasing engagement of local people with the village councils. State governments often saw the local institutions as rivals and withdrew their powers and restricted funding.[17] In many cases, there was a failure to hold regular elections.[18] The Ashok Mehta Committee, appointed to review the state of the panchayati raj system in 1978 (it described the period between 1965–69 as one of 'stagnation' and that between 1969–77 as one of 'decline') sought ways to revitalise and strengthen that system so that it could contribute effectively to development programs.[19] The Committee proposed a two-tier system, moving more power to the district level panchayat.[20] Reforms in the 1980s sought to ally the local government institutions with the poverty alleviation policies being pursued at

13 Government of India, 'Report of the Team for the Study of Community Projects', pp. 10, 15, 20–21.
14 Ibid., pp. 20–1.
15 Biju, *Resurgent Rural India*, pp. 22–3.
16 Singh, 'Constitutional Base', p. 819 (his emphasis). *Gram swaraj* means village self-rule.
17 Ibid., p. 821.
18 Ibid., p. 819.
19 Government of India, 'Report of the Committee on Panchayati Raj Institutions' (Chairperson: Ashok Mehta), New Delhi: Government of India, 1978, p. 4.
20 Ibid., 37–56; see Singh, 'Constitutional Base', p. 819; see also Biju, *Resurgent Rural India*, p. 25.

the time.[21] Again, however, the emphasis was on the higher-level councils rather than the village.

In 1989, the government of Rajiv Gandhi introduced a bill seeking to amend the Indian Constitution to provide for a more effective devolution of powers to the local level. The bill failed to pass at its first attempt, but was subsequently enacted in 1992, the year after Rajiv Gandhi's assassination. Taking effect in 1993, the Constitution (Seventy-Third Amendment) Act 1992 still left determination of the precise scope of panchayat powers to the states, but prescribed a more detailed organisational and electoral structure consistent with the three-tier approach.[22] Significantly, while each panchayat level is to be directly elected by the constituency within its territorial scope, seats are reserved for women, Scheduled Tribes and Scheduled Castes.[23] And while the formula from Article 40 remained (that the powers vested in panchayats be those 'necessary to enable them to function as institutions of self-government'[24]), the new provisions went on to list areas in respect of which state legislatures could vest power in the panchayats 'at the appropriate level'.[25] These include 'the preparation of plans for economic and social justice' and a variety of specific heads listed in the Eleventh Schedule.[26] The most significant of these for the concept of traditional knowledge is 'the maintenance of community assets'.[27] The Constitution also provides that states may vest revenue-raising powers in the panchayats. The intention with this measure was to enable the panchayats to have more effective control of their finances so as to have

21 See Singh, 'Constitutional Base', pp. 819–20, citing Government of India, 'Report of the Committee to Review the Existing Administrative Arrangements for Rural Development and Poverty Alleviation Programmes (CAARD)' (Chairperson: G. V. K. Rao), Department of Rural Development, Ministry of Agriculture, New Delhi: Government of India, 1985.

22 See Constitution of India, arts 243-B, 243-C.

23 Ibid., art 243-D.

24 Ibid., art 243-G.

25 Ibid.

26 Ibid., art 243-G; Eleventh Schedule.

27 Ibid.

more effective control over developing and implementing policy. The amendments have been widely hailed for providing for the institution of the gram sabha within the Constitution.[28] However, apart from providing a definition and enabling gram sabhas to 'exercise such powers and perform such functions at the village level as the Legislature of a State may, by law, provide',[29] the Constitution sets out no further details on the role of the gram sabha. Nonetheless, consistent with the Constitution having provided that the gram sabha is made up of the constituency which elects the village panchayat, most States, whether by convention or consensus, have enacted provisions vesting oversight of the village panchayat with the gram sabha and requiring it to meet at regular intervals (normally once or twice a year).[30] However, as to the vesting of the powers listed in the Eleventh Schedule, most States have failed to do so in a meaningful way.[31]

Initially, the panchayati raj structure established by the constitutional amendments did not apply in the 'Scheduled Areas'. These are areas which mainly contain tribal populations and which the government considers require special measures and certain protections. (The relative isolation of these communities and the particularly close relationship they enjoy with their environments has made tribal peoples a key source of traditional knowledge.) Formally, Scheduled Areas are those areas designated by the President under article 244, according to the procedure in paragraph 6 of the Fifth Schedule. This procedure enables the President to make the initial designation of a Scheduled Area, but any changes to it can only be made in consultation with the relevant state Governor. While the Constitution does not set out precisely the criteria for a Scheduled Area, these have become

28 See, e.g., Biju, *Resurgent Rural India*, ch. 2; see generally L. C. Jain (ed.), *Decentralisation and Local Governance*.

29 'In this Part: ... "Gram Sabha" means a body consisting of persons registered in the electoral rolls relating to a village comprised within the area of Panchayat at the village level': Constitution of India, art 243.

30 See Biju, *Resurgent Rural India*, pp. 70–1. Elections are to be held once every five years: Constitution of India, art 243-E.

31 See Biju, *Resurgent Rural India*, p. 92.

well established by convention.[32] They are: a 'preponderance of tribal population, compactness and reasonable size of the area; under-developed nature of the area; and marked disparity in [the] economic standard of the people.'[33] Article 243-M of the Constitution excluded Scheduled Areas from the new panchayat structure but also provided that the scheme could be extended to them by an Act of Parliament, subject to exceptions and modifications made by that Act.

In 1994, the Bhuria Committee was established to make recommendations on how best to extend the scheme to the Scheduled Areas. In its report, the Committee emphasised the need to respect traditional local governing practices. The report stated that 'many tribal societies have had their own customary laws, traditional practices, community ethos, political and administrative systems etc.'[34] It further argued that since

> many tribal communities have been living autonomously cut off from the rest of the society, they have exercised control over and had access to natural resources moulding their institutions. Their Gram Sabhas and village councils have been vibrant institutions in the administrative, religious, political, economic, justice etc. fields.[35]

In light of these characteristics, the Committee proposed that in 'shaping the new Panchayati Raj structure in tribal areas, it is desirable to blend the traditional with the modern by treating the traditional institutions as the foundation on which the modern

32 See P. S. K. Menon and Bakshi Sinha, *Panchayati Raj in Scheduled Areas: A Critical Study*, New Delhi: Concept Publishing, 2003, p. 7.

33 Ibid. See Government of India, Ministry of Tribal Affairs, 'Definition of Scheduled Areas' at: http://tribal.gov.in/index3.asp?subsublinkid=305&langid=1 (last accessed 6 December 2011).

34 Dileep Singh Bhuria *et al.*, 'Report of the Committee of MPs and Experts to Make Recommendations on the Salient Features of the Law for Extending Provisions of the Constitutions (73rd) Amendment Act, 1992 to the Scheduled Areas, 1995', in Menon and Sinha, *Panchayati Raj*, pp. 139–40.

35 Ibid., p. 140.

supra-structure [*sic*] should be built.'[36] In particular, the Committee proposed that '[t]ime-honoured customary usages and arrangements in tribal areas should be respected and allowed to continue. Traditional tribal conventions and laws should continue to hold validity.'[37] The Committee also emphasised that tribal communities should have control over natural resources in their areas. The references to particular resources focus on land, forest produce, grazing, agriculture and water.[38] It is not clear whether the Committee considered if knowledge might be a 'resource' for these purposes. However, the overall emphasis is that tribal communities should have control over the resources that are traditionally held locally by the community, and this would at least potentially include intellectual resources.

The Panchayats (Extension to the Scheduled Areas) Act 1996 incorporated many of the recommendations of the Bhuria Committee. The Act provides that 'State legislation on the Panchayats ... shall be made in consonance with the customary law, social and religious practices and traditional management practices of community resources.'[39] It also provides that 'every Gram Sabha shall be competent to safeguard and preserve the traditions and customs of the people, their cultural identity, community resources and the customary mode of dispute resolution'.[40] In their review of the implementation of the Act in the states containing Scheduled Areas, Menon and Sinha noted that the states have generally been reluctant to enact the mandated provisions in a form which gives them full effect, but remained hopeful that this could occur (and indeed observed that it was beginning to occur).[41] Further, they found that even where the provisions of state legislation failed to live up to the promise in the Panchayats (Extension to the Scheduled Areas) Act 1996, the awareness of

36 Ibid. (my emphasis).
37 Ibid.
38 Ibid., pp. 150–2 (annexure 'A' to the report).
39 Panchayats (Extension to the Scheduled Areas) Act 1996 (India), s 4(a).
40 Ibid., s 4(d).
41 Menon and Sinha, *Panchayati Raj*, pp. xvii–xix, 92–5.

local groups of the rights contained within it (fostered by NGOs) had a positive effect on local campaigns.[42]

The national and various state laws providing for local autonomy provide part of the basis for the claims made by and for local communities for sovereignty over traditional knowledge. As Shiva and her colleagues argue, much of the impetus for the claims stems from the 'political climate of decentralisation' that these laws are intended to put into place.[43] It is also evident from the various memoranda issued through the Campaign for Community Control over Biodiversity, that the participants rely on the panchayat structure established under the Constitution. As we saw in Chapter 2, it is the village panchayats whose signature authorises the Memorandum and which issue the resolutions directed at the Prime Minister.[44] Rather than rejecting entirely the state's claim to incorporate local governing structures within the overall national legal framework, claimants draw specifically on, and seek to extend, the effect of these laws. This is particularly true of the Panchayats (Extension to the Scheduled Areas) Act 1996, which though it only applies to tribal people in Scheduled Areas, is often taken as a model which should apply to all tribal peoples and even beyond tribal peoples to include all villages.[45] Moreover, it has been convincingly shown that categories constructed by state institutions can have a profound effect on the self-perception and identity of groups whose existence preceded the state itself.[46]

42 Ibid., pp. xvii, 75.

43 Shiva, Jafri, Bedi and Holla-Bhar, *Enclosure and Recovery of the Commons*, p. 159.

44 'Community Control over Biodiversity: Memorandum to the Government of India', 8 December 2004, submitted by 200 Gram Panchayats and gram sabhas of Chhattisgarh, Madhya Pradesh, Andhra Pradesh, Karnataka, Tamil Nadu, and Uttaranchal, along with Kalpavriksh, Gene Campaign, People's Alliance for Livelihood Rights, Deccan Development Society, Centre For World Solidarity, Green Foundation, Delhi Forum and Beej Bachao Andolan, on behalf of the Campaign on Community Control over Biodiversity, at: http://www.ddsindia.com/www/Biodiversity rules rally report_link MoEF.htm (last accessed 6 December 2011). See Chapter 2, text accompanying notes 165–73.

45 See above note 8 and accompanying text.

46 An example would be Kapila's work on the Gaddi and their attempt to be recognised as a Scheduled Tribe: see Kriti Kapila, 'The Measure of a Tribe: the

Because of their reliance on national law, the claims by local communities seem to do two contradictory things. It might appear that local communities (or those who advocate on their behalf) are seeking to vest ultimate authority in the community against the state, while at the same time relying on national law to ground their claim. This apparent duality can be seen in two adjoining paragraphs in Shiva *et al.*'s *The Enclosure and Recovery of the Commons*, a text I have used already as an example of claims to vest sovereignty over traditional knowledge in local communities. In one paragraph, the authors set out descriptions of various attempts by local tribal communities to resist the imposition of national laws over forests and resources. They write, for example, that the 'people of Kolkan are sticking to their traditional system of self-management and are not prepared to surrender their rights in favour of new formal institutions established by the state.'[47] In the very next paragraph, Shiva and her colleagues refer to the Panchayats (Extension to Scheduled Areas) Act 1996 in very different terms. About this Act, they say that 'the deep rooted aspirations of the people for self-government has been given formal recognition by the Parliament of India through a legislation [*sic*] accepting the communities as the real sovereign'.[48]

At one level, it can be seen that Shiva and her colleagues are distinguishing between laws based on their content. That is, they criticise those national laws which remove community control over resources and praise those that restore it. Using the language of sovereignty, however, would seem to make this problematic. As I noted in the Introduction, the concept of sovereignty often sits uneasily with political arguments about the particular content of a law (i.e. that a law providing for X is a denial of a sovereignty), because it assumes a certain uniformity and stability to the choice that would be exercised by the entity whose sovereignty is

Cultural Politics of Constitutional Reclassification in North India', *Journal of the Royal Anthropological Institute*, 14, 2008, 117. See also Marc Galanter, *Competing Equalities: Law and the Backward Classes in India*, Berkeley: University of California Press, 1984.

47 Shiva, Jafri, Bedi and Holla-Bhar, *Enclosure and Recovery of the Commons*, p. 126.

48 Ibid.

apparently being denied (i.e., that if given the choice the purported sovereign would choose Y). And while at least here the question is between laws which either increase or decrease community autonomy (and is thus closer to a question of sovereignty than, for example, whether patents should apply to medicines) it would appear that in endorsing the Panchayats (Extension to the Scheduled Areas) Act 1996, Shiva and her colleagues are not putting in question the authority of the state to legislate for communities and determine their character. It may seem that their concern is with what the national sovereign should do, rather than whether it in fact holds legitimate power to do it. This focus could be seen to undermine the claim for a sovereignty vested in the community itself which is not ultimately derived from the state.

However, rather than exposing a contradiction in the claims to sovereignty by local communities, I argue that the duality expressly evident in Shiva *et al.*'s text, and more generally evidenced by the fact that the claims to sovereignty made through the Campaign for Community Control over Biodiversity are made by bodies constituted according to national and state law, is one which exposes the complexity of sovereignty and, in particular, of the relationship between local and national grounds of authority in India. In the next section, I will argue that while the gram sabha and panchayat may well be features of Indian national law, they are not creatures of it. Indeed, the question of derivation will become inverted. Rather than local authority being something derived solely from national law, I will argue that the national law concerning local authority is derived, to a significant degree, from local authority structures and traditions. Viewed this way, it is possible to see both national sovereignty and local sovereignty as dependent on each other.

2 The Constitutive Dependence of National Sovereignty on Local Community Sovereignty

I have shown above that despite the attempt to ground authority solely in the community, the claims of local communities depend at least partly on the authority of the state. But if, as I argued in Chapter 3, a sovereign position is one which can only be held in relation to other sites of authority, then any sovereign will depend at least in part on the recognition of other sites of authority and its relation with them. As such, this partial dependence is not one which necessarily compromises the sovereign character of the claims in question. In this section, I will seek to show that just as the sovereignty of local communities is dependent to some degree on the sovereignty of the Indian state, the reverse is also true. I will show this dependence of the state on local forms of sovereignty in two ways. First, I will show how the modern Indian state constituted its sovereignty by setting itself against local forms of authority, particularly in the period immediately before and after independence. Second, I will show how despite seeking to set itself against local authority, the Indian state has also tried to draw that authority within itself. For the state to rely on local forms of authority in these ways, it is necessary that they are independent of and not wholly derived from, the state.

2.1 The dependence of the state on its opposition to local forms of authority

The creation of a modern Indian nation-state was not simply an effort directed at overcoming an external colonial power. The formation of a unitary modern state also required the overcoming of internal particularity – of caste, religious, linguistic and cultural differences. This process was well underway during colonial times and was continued as India gained independence. The colonialists' contribution to the process of overcoming internal particularities was achieved not only by their assertion of power over the whole territory of the colony (thus constituting it as a single entity), but by their making civic subjects out of the colonial population. By the late nineteenth century in India, the colonialists' obsession with ethnographic surveys and censuses generated a kind of knowledge in which the colonial subject could be classified in increasingly specific ways – into 'groups, households and individuals'[49] and re-aggregated into an 'objective and culturally neutral classificatory system of individuals, households, occupations', making it 'available to more extensive administrative penetration.'[50] This had two significant effects. First, it enabled the individual to be counted as a colonial subject outside of its connection to other forms of community – ethnic, religious, caste, linguistic (to which it would still also belong). Second, it required the demarcation and classification of these very traits from which the individual would be both included and detached. Prior to colonisation, as Randeria argues, 'multiple identities based on cultural differences in … India were fluid and flexible rather than exclusive and exhaustive partitions of the world.'[51] But in the process of the 'enumeration of communities', such identities were used by the colonial administrators not only for their own records but also to determine quotas for civil service jobs and seats in governing bodies.[52] All of which was meant to facilitate the overcoming of various forms of inequality between colonial subjects with a view to their becoming citizens. But in practice it also led to the essentialisation and encapsulation of difference in bureaucratic language – and identification with these demarcations by those to whom they applied because of the rights which attached to them.[53]

These two effects carried over into the newly independent Indian nation-state. The individual's classification as a colonial subject distinct from other ties set the scene for its demarcation as

49 Gyan Prakash, 'Writing Post-Orientalist Histories of the Third World: Perspectives from Indian Historiography', *Comparative Studies in Society and History* 32, 1990, 383, 387.

50 Ibid.

51 Shalini Randeria, 'Entangled Histories of Uneven Modernities: Civil Society, Caste Solidarities and Legal Pluralism in Post-Colonial India' in Yehuda Elkana *et al.* (eds), *Unraveling Ties: From Social Cohesion to New Practices of Connectedness*, New York: Campus Verlag, 2002, p. 296.

52 Ibid.; Partha Chatterjee also uses 'enumerated' communities: *The Nation and Its Fragments: Colonial and Postcolonial Histories*, Princeton: Princeton University Press, 1993, pp. 223–4.

53 Randeria, 'Entangled Histories', p. 295. See also, Chatterjee, '*The Nation and Its Fragments*', pp. 220–39. See also Kapila, 'Measure of a Tribe', p. 117.

a citizen of the nation. Nation was viewed by both the colonialist and the nationalist as the bringer and the marker of modernity and both set the nation against local, caste, religious, linguistic and other such ties. As Randeria argues, '[a]ffiliations of caste, solidarities of religious communities, parochial loyalties of language or region were seen as signs of backwardness. It was considered imperative in the interest of national progress and prosperity that Brahmins, Bengalis or Muslims be turned into Indians.'[54] As such, Indian nationalists inherited and agreed 'to the notion of an India essentialized in relation to Europe', and assumed 'that India was an undivided entity' but, in contrast to the colonialist[55] 'attributed to it a sovereign and unitary will' of its own.[56] Thus what distinguished the colonialist and the Indian nationalist was not the question of whether the Indian nation was unitary, but who could speak for it.

The demarcation of communities and minorities as fixed and stable identities for bureaucratic purposes also continued in post-independence India – still with the ostensible purpose of overcoming difference and inequality, and still with the same effect of essentialising it. Indeed, the post-independence concern with legitimacy based on numerical majority meant that in the new nation it remained 'imperative to define and draw precisely the boundaries of nations and of regions and communities within it.'[57] In this way, the nation was not only set against the local and the particular, but also constituted so as to bring these things within it and contain them. Indeed, just as the Indian nation is set against local and particular traits, its own particularity is dependent on them – the Indian nation conceived as the sole entity capable of bringing these various cultures, languages and castes together and surpassing them to form a unitary whole.

54 Randeria, 'Entangled Histories', p. 284.

55 Strictly, for Prakash, who is talking about historical approaches, it is the 'orientalist' who, along with the nationalist, assumes India's unity: Prakash, 'Post-Orientalist Histories', p. 390.

56 Ibid.

57 Randeria, 'Entangled Histories', p. 297.

However, consistent with the arguments advanced in Chapters 2 and 3 about the impossibility of containing community, the formation of a unitary whole can never be fully and finally achieved. More specifically, despite ostensible attempts to contain questions of identity within firmly established hierarchies, the reality of local Indian politics and law is one in which identity and affiliation is highly contextual and contingent. As Randeria writes, 'even in a world of enumerated collectivities, many castes continue to function as local territorially-demarcated groups with their own norms, procedures and practices of self-government, which they jealously guard against state intervention.'[58] But importantly this does not mean that the people in local communities reject all forms of state law or rights. Rather, 'different kinds of ties based on different logics of connectedness are deployed by caste members in different contexts.'[59] Even in relation to single disputes, multiple legal fora (both those which form part of the state and those separate to it) may be used simultaneously.[60] Claims to sovereignty over traditional knowledge form a particularly cogent example of such divided collective identities.

Moreover, the case of India provides an excellent example of the process by which the constitution of the state in relation to that which it is not, remains an ongoing process – and, in particular, how this demonstrates the way in which singularities co-appear, to use Nancy's term, in the course of their relation with each other. As much as the state seeks to define and bring within itself the communities which make it up, it also sets itself against them in its claim to transcend such particularity. What this also shows is the way in which the actions of the state influence the nature of the local communities to which it is opposed and how

58 Ibid.
59 Ibid.
60 And so, in Randeria's account of the resolution of disputes concerning familial matters in Gujurati local caste councils, we find that while a high degree of legal autonomy in the local councils, the particular dynamics of any dispute may find state courts used as a means of delaying resolution of the dispute within the community or to 'demonstrate one's networks of influence outside the caste': ibid., p. 307.

this reflects back on the state. In its bureaucratic classification and bestowing of rights on the basis of membership of a group or the bearing of certain characteristics, such groups tend to become more rigid and membership claimed to be more exclusive and so on. But since these forms of community have a life of their own outside the dictates of the state, attempts at determining such boundaries (whether as a result of state measures or by the actions of members of the group themselves in response to such measures) are always contested and unresolved. And if the content and character of these groups is in a state of flux, it follows that the nation-state which constitutes itself in opposition to them is also forced to continually re-position itself in response. In this way, it is possible to see how local forms of community and authority co-appear with the nation-state, not in a strict temporal sense, but, as argued in Chapter 3, in the sense that they are involved in a dynamic in which their self or autoposition must constantly be re-appropriated 'in the simultaneity of an assemblage or assembly, being together, or "living together",' to quote Derrida once more.[61] This dynamic of re-positioning is further evidenced in the attempts by the state to absorb within itself the authority claimed by local communities, to which I will now turn.

2.2 The dependence of the state on its attempt to absorb local forms of authority

The 1992 constitutional reforms and the Panchayats (Extension to the Scheduled Areas) Act 1996, like their predecessors in post-independence India and even in the colonial period, attempted to institutionalise the gram sabha or panchayat into national (or, in respect of those predecessors, colonial) law. They did not create the idea of the gram sabha or panchayat. Nor did they seek simply to adopt old words for local government and apply them to fundamentally different forms. Rather, they expressly attempted to

61 Jacques Derrida, *Rogues: Two Essays on Reason*, trs Pascale-Anne Brault and Michael Naas, Stanford: Stanford University Press, 2005, p. 11.

bring into the dominant legal framework an authority structure which existed before and had its own independent life. To be sure, the mode of doing so has generally been one which seeks also to subordinate that authority structure to the dominant law, but it is wrong to treat it as the creation of that dominant law. As such, despite the fact that the modern form of the gram sabha and panchayat is shaped to a large extent by the state, the various attempts to institutionalise it within the state governing apparatus have not exhausted or obliterated this life. Indeed, to do so would be counter-productive to what the state is trying to do when it institutionalises these forms of government. The state explicitly tries to co-opt the ancient tradition of the gram sabha and panchayat within the state system, to draw on the respect that local people have for the ancient institution. Indeed, the panchayats have been regarded as least effective when seen by local people simply as an arm of the state rather than as a meaningful institution in their own right. The imperative of engaging local people in the institutions through increased autonomy has been the guiding principle of the more recent reforms.[62] This principle has been accompanied by a rhetoric in which the national law is seen not to *create*, but to *restore* the power and autonomy of gram sabhas and panchayats. Some claimants go further and seem to deny the state any generative role in respect of the authority of the local communities – reducing the legislation to a belated recognition of something which has always existed.

The rhetoric of restoration has much material on which to draw. Biju writes that '[p]anchayats or village councils are as old as India's history'.[63] The idea of village self-governance has been traced back to the Rig Vedic period (around 1200 BC) and village councils are mentioned as the basic unit of political life in the famous Sanskrit epic poem *Mahabharata*, composed between the eighth century BC and the fourth century AD. But as if to demonstrate at its earliest moment the tension between central and local authority, the poem also records the creation of the first

62 See, e.g., Bhuria *et al.*, 'Report of the Committee'.
63 Biju, *Resurgent Rural India*, pp. 10–11.

sovereign, King Prithu.[64] In Biju's account of the poem, the 'sabhas' and 'samitis', 'democratic bodies at the local level ... played a part in controlling the decisions of the king.'[65] Nehru writes that in a tenth-century book, the Nitisara, 'the village panchayat or elected council' was described as having 'large powers both executive and judicial and its members were treated with the greatest respect by the King's officers.'[66]

Testaments to the ancient quality of the self-government of village communities can be seen in the work of British colonial officials and scholars in the nineteenth century. Charles Metcalfe wrote in 1830: 'They seem to last when nothing else lasts. Dynasty after dynasty tumbles down; revolution succeeds to revolution; Hindu, Pathan, Mahratta, Sikh, English are masters in turn; but the village communities remain the same.'[67] In 1883, Sir Monier Monier-Williams, a professor of Sanskrit at Oxford University, referred to panchayats being 'a most ancient Indian institution,' having 'existed unaltered ... from time immemorial' and surviving 'all changes, all political, religious, and physical convulsions – all wars, massacres, pestilences, and famines – in a word all the external and internal disturbing forces that have swept over and agitated the country for more than three thousand years.'[68] This persistence was accounted for in large part by the esteem in which the villagers themselves were held to regard the institution.

64 See Alok Pant, 'Panchayats – An Institutional Myth or Viable Reality' in M. P. Dubey and Munny Padalia (eds), *Democratic Decentralisation and Panchayati Raj in India*, New Delhi: Anamika, 2002, pp. 77–80, p. 77.

65 Biju, *Resurgent Rural India*, p. 12.

66 Jawaharlal Nehru, *The Discovery of India*, New Delhi: Penguin, 2004, p. 266; see also Meenakshisundaram, 'Rural Development', p. 418.

67 Cited in Lalit Joshi, 'The Myth of Decentralisation: Village Panchayats in Colonial India' in Dubey and Padalia (eds), *Democratic Decentralisation*, pp. 64–76, p. 65.

68 Monier Monier-Williams, *Modern India and the Indians: Being a Series of Impressions, Notes and Essays*, 3rd ed., 1879, Delhi: Oriental Publishers, 1971, pp. 40–3.

Monier-Williams noted that 'a common proverb is current throughout India that "the voice of God is in the five."'[69]

To colonial administrators, the esteem the locals had for the panchayats related directly to their legal function. In 1807, Sir Thomas Munro wrote that 'there can be no doubt that the trial by panchayat is as much the common law of India in civil matters, as that by jury is of England. No native thinks that justice is done where it is not adopted.'[70] A report by a commission chaired by Munro in 1816 prompted a regulation granting recognition to the panchayat system for the purpose of resolving village disputes.[71] A similar regard for the efficacy of panchayats in resolving local disputes is evident in Mountstuart Elphinstone's report in 1819, in which the then soon to be Governor of Bombay proposed:

> that the native system should still be preserved and means taken to remove its abuses and revive its energy.... Our principal instrument must continue to be the Panchayat, and that must continue to be exempt from all new forms, interference, and regulation, on our part.[72]

Elphinstone's report demonstrates a recognition of the persistence of panchayats and that they had an 'energy' of their own. But it also proceeds on the basis that the colonial administration had the capacity to preserve or destroy panchayats and therefore needed to take positive steps to ensure their survival.

69 Ibid., 43. Recall that the term 'panchayat' derives from the Sanskrit term 'Panchayatan', meaning a group of five appointed or elected to govern the village: see Chapter 2, text accompanying note 175.

70 Thomas Munro, 'Trial by Panchayat', minute of 15 August 1807, in Alexander Arbuthnot (ed.), *Major General Sir Thomas Munro: Selections from his Minutes and Other Official Writings*, London: Kegan Paul and Co, 1881, vol. II, p. 4.

71 Joshi, 'Myth of Decentralisation', pp. 66–7.

72 Mountstuart Elphinstone, 'Report on the Territories Conquered from the Peshwa' in George Forrest (ed.), *Selections from the Minutes and Other Official Writings of the Honourable Mountstuart Elphinstone, Governor of Bombay*, London: Richard Bentley and Son, 1884, pp. 358–9.

Whatever steps were taken by the British to preserve the panchayats, to Indian nationalists their effect was the opposite. In the nationalist view, bringing the panchayats into the colonial structure inverted the basis of power on which the panchayats historically functioned – that is, as a corporate body working together for the benefit of the community. The colonialists also took away key functions which had previously been exercised at the village level.[73] Lamenting these two consequences, R. C. Dutt wrote that of the

> many changes which India has witnessed with the advent of the British Rule ... the saddest change is the virtual extinction of the old forms of self-government, and the disappearance of those ancient Village Communities of which India was the first home among all the countries of the earth.[74]

As this quote shows, the nationalists' concern for the lost vitality of village self-government was not simply one which related to the villages themselves, but to India's *national* identity. This view provided the basis for some nationalists to look to the revival of village self-government as a ground on which to fight British rule.

The idea of village self-rule as a mode of national resistance to colonisation was taken to its furthest by Gandhi. In a famous article entitled 'Village Swaraj', Gandhi set out a vision of a village which was 'a complete republic, independent of all its neighbours for its vital wants, and yet interdependent for many others in which dependence is a necessity.'[75] In terms of its operation, village self-government, would 'be conducted by a Panchayat of five persons annually elected by the adult villagers, male and female'

73 Joshi, 'Myth of Decentralisation', p. 71.

74 R. C. Dutt, *Economic History of India Under Early British Rule: From the Rise of the British Power in 1757 to the Accession of Queen Victoria in 1837*, London: Kegan Paul, Trench Trübner, 1902, pp. 151–2.

75 Mahatma Gandhi, 'Village Swaraj' in Mahatma Ghandi, *The Collected Works of Mahatma Ghandi*, Vol 83 (7 June 1942 – 26 January 1944), at: http://www.gandhiserve.org/cwmg/cwmg.html (last accessed 6 December 2011), p. 113.

having 'all the authority and jurisdiction required.'[76] Ruled by the law of non-violence, the villager and their village 'are able to defy the might of a world.'[77] In this thinking, Gandhi drew explicitly on the idea of village self-government as ancient and put it (and its virtues) in opposition to the modern state. Chatterjee argues that Gandhi's 'plea for a return to the simple self-sufficiency of "traditional" village life [was] based on the idea that it was the very changelessness of Indian civilisation, its timeless ahistoricity, which was proof of its truth.'[78] In support, Chatterjee cites Gandhi's statement that:

> It is a charge against India that her people are so uncivilised, ignorant and stolid, that it is not possible to induce them to adopt any changes. It is a charge really against our merit. What we have tested and found true on the anvil of experience, we dare not change.[79]

Gandhi's conception of village self-rule, of course, fitted within a broader political, social and economic theory which opposed not only centralised British rule, but centralised rule in general. And as is very well known, Gandhi's views on the form that a post-independence Indian state should take did not win out in the debates within the Congress, and what resulted was a strong, centralised, state (albeit a federation).[80]

The recent reforms draw explicitly on the legacy of Gandhi's thought on village self-rule. In advance of the constitutional reforms, then Prime Minister Rajiv Gandhi told Parliament that

76 Ibid.
77 Ibid.
78 Partha Chatterjee, *Nationalist Thought and the Colonial World: A Derivative Discourse*, London: Zed Books, 1986, p. 103.
79 Mahatma Gandhi, 'What is True Civilisation?' in Mahatma Ghandi, *Collected Works*, Vol 10 (5 August 1909 – 9 April 1910), p. 279; see ibid.
80 In the words of B. R. Ambedkar (Chairman of the constitution drafting committee), 'I like a strong united centre, much stronger than the centre we had created under the Government of India Act 1935': see Biju, *Resurgent Rural India*, p. vi.

his government was 'determined to realise Gandhiji's dreams of democracy commencing from the villages.'[81] In further promoting the first set of bills (which as we saw above, did not pass), Rajiv Gandhi argued that they did indeed 'represent the realisation of Mahatma Gandhi's vision.'[82] Most recently, in referring to his government's efforts to strengthen the panchayat institutions, Indian Prime Minister Manmohan Singh stated that he had 'every confidence that Panchayati Raj will truly bloom within the next few years so that even as our economy gallops forward, rural India sees the blossoming of the dream of Gram Swaraj that has inspired our leaders from Mahatma Gandhi to Rajiv Gandhi.'[83] Invoking Mahatma Gandhi provides a mode by which national and state politicians can draw on the ancient concept of village autonomy on the one hand, while also linking it to a distinctly nationalist tradition. As such, the nation is at once able to set itself against the particularity of the village while simultaneously embracing it. Nowhere is this clearer than in Rajiv Gandhi's speech on the panchayati raj bills. In defending the uniform requirements for participation of women and scheduled castes and tribes in the panchayat system, he also emphasised that 'we are one country.'[84] And yet he also recognised that 'in a country like India, the *only* unity that is possible is by a large-hearted acceptance of diversity.'[85]

The references to Gandhi's dream evoke a sense of restoration – of the recovery of something which existed before but which had been lost. To the extent that the constitutional reforms linked to Gandhi's vision of village self-rule and that his vision drew explicitly on ancient forms and ideas, one can observe a link between the newly reformed panchayats and those ancient forms.

81 Rajiv Gandhi, 'Realisation of Gandhiji's Dreams' in M. C. Shah (ed.), *Rajiv Gandhi in Parliament*, Delhi: Shipra, 1991, p. 139.

82 Rajiv Gandhi, 'Power to the People' in M. C. Shah (ed.), *Rajiv Gandhi*, p. 170.

83 Manmohan Singh, 'PM's speech at the conference on "The State of the Panchayats"', 22 November 2006, New Delhi, at: http://pmindia.nic.in/speeches.htm (last accessed 6 December 2011).

84 Rajiv Gandhi, 'Power to the People', p. 162.

85 Ibid. (my emphasis).

But in the claims made by and for local communities, the link to the ancient forms arises not only through the mediation of Gandhi's august authority. Instead (or in some cases, in addition), the claim in respect of the recent reforms is for the recognition of something which has continued as a living reality despite the failure of the state previously to recognise it. For Shiva and her colleagues, in passing the Panchayats (Extension to the Scheduled Areas) Act 1996, the Indian Parliament did not create community rights but, after a long period in which they were denied, finally recognised them. On this view, the rights of the community – rights we have seen are phrased in terms of sovereignty – pre-existed their recognition by the state and are not derived from it. This sense of recognition rather than creation (or even restoration) is captured in the following passage:

> A tradition of communities' control over common resources and a culture of equity and equal benefit has always been a part of the common law in India *irrespective of the formal legal recognition to it....* The recognition of the community by the state [in the Panchayats (Extension to the Scheduled Areas) Act 1996], which [up until] now has refused to acknowledge it ... and their control over their resources ... is not in isolation but in relation to the cultural identity of the people. Though this Act applies to the scheduled areas, we envisage it acting as a precedent for the wider interpretation of communities in the rest of India.[86]

In the terms used by Shiva and her colleagues, the state is in a position merely to recognise local sovereignty – in a mode analogous, but not identical, to the recognition by one state of another's sovereignty. As we saw in Chapter 3, the recognition by states of each other is a crucial component in the constitution of their sovereignty, but it is not the case that the recognition is wholly constitutive such that the sovereignty of the recognised entity is

86 Shiva, Jafri, Bedi and Holla-Bhar, *Enclosure and Recovery of the Commons*, p. 139 (my emphasis).

derived from it. In this way, the reliance by traditional knowledge holders on the terms of national law, and the desire for more extensive reforms to it, is not inconsistent with their claims for sovereignty and does not mean that their claims are wholly based on the sovereignty of the state. Rather, it is consistent with an autopositioned sovereign claim – one in which authority is vested in the community for which the sovereign claims to speak – but which can exist only in relation to other sites of sovereign authority.

It is in this context that one should read the conclusion of the Bhuria Committee to which I referred above, that in 'shaping the new Panchayati Raj structure in tribal areas, it is desirable to blend the traditional with the modern by treating the traditional institutions *as the foundation* on which the modern supra-structure [*sic*] should be built.'[87] If the national law concerning local government is a super-structure whose foundation lies in the ancient and traditional forms of governance which it seeks to recognise and to give effect, then one finds the national law to be dependent on the authority of the local community. This goes beyond the recognition that the authority of the local community has (so far as it concerns itself) a life of its own which is not derived from the state. Reversing the orientation, it shows that the state itself is dependent on the local community. And it is dependent on it being not simply vital, but also *sovereign*. If the authority of the local community did not have this character – if its authority was always and already derived from and dependent on the dispensation of the state – the state could not rely on it as a foundation for the very provisions of the Constitution and the national legislation applicable to those communities. Moreover, the Indian state can be seen not only to rely on local communities in constituting its sovereignty over them, but in its sovereignty generally. In Rajiv Gandhi's terms, the panchayati raj constitutional reforms were 'designed to entrench democracy in the *very foundations of our polity* so that the superstructure of democracy in State capitals

87 Bhuria *et al.*, 'Report of the Committee', p. 140 (my emphasis).

and the national capital might be stable, sound and well-founded.'[88]

Conclusion

Claims by local communities to sovereignty over traditional knowledge present a radical challenge to the notion that the nation-state is the exclusive and originary site of sovereignty in modernity. Claims over traditional knowledge in India provide an interesting example of this challenge precisely because of the extent to which the state has tried to bring them within national law. However, as I explained in the Introduction, there is a tension between traditional knowledge being the subject of rights under national legislation on intellectual property (such rights then capable of being licensed), and their being part of a wider cultural context which cannot be reduced to a mere property or economic right. The legal and cultural context within which claims to determine the law over traditional knowledge are made is incompatible with the framework within which the state understands and protects knowledge as property. In substance, the interaction between the Indian state and traditional knowledge holders is one between incommensurable forms of life and law. This incommensurability gives substance to the formal position taken by local communities in relation to the state – the position of a claim to sovereignty. And while this interaction is clearly and vibrantly evident in India, we lack the tools to understand it if we strictly adhere to the idea of the exclusive sovereignty and ultimate unity of the nation-state. Instead, we require a concept of sovereignty which recognises the contingent nature of the sovereign position and its dependence on relation with other sites of authority. Such a concept will not 'solve' the problem of the incommensurability of national sovereignty and the claims of local communities, but it does help to understand how and why the claims exist and how they interact with the sovereignty of the state.

88 Rajiv Gandhi, 'Power to the People', p. 170 (my emphasis).

If the nation-state was the only form of sovereignty possible in modernity, then the claims by local communities would easily be dismissed. However, as we have seen, they have a certain life and vitality which means they are not easily dismissed. Understanding and coming to terms with why these claims seem to have such vitality has been one of the aims of this chapter. The complex relation between the authority of local communities and the Indian state reveals each to hold a self-grounded position apart from the other while at the same time being dependent on their relation with the other. Claims to sovereignty by local communities over traditional knowledge ground their authority in the community itself. But the form that this community frequently takes, and at least some of the authority it holds, is expressly derived from Indian national law, most conspicuously, the Indian Constitution. These claims thus rely on the sovereignty of the state. And yet, despite this derivation, the sovereign authority asserted by local communities has a life of its own which is not reducible to the provisions of national law and is not wholly derived from them. Indeed, reversing the orientation, we also found that the Indian state itself relies on this 'life' in constituting its own authority to establish the national law concerning local government and perhaps even the very foundations of its democracy. In particular, India's national sovereignty has been constituted in the attempt to set itself against local and particular institutions. However, this constitution by opposition has not occurred in a stark or simple way. The nation has been presented as a singular entity capable of embracing the diversity (including a diversity of forms of authority) it seeks to hold within. In order to do that, it cannot also be the origin of that authority or obliterate it in the process of embracing it. Rather, the nation relies on local sovereignty even as it purports to absorb its life by institutionalising it within national law.

These sovereignties are not diametrically opposed and separated by clear borders, but are mutually constitutive. Like the intricate relationship between the WTO and the Indian state which I attempted to reveal in Chapter 4 by a detailed analysis of the Indian Patents Act 1970, the relation of the state and the sovereignty of local communities is also a close one. It takes place within the lines of text which make up India's Constitution and its laws concerning biological diversity and local government, in the memoranda, letters and petitions of local communities, in the speeches of ministers and prime ministers and in the traditional practices lived and developed in local communities. But despite this closeness, there is also a distance. Indeed, distance is required so that closeness does not become dissolution. The incommensurability of the claims to sovereignty means that they can never be fully resolved. This creates a tension which we can observe as the operative dynamic of the politics surrounding traditional knowledge and its protection. But we cannot make sense of this tension unless we find a way of understanding sovereignty which does not cast the sovereignty of the nation-state (or any other single form of community) as exclusive, originary and ultimate.

As such, a theory of sovereign autopositioning provides a better way of understanding the nature of the claims to sovereignty by local communities than those theories which posit the nation-state as the ultimate source of all legal authority. It helps to explain the persistence of these claims despite the conceptual and practical hurdles put in their way. Close attention to the sovereign character of the claims made by local communities (and their implications for the sovereignty of the state) may also reveal something significant about the potential of the claims. Their potential lies in their ability to put in question the conceptual foundations of the national legal authority which seeks to speak for or to them through such legislation as the Biological Diversity Act 2002; to question whether the state *really* does have the authority to legislate with respect to traditional knowledge. Recognising that the nation-state does not exercise its power *over* local communities but *in relation* to them, means that one would need to treat the current national law as a re-solution for the time being between two rival sites of authority, not the sole product of one of them. This would make the relation between local communities and the Indian state similar in nature to the relation between the state and the WTO.

Crucially, such an approach is not blind to the relative power of the entities claiming sovereignty. It is likely that in most cases the sovereignty of the state will, in situations where a clear choice between them must be made, prevail in any single instant. However, what the theory of sovereign autopositioning reveals when applied to the relation between local communities and the state is that, however extensive its power, the state remains strangely dependent on the local community. Each requires the tension of its relation with the other in order to hold its position. Thus, the state cannot rely on its practical power, or its own self-grounded claim to sovereign authority, to deny the potential of the sovereign claims of local communities to call national sovereignty into question and to demand, and perhaps even live, a new, and yet always provisional, re-solution of these rival sovereign positions.

Conclusion

> 'The whole problem, if there is a problem, is of knowing if the execution, the finish, is finite or infinite, and in what sense of these words.'[1]

A recurring theme in this book has been the nature of modern sovereignty as both imperative and impossible. In keeping with that theme, an appropriate conclusion would somehow provide a determinate concentration of its argument while at the same time leaving its implications open. As such, I will conclude by presenting the argument as one which seeks an opening rather than a closure; it seeks to work towards a more flexible and dynamic notion of modern sovereignty than the one provided by standard accounts of international law.

I have taken the example of particular challenges to national sovereignty in India from the international and local levels as a provocation to undertake this theoretical work and to provide a context within which to trace its implications. It is common ground that the World Trade Organisation and local and indigenous communities present a challenge to the sovereignty of the state. Most frequently these challenges (especially that posed by the WTO)

1 Jean-Luc Nancy, *Being Singular Plural*, trs Robert Richardson and Anne O'Byrne, Stanford: Stanford University Press, 2000, p. 118.

are characterised as marking the 'decline' of sovereign statehood. Because modern sovereignty is associated so closely (most often, exclusively) with the nation-state, this decline appears to be one of sovereignty itself. But characterising the issue as one of decline is unsatisfactory for at least three reasons. The first reason flows from the fact that talk of the decline of the sovereignty of the state is dependent on an image of a past (or perhaps soon-to-be past) condition in which all authority in the world flowed from the nation-state, from which this decline can be marked. Whether the apparent decline is celebrated or opposed, the fixation on this image obscures the problems with (and contradictions inherent in) this conception of sovereignty itself. This leads to the second problem, which is that an attachment to the idea that all legal authority flows from the state leaves us with limited tools to understand the complex interaction between claims to determine law at the local, national and international levels, of which the question of control over Indian patent law and traditional knowledge is but an example. The third reason is that it is not possible to abandon the concept of sovereignty in general without at the same time threatening the concepts of responsibility and autonomy (individual and collective).[2] Abandoning the concept would also take us further away from the task of coming to terms with the absence of a solid foundation of law and community, since it is the problem of sovereignty which forces us to confront this absence.

This book has argued that the challenges exemplified by the WTO and local communities in India are not evidence of a decline in modern sovereignty, but prompt a reconception of modern sovereignty itself. However, the aim was not to create a new conception of sovereignty to suit a particular use to which it might be put (i.e. to challenge or defend the authority of the state, or of the WTO, or of local communities). Instead, the aim was to challenge modern sovereignty from the inside, as it were;

2 Jacques Derrida, *Without Alibi*, tr. Peggy Kamuf, Stanford: Stanford University Press, 2002, p. xix; Jacques Derrida, *Rogues: Two Essays on Reason*, trs Pascale-Anne Brault and Michael Naas, Stanford: Stanford University Press, 2005, p. 158.

to examine its constituent characteristics and push them to their limits. This has enabled a reconception which remains (and indeed is perhaps more) faithful to those characteristics. At its heart, the approach taken in this book has been to push to its limit the simple idea that a sovereign is the highest legal authority within a certain space and that its authority is not derived from or subject to any other. It then sought to consider the implications of this idea for the concepts of community and law, and for the way different forms of authority relate to each other. Before presenting some concluding remarks, I will briefly retrace the steps of my argument.

Chapter 1 sought to test the notion that the nation-state is the exclusive site of modern sovereignty. It took Jean Bodin's famous statements on the characteristics of modern sovereignty and found that irresolution was embedded within each of them. Each was found to be both a necessary and impossible characteristic of modern sovereignty. It was then suggested that if the nation-state could somehow resolve these points of irresolution, then a good claim could be made to it being the exclusive occupant of the sovereign position in modernity. However, we saw that the nation failed to resolve these points of irresolution and in fact showed that modern sovereignty lacks a stable ground.

In Chapter 2, I argued that the failure of nation as a ground for sovereignty leads to a thought of modern sovereignty as necessarily self-grounded. In doing so, I sought to develop in more detail Derrida's notion of sovereign 'autopositioning'. This analysis found that a simple self-designation of authority is not enough. Instead, autopositioned sovereignty depends on a relation to law and to the community for which that sovereign claims to speak. Drawing on Jean-Luc Nancy's work on community and Peter Fitzpatrick's work on law, these two concepts were shown to ground sovereignty not only by what they bring to it, but also by what they lack. And this lack in community and in law (their vacuity) was shown to create a need for autopositioned sovereignty. Based on this analysis, it was argued that a theory of sovereign autopositioning shows that the sovereign position is open to an entity capable of making a self-grounded claim to ultimate authority to determine the law of a community. And since the national community is not the only form of community, and national law is not the only form of law, it was suggested that the nation-state could not be the only site of sovereignty in modernity. I then set out how the WTO and local and indigenous communities in India can each be seen to make autopositioned sovereign claims.

Chapter 3 sought to expand on the notion of sovereign autopositioning by analysing the relation between sovereign positions. This served two main purposes. The first was to demonstrate the importance of relation to the creation and constitution of a sovereign position. This served to show the impossibility of a pure origin on which law, community or sovereignty might be based. The second was to provide a framework for understanding how sovereignties, once 'positioned', might relate to one another. As the analysis proceeded, it became evident that these two issues are linked. Drawing on Nancy's work on the limits of singularity, we saw that the maintenance of a sovereign position requires not only an assertion of that position, but a reassertion in response to changing circumstances (in particular, those prompted by rival claims to authority). Again using the classic notion of the exclusive sovereignty of the nation-state to illustrate the point, I tried to show how this dynamic (and its necessity) could be observed in the work of classic theorists of modern sovereignty and international law, from Vitoria to Rousseau, and in the event taken most frequently to mark the 'origin' of the nation-state, the Peace of Westphalia. The sovereignty of states was found to be dependent on their relation with each other and with that from which they could be opposed. Together with Chapters 1 and 2, the analysis in this chapter set the scene for the new interpretation of the relationship between the authority claimed by the WTO, the Indian State and local communities in India set out in Chapters 4 and 5.

Chapter 4 examined the relationship between the Indian state and the WTO in the area of patent law. The theory of sovereign autopositioning was found to provide space for understanding this relation as something other than a simple imposition on, or exercise of, India's sovereignty. It was argued that the WTO can be seen to make a sovereign claim over (among other things) the patent law of its member states. This claim did not completely overcome the claim of the state, however, but established the two sites as rival sovereign positions. From there, India's patent law could be seen as the result not of singular sovereign determination, but as the result of the dynamic relation between these rival positions.

Chapter 5 examined the relationship between the Indian state and claims by local communities to sovereignty over traditional knowledge. These claims do not fit the model of 'self-determination' as it is understood in international law. If, in modernity only states are sovereign (and only aspiring states can aspire to sovereignty) such claims should be impossible. And yet they have a certain potency which would deny this conclusion. As I argued in the Introduction, traditional knowledge is regarded by its custodians as integral to the context in which it is developed. As such, it cannot be commodified in order to be brought within the dominant system of intellectual property law without losing something essential to it. This means that it is impossible to assimilate the claims of traditional knowledge to, or bring them fully within, the law of the state. In turn, this creates an impetus for them to take the form of an autopositioned sovereign claim. Having set out the terms of these claims in Chapter 2, Chapter 5 focused on their relation to the state in light of the provisions of India's Constitution (and of closely-related legislation) which provide for a certain degree of autonomy for local communities. This approach allows the claims of local communities to be taken seriously and also sheds light on the nature of the sovereignty of the Indian state and its constitutive dependence on the authority of those very communities. In this way, the theory of sovereign autopositioning shows that claims by local communities are not an aberration afflicting India's national sovereignty but are integral to it.

Drawing its themes together, this book has attempted to develop a theory of modern sovereignty which provides a different perspective on the so-called decline of national sovereignty brought about by globalisation or the increasing recognition of local or indigenous claims to authority. Eschewing a fruitless search for pure origins and stable grounds, it has tried to show that there is, in any setting, as much sovereignty (and as much community and law) as there is. Any particular sovereign, then, has as much sovereignty as it has. And as the scope of its authority ebbs and flows according to the dynamic of the relation between it and other sites of authority, there is nothing to be impinged on or denied. Instead, all we have is a relation between rival sites of authority in which the scope of a sovereign's authority is always subject to the possibility of change and requires constant reassertion and adaptation.

This approach allows us to look differently at the relationship between the state and other sites of authority. In the case of the WTO, this theory works with, rather than against, the complexity inherent in its both drawing on and limiting the authority of states to legislate in their national interests. It also allows a more nuanced understanding of the responsibility of each entity for the content of the law which results from this relationship. In the case of local communities, it contributes towards a way of thinking through the problem of how incommensurable systems of law relate to each other. It helps explain the persistence of sovereign claims by local communities; claims which were meant to have been brought within or superseded by the sovereignty of the state.

In pushing the concept of sovereignty to its limits, instead of abandoning it, and by finding it to be intimately connected to community and law, the theory developed here keeps alive a focus on the relationship between authority and responsibility, autonomy and legitimacy. But what it does not do, is guarantee these concepts or prescribe a correct mode of their application. And so, this book has not sought to set out a policy or prescription for action. It has not suggested a particular way of managing the question of intellectual property protection on a global scale, nor a blueprint for the recognition of the rights of local communities. It has, along the way, touched on certain implications for policy or politics, but these are necessarily general. For example, the analysis in Chapter 4 might suggest that too much attention has been placed on casting the WTO as a denier of national sovereignty in the context of intellectual property rights, and too little attention placed on developing countries exercising the full scope of the flexibility within TRIPS to create their own interpretations of its requirements.[3] Some steps towards this approach can be seen in the language of the Doha Declaration on TRIPS and Public Health, although it remains to be seen how this will play out in practice.

In the case of traditional knowledge, this book would offer the suggestion that taking its protection seriously requires us to think about creating conditions of possibility for the way of life in which that knowledge has been created and developed to continue. A reconception of sovereignty, and of local peoples' relationship to law and community in India and other countries facing similar issues, may help contribute to thought along these lines. But it would not tell us what to do. Indeed, it leaves many questions open, unresolved. It does not provide us with tools to definitively determine which claims to authority are legitimate and which are not, what the sensible boundaries of and between communities should be, or what law best represents the interests and character of any community. Modern sovereignty, drawing as it does on the vacuity of community and law (and with it a Derridean notion of justice), always leaves open the risk of its being appropriated for bad ends.[4] But if, as this book has argued, embedded within modern sovereignty is a promise of a continuing openness to new and different possibilities of community, of law, and of life, that risk is inseparable from this promise.

3 For examples of commentators attuned to the possibility of exploring the flexibility within TRIPS, see Jayasharee Watal, 'Implementing the TRIPS Agreement: Policy Options Open to India', *Economic and Political Weekly* 32(39), 1997, 2461–8, and Carlos Correa, *Intellectual Property Rights, the WTO and Developing Countries: The TRIPS Agreement and Policy Options*, New York: Zed Books, 2000.

4 Jacques Derrida, 'Force of Law: The Mystical Foundation of Authority', tr. Mary Quaintance, in Jacques Derrida, *Acts of Religion*, ed. Gil Anidjar, New York: Routledge, 2002, p. 257.

Bibliography

Abbott, Frederick and Reichman, Jerome, 'The Doha Round's Public Health Legacy: Strategies for the Production and Diffusion of Patented Medicines under the Amended TRIPS Provisions', *Journal of International Economic Law* 10, 2007, 921.

Agamben, Giorgio, *Homo Sacer: Sovereign Power and Bare Life*, tr. Daniel Heller-Roazen, Stanford: Stanford University Press, 1998.

Agamben, Giorgio, *State of Exception*, tr. Keven Attel, Chicago: University of Chicago Press, 2005.

Ahmad, Khabir, 'India's New Patent Bill Threatens Generic Industry', *The Lancet Infectious Diseases*, 5, 2005, 265.

Alvarez, Jose, *International Organizations as Law-makers*, Oxford: Oxford University Press, 2005.

Anderson, Benedict, *Imagined Communities*, London: Verso, 1991.

Anghie, Antony, *Imperialism, Sovereignty and the Making of International Law*, Cambridge: Cambridge University Press, 2005.

Arbuthnot, Alexander, (ed.), *Major General Sir Thomas Munro: Selections from his Minutes and Other Official Writings*, London: C. Kegan Paul and Co, 1881.

Aristotle, *The Nicomachean Ethics*, New York: Oxford University Press, 1980.

Austin, John, *Province of Jurisprudence Determined*, ed. Wilfred Rumble, Cambridge: Cambridge University Press, 1995.

Ayyangar, N. Rajagopala, *Report on the Revision of the Patents Law*, New Delhi: Government of India, 1959.

Bandyopadhyay, D., 'Rajiv Gandhi and the Third Tier of Governance' in L. C. Jain (ed.), *Decentralisation and Local Governance: Essays for George Mathew*, Hyderabad: Orient Longman, 2005.

Barbour, Charles and Pavlich, George (eds), *After Sovereignty: On the Question of Political Beginnings*, Abingdon: Routledge, 2010.

Bartleson, Jens, *A Genealogy of Sovereignty*, Cambridge: Cambridge University Press, 1995.

Bataille, Georges, *Literature and Evil*, tr. Alastair Hamilton, London: Marion Boyars, 1973.

Bataille, Georges, *The Accursed Share: Volumes II and III*, tr. Robert Hurley, New York: Zone Books, 1991.

Beaulac, Stephane, 'The Westphalian Model in Defining International Law: Challenging the Myth', *Australian Journal of Legal History* 8, 2004, 181.

Bhuria, Dileep Singh, *et al.*, 'Report of the Committee of MPs and Experts to Make Recommendations on the Salient Features of the Law for Extending Provisions of the Constitutions (73rd) Amendment Act, 1992 to the Scheduled Areas, 1995', in P. S. K. Menon and Bakshi Sinha, *Panchayati Raj in Scheduled Areas: A Critical Study*, New Delhi: Concept Publishing, 2003, annexure IV.

Biju, M. R., *Resurgent Rural India: Decade after the Constitutionalisation of Panchayati Raj*, Delhi: Authors Press, 2007.

Blakeney, Michael, *Trade Related Aspects of Intellectual Property Rights: A Concise Guide to the TRIPS Agreement*, London: Sweet and Maxwell, 1996.

Blakeney, Michael, 'The Protection of Traditional Knowledge Under Intellectual Property Law', *European Intellectual Property Review* 22, 2000, 251.

Blakeney, Michael, 'Hans Christian Andersen and the Protection of Traditional Cultural Expressions' in H. Porsdam (ed.), *Copyright and Other Fairytales: The Commodification of Creativity*, Cheltenham: Edward Elgar, 2005.

Blanchot, Maurice, 'The Madness of the Day' in Maurice Blanchot, *The Station Hill Blanchot Reader: Fiction and Literary Essays*, Barrytown: Station Hill Press, 1998.

Bodin, Jean, *Six Books of the Commonwealth*, tr. R. Knolles, London: Bishop, 1606.

Bodin, Jean, *Method for the Easy Comprehension of History*, tr. Beatrice Reynolds, New York: Columbia University Press, 1945.

Bodin, Jean, *On Sovereignty: Four Chapters from the Six Books of the Commonwealth*, ed. and tr. Julian Franklin, Cambridge: Cambridge University Press, 1992.

Bolivia, Brazil, Cuba, Ecuador, India, Pakistan, Peru, Thailand and Venezuela, 'The Relationship Between the TRIPS Agreement and the Convention on Biological Diversity and the Protection of

Traditional Knowledge', submission to the Council for Trade-Related Aspects of Intellectual Property Rights, World Trade Organisation (IP/C/W/403), 24 June 2003.

Bolivia, Brazil, Cuba, Ecuador, India, Pakistan, Peru, Thailand and Venezuela, 'The Relationship Between the TRIPS Agreement and the Convention on Biological Diversity (CBD) and the Protection of Traditional Knowledge: Elements of the Obligation to Disclose Evidence of Prior Informed Consent under the Relevant National Regime', submission to the Council for Trade-Related Aspects of Intellectual Property Rights, World Trade Organisation (IP/C/W/438), 10 December 2004.

Borradori, Giovanna, *Philosophy in a Time of Terror: Dialogues with Jurgen Habermas and Jacques Derrida*, Chicago: University of Chicago Press, 2003.

Brazil, China, Colombia, Cuba, Dominican Republic, Ecuador, India, Indonesia, Pakistan, Paraguay, Peru, South Africa, Tanzania, Thailand, Venezuela, LDC Group and ACP Group, 'Doha Work Programme – Relationship Between the TRIPS Agreement and the Convention on Biological Diversity', submission to the Council for Trade-Related Aspects of Intellectual Property Rights, World Trade Organisation (WT/GC/W/590), 28 May 2008.

Brazil, China, Colombia, Cuba, India, Pakistan, Peru, Thailand and Tanzania, 'Doha Work Programme – The Outstanding Implementation Issue on the Relationship Between the TRIPS Agreement and the Convention on Biological Diversity', submission to the Council for Trade-Related Aspects of Intellectual Property Rights, World Trade Organisation (WT/GC/W/564/Rev.2) 5 July 2006.

Brazil, China, Colombia, Ecuador, India, Indonesia, Peru, Thailand, the ACP Group, and the African Group, 'Draft Decision To Enhance Mutual Supportiveness Between the TRIPS Agreement and the Convention on Biological Diversity', submission to the Council for Trade-Related Aspects of Intellectual Property Rights, World Trade Organisation (TN/C/W/59) 19 April 2011.

Brazil and India, 'The Relationship between the TRIPS Agreement and the Convention on Biological Diversity (CBD) and the Protection of Traditional Knowledge: Technical Observations on Issues raised in a Communication by the United States', submission to the Council for Trade-Related Aspects of Intellectual Property Rights, World Trade Organisation (IP/C/W/434), 18 March 2005.

Brownlie, Ian, *Principles of Public International Law*, 6th ed., Oxford: Oxford University Press, 2003.

Bush, George W., *The National Security Strategy of the United States of America*, Washington: Office of the President of the United States, 2002.

Bush, George W., *The National Security Strategy of the United States of America*, Washington: Office of the President of the United States, 2006.

Campaign for Community Control over Biodiversity, 'Laws and Flaws: Farmers' Questions, Farmers' Answers', Report of a Workshop in Zaheerabad, Medak District, Andhra Pradesh, 14–16 January 2007, at: http://www.kalpavriksh.org/f1/f1.1/bdbdcamp (last accessed 15 May 2009, copy on file).

Campaign for Community Control over Biodiversity, 'Letter to the Prime Minister of India', 27 April 2007, at: www.ddsindia.com/www/Campaign letter to the PM.pdf (last accessed 6 December 2011).

Campaign for Community Control over Biodiversity, 'Resolution Regarding the Biological Diversity Rules 2004', provided to the author by Kanchi Kohli of Kalpavriksh, copy on file.

Canada, 'Notification under Paragraph 2(C) of the Decision of 30 August 2003 on the Implementation of Paragraph 6 of the Doha Declaration on the TRIPS Agreement and Public Health' (IP/N/10/CAN/1), 8 October 2007.

Castells, Manuel, *The Rise of the Network Society*, 2nd ed., Chichester: Wiley-Blackwell, 2010.

Cavallar, George, *The Rights of Strangers: Theories of International Hospitality, the Global Community, and Political Justice since Vitoria*, Aldershot: Ashgate, 2002.

Chatterjee, Partha, *Nationalist Thought and the Colonial World: A Derivative Discourse*, London: Zed Books, 1986.

Chatterjee, Partha, *The Nation and Its Fragments: Colonial and Postcolonial Histories*, Princeton: Princeton University Press, 1993.

Chaturvedi, Sachin, 'Kani Case: A Report for GenBenefit', 2007, at: www.uclan.ac.uk/schools/school_of_health/research_projects/files/health_genbeneift_kani_case.pdf (last accessed 6 December 2011).

Chaudhuri, Sudip, *The WTO and India's Pharmaceuticals Industry: Patent Protection, TRIPS and Developing Countries*, New Delhi: Oxford University Press, 2005.

'Community Control over Biodiversity: Memorandum to the Government of India', 8 December 2004, submitted by 200 Gram Panchayats and gram sabhas of Chhattisgarh, Madhya Pradesh, Andhra Pradesh, Karnataka, Tamil Nadu, and Uttaranchal, along with Kalpavriksh, Gene Campaign, People's Alliance for Livelihood Rights, Deccan Development Society, Centre For World Solidarity, Green Foundation,

Delhi Forum and Beej Bachao Andolan, on behalf of the Campaign on Community Control over Biodiversity, at: http://www.ddsindia.com/www/Biodiversity rules rally report_link MoEF.htm (last accessed 6 December 2011).

Correa, Carlos, *Intellectual Property Rights, the WTO and Developing Countries: The TRIPS Agreement and Policy Options*, New York: Zed Books, 2000.

Correa, Carlos, 'Public Health and Patent Legislation in Developing Countries' *Tulane Journal of Technology and Intellectual Property* 3, 2001, 1.

Correa, Carlos, 'Implications of the Doha Declaration on the TRIPS Agreement and Public Health', World Health Organisation: WHO/EDM/PAR/2002.3, 2002.

Correa, Carlos, 'Bilateralism in Intellectual Property: Defeating the WTO System for Access to Medicines', *Case Western Reserve Journal of International Law* 36, 2004, 79.

Correa, Carlos, 'Investment Protection in Bilateral and Free Trade Agreements: Implications for the Granting of Compulsory Licences', *Michigan Journal of International Law* 26, 2004, 31.

Crawford, James, *The Creation of States in International Law*, 2nd ed., Oxford: Clarendon Press, 2006.

Derrida, Jacques, 'Declarations of Independence', *New Political Science* 7, 1986, 7.

Derrida, Jacques, 'The Laws of Reflection: Nelson Mandela, In Admiration', trs M. Caws and I. Loenz in Jacques Derrida and Mustapha Tlili (eds.), *For Nelson Mandela*, New York: Seaver Books, 1987.

Derrida, Jacques, *Spectres of Marx: The State of the Debt, the Work of Mourning and the New International*, tr. Peggy Kamuf, New York: Routledge, 1994.

Derrida, Jacques, 'Remarks on Deconstruction and Pragmatism', tr. Simon Critchley, in Simon Critchley, Jacques Derrida, Ernesto Laclau and Richard Rorty, *Deconstruction and Pragmatism*, London: Routledge, 1996.

Derrida, Jacques and Dufourmantelle, Anne, *Of Hospitality (Cultural Memory in the Present)*, tr. Rachel Bowlby, Stanford: Stanford University Press, 2000.

Derrida, Jacques, *Acts of Religion*, ed. Gil Anidjar, New York: Routledge, 2002.

Derrida, Jacques, *Without Alibi*, tr. Peggy Kamuf, Stanford: Stanford University Press, 2002.

Derrida, Jacques, *Rogues: Two Essays on Reason*, trs Pascale-Anne Brault and Michael Naas, Stanford: Stanford University Press, 2005.

Derrida, Jacques, *Sovereignties in Question: The Poetics of Paul Celan*, ed. Thomas Dutoit and Outi Pasanen, New York: Fordham University Press, 2005.

Derrida, Jacques, *The Politics of Friendship*, tr. George Collins, London: Verso, 2005.

Derrida, Jacques, *The Beast and the Sovereign (Volume I)*, tr. Geoffrey Bennington, Chicago: University of Chicago Press, 2009.

Derrida, Jacques, *The Beast and the Sovereign (Volume II)*, tr. Geoffrey Bennington, Chicago: University of Chicago Press, 2011.

Drahos, Peter, 'Global Property Rights in Information: The Story of TRIPS at the GATT', *Prometheus* 13, 1995, 6.

Drahos, Peter, 'Indigenous Knowledge and the Duties of Intellectual Property Owners', *Intellectual Property Journal* 11, 1997, 179.

Drahos, Peter, 'BITS and BIPS: Bilateralism in Intellectual Property', *Journal of World Intellectual Property* 4, 2001, 791.

Drahos, Peter, 'Developing Countries and Intellectual Property Standard-Setting', *Journal of World Intellectual Property* 5, 2002, 765.

Drahos, Peter, 'Towards an International Framework for the Protection of Traditional Group Knowledge and Practice', paper prepared for the *UNCTAD-Commonwealth Secretariat Workshop on Elements of National Sui Generis Systems for the Preservation, Protection and Promotion of Traditional Knowledge, Innovations and Practices and Options for an International Framework*, Geneva, 4–6 February 2004.

Drahos, Peter, 'Weaving Webs of Influence: The United States, Free Trade Agreements and Dispute Resolution', *Journal of World Trade* 41, 2007, 191.

Dutfield, Graham, *Intellectual Property, Biogenic Resources and Traditional Knowledge*, London: Earthscan, 2004.

Dutt, R. C., *Economic History of India Under Early British Rule: From the Rise of the British Power in 1757 to the Accession of Queen Victoria in 1837*, London: Kegan Paul, Trench Trübner, 1902.

Economist, 'The Great Unravelling: Is Globalisation Killing India's Cotton Farmers?', *Economist* 382, 20 January 2007.

Fell, A. London, *Origins of Legislative Sovereignty and the Legislative State: Volume Three: Bodin's Humanistic Legal System and Rejection of 'Medieval Political Theology'*, Boston: Oelgeschlager, Gunn & Hain, 1987.

Fisher, Matthew, *Fundamentals of Patent Law: Interpretation and Scope of Protection*, Oxford: Hart, 2007.

Fitzpatrick, Peter, *Modernism and the Grounds of Law*, Cambridge: Cambridge University Press, 2001.

Fitzpatrick, Peter, '"Gods Would Be Needed…": American Empire and the Rule of (International) Law', *Leiden Journal of International Law* 16, 2003, 429.

Fitzpatrick, Peter, 'We Know What It Is When You Do Not Ask Us: The Unchallengable Nation', *Finnish Yearbook of International Law* 15, 2004, 129.

Fitzpatrick, Peter, 'Access as Justice', *Windsor Yearbook of Access to Justice* 23, 2005, 3.

Fitzpatrick, Peter, 'What are the Gods to Us Now?: Secular Theology and the Modernity of Law', *Theoretical Inquiries in Law* 8, 2007, 161.

Fitzpatrick, Peter, 'Is Humanity Enough? The Secular Theology of Human Rights', *Law, Social Justice and Global Development* 1, 2007, at: http://www2.warwick.ac.uk/fac/soc/law/elj/lgd/2007_1/fitzpatrick (last accessed 6 December 2011).

Fitzpatrick, Peter, 'Latin Roots: Imperialism and the Formation of Modern Law' in Peter Fitzpatrick, *Law as Resistance: Modernism, Imperialism, Legalism*, Aldershot: Ashgate, 2008.

Fitzpatrick, Peter, 'Making Difference: Modernity and the Political Formations of Death' in Austin Sarat and Charles J. Ogletree Jr (eds), *The Road to Abolition: The Future of Capital Punishment in the United States*, New York: New York University Press, 2009.

Fitzpatrick, Peter, 'Leveraging Leviathan' in Charles Barbour and George Pavlich (eds), *After Sovereignty: On the Question of Political Beginnings*, Abingdon: Routledge, 2010.

Fitzpatrick, Peter, 'Surpassing Sovereignty', in Julie Evans *et al.* (eds), *New Worlds, New Sovereignties: Frontiers of Possibility in the Emerging Global Order*, Honolulu: University of Hawai'i Press, forthcoming.

Fitzpatrick, Peter and Joyce, Richard, 'Copying Right: Cultural Property and the Limits of (Occidental) Law' in Fiona Macmillan (ed.), *New Directions in Copyright Law: Volume 4: Protection of Traditional Knowledge and Culture*, Cheltenham: Edward Elgar, 2007.

Fitzpatrick, Peter and Joyce, Richard, 'The Normality of the Exception in Democracy's Empire', *Journal of Law and Society* 34, 2007, 64.

Forrest, George (ed.), *Selections from the Minutes and Other Official Writings of the Honourable Mountstuart Elphinstone, Governor of Bombay*, London: Richard Bentley and Son, 1884.

Foster, George, 'Opposing Forces in a Revolution in International Patent Protection: The US and India in the Uruguay Round and its Aftermath', *U.C.L.A. Journal of International Law and Foreign Affairs* 3, 1998, 283.

Foucault, Michel, 'Maurice Blanchot: The Thought from the Outside', tr. Brian Massumi, in Maurice Blanchot and Michel Foucault, *Foucault/ Blanchot*, New York: Zone Books, 1987.

Franklin, Julian, *Jean Bodin and the Sixteenth Century Revolution in the Methodology of Law and History*, New York: Columbia University Press, 1963.

Fulcher, James, 'Globalisation, the Nation-State and Global Society', *The Sociological Review* 48, 2000, 522–43.

Galanter, Marc, *Competing Equalities: Law and the Backward Classes in India*, Berkeley: University of California Press, 1984.

Gene Campaign, 'Farmers' Rights and IPR' at: http://www.genecampaign.org/Sub%20pages/wws-ID9.htm (last accessed 6 December 2011).

Gervais, Daniel, 'Traditional Knowledge & Intellectual Property: A TRIPS-Compatible Approach', *Michigan State Law Review* 2005, 137.

Gervais, Daniel, *The TRIPS Agreement: Drafting History and Analysis*, 3rd ed., London: Sweet and Maxwell, 2008.

Mahatma Ghandi, *The Collected Works of Mahatma Ghandi*, at: http://www.gandhiserve.org/cwmg/cwmg.html (last accessed 6 December 2011).

Gibson, Johanna, *Community Resources: Intellectual Property, International Trade and Protection of Traditional Knowledge*, Aldershot: Ashgate, 2005.

Gibson, Johanna, *Creating Selves: Intellectual Property and the Narration of Culture*, Aldershot: Ashgate, 2006.

Gopalakrishnan, N. S., 'Protection of Traditional Knowledge: The Need for a *Sui Generis* Law in India', *Journal of World Intellectual Property* 5, 2002, 725.

Government of India, 'Report of the Team for the Study of Community Projects and National Extension Service' (Chairperson: Balvantray Mehta), Committee on Plan Projects, National Development Council, New Delhi: Government of India, 1957.

Government of India, 'Report of the Committee on Panchayati Raj Institutions' (Chairperson: Ashok Mehta), New Delhi: Government of India, 1978.

Government of India, Ministry of Tribal Affairs, 'Definition of Scheduled Areas' at: http://tribal.gov.in/index3.asp?subsublinkid=305&langid=1 (last accessed 6 December 2011).

Gross, Leo, 'The Peace of Westphalia: 1648–1948', *American Journal of International Law* 42, 1948, 20.

Grotius, Hugo, *The Free Sea*, tr. Richard Hakluyt, ed. David Armitage, Indianapolis: Liberty Fund, 2004.

Grotius, Hugo, *The Rights of War and Peace*, ed. Richard Tuck, Indianapolis: Liberty Fund, 2004.

Grotius, Hugo, *Commentary on the Law of Prize and Booty*, ed. Martine Julia van Ittersum, Indianapolis: Liberty Fund, 2006.

Gruère, Guillame, Metha-Bhatt, Purvi and Sengupta, Deblotta, 'Bt Cotton and Farmer Suicides', IFPRI Discussion Paper 00808, International Food Policy Research Institute, October 2008.

Gupta, Anil, *WIPO-UNEP Study on the Role of Intellectual Property Rights in the Sharing of Benefits Arising from the Use of Biological Resources and Associated Traditional Knowledge*, WIPO-UNEP: 2004, at: www.wipo.int/tk/en/publications/769e_unep_tk.pdf (last accessed 6 December 2011).

Held, David and McGrew, Anthony, *Globalisation/Anti-Globalisation: Beyond the Great Divide*, 2nd ed., Cambridge: Polity Press, 2007.

Higgins, Rosalyn, *The Development of International Law through the Political Organs of the UN*, London: Oxford University Press, 1963.

The Hindu, 'Biodiversity Act, Rules opposed' in *The Hindu*, 8 December 2004, at: http://www.hindu.com/2004/12/08/stories/2004120815390300.htm (last accessed 6 December 2011).

Hinsley, F. H., *Sovereignty*, Cambridge: Cambridge University Press, 1986.

Hobbes, Thomas, *Leviathan*, London: Penguin, 1968.

Hobbes, Thomas, *The Elements of Law Natural and Politic*, Whitefish: Kessinger Publishing, 2004.

Howard, John, 'The Right Time', Address to the Sydney Institute, 11 October 2007, printed in *The Age*, 11 October 2007, at: http://www.theage.com.au/articles/2007/10/11/1191696077007.html (last accessed 6 December 2011).

India, 'Protection of Biodiversity and Traditional Knowledge – The Indian Experience', submission to the Committee on Trade and Environment Council for Trade-Related Aspects of Intellectual Property Rights (WT/CTE/W/156), 14 July 2000.

Intergovernmental Committee on Intellectual Property and Genetic Resources, Traditional Knowledge and Folklore, World Intellectual Property Organisation, 'The Protection of Traditional Knowledge: Draft Articles', Annex to Document WIPO/GRTKF/IC/21/4, 18 January 2012, at http://www.wipo.int/tk/en/igc/ (last accessed 20 April 2012). Previous iterations of the draft articles were also consulted. These can be found at http://www.wipo.int/meetings/en/topic.jsp?group_id=110 (last accessed 20 April 2012).

International Law Commission, 'Draft Articles on the Law of Treaties, with Commentaries' (1966) *Yearbook of the International Law Commission*, at: http://untreaty.un.org/ilc/texts/instruments/english/commentaries/1_1_1966.pdf (last accessed 6 December 2011).

Iyer, V. R. Krishna, 'Human Health and Patent Law', *Frontline* 17(21), 2000, at: http://www.frontline.in/fl1721/17210790.htm (last accessed 6 December 2011).

Iyer, V. R. Krishna, 'The Doha-Delhi Odyssey' *Frontline* 19(6), 2002, at: http://www.hindu.com/fline/fl1906/19060900.htm (last accessed 6 December 2011).

Iyer, V. R. Krishna, Reddy, O. Chinappa, Desai, D. A. and Sachar, Rajinder, *Peoples' Commission on GATT: On the Constitutional Implications of the Final Act Embodying the Results of the Uruguay Round of Multilateral Trade Negotiations*, New Delhi: Centre for Study of Global Trade System and Development, 1996.

Jackson, John, 'The Great 1994 Sovereignty Debate: United States Acceptance and Implementation of the Uruguay Round Results', *Columbia Journal of Transnational Law* 36, 1997, 157.

Jackson, Robert, *Quasi-states: Sovereignty, International Relations and the Third World*, Cambridge: Cambridge University Press, 1990.

Johnson, Martha, 'Research on Traditional Environmental Knowledge: its Development and its Role' in Martha Johnson (ed.), *Lore: Capturing Traditional Environmental Knowledge*, Ottowa: International Development Research Centre, 1992.

Joshi, Lalit, 'The Myth of Decentralisation: Village Panchayats in Colonial India' in M. P. Dubey and Munny Padalia (eds), *Democratic Decentralisation and Panchayati Raj in India*, New Delhi: Anamika, 2002.

Joyce, Richard, 'Westphalia: Event, Memory, Myth' in Fleur Johns, Richard Joyce and Sundhya Pahuja (eds), *Events: The Force of International Law*, Abingdon: Routledge, 2011.

Kafka, Franz, *The Trial*, trs Willa and Edwin Muir, London: David Campbell, 1992.

Kant, Immanuel, *The Metaphysics of Morals*, ed. and tr. Mary Gregor, Cambridge: Cambridge University Press, 1996.

Kantorowicz, Ernst, *The King's Two Bodies: A Study in Medieval Political Theology*, Princeton: Princeton University Press, 1957.

Kapila, Kriti, 'The Measure of a Tribe: the Cultural Politics of Constitutional Reclassification in North India', *Journal of the Royal Anthropological Institute* 14, 2008, 117.

Keayla, B. K., 'Amended Patents Act: A Critique', *Combat Law* 4(2), 2005, India Together, at: http://www.indiatogether.org/combatlaw/vol4/issue2/patents.htm (last accessed 6 December 2011).

Knop, Karen, *Diversity and Self-Determination in International Law*, Cambridge: Cambridge University Press, 2002.

Krasner, Stephen, 'Westphalia and All That' in Judith Goldstein and Robert O. Keohane (eds), *Ideas and Foreign Policy: Beliefs, Institutions and Political Change*, Ithica: Cornell University Press, 1993.

Krasner, Stephen, *Sovereignty: Organized Hypocrisy*, Princeton: Princeton University Press, 1999.

Liddell, Henry, Scott, Robert and Jones, Henry, *A Greek-English Lexicon*, Oxford: Clarendon Press, 1968.

Lindahl, Hans, 'Constituent Power and Reflexive Identity: Towards an Ontology of Collective Selfhood', in Martin Loughlin and Neil Walker (eds), *The Paradox of Constitutionalism: Constituent Power and Constitutional Form*, Oxford: Oxford University Press, 2007.

Macmillan, Fiona, *WTO and the Environment*, London: Sweet and Maxwell, 2001.

Macmillan, Fiona, 'International Economic Law and Public International Law' *International Trade Law and Regulation* 6, 2004, 115.

Macmillan, Fiona, 'Commodification and Cultural Ownership' in Jonathan Griffiths and Uma Suthersanen (eds), *Copyright and Free Speech: Comparative and International Analyses*, Oxford: Oxford University Press, 2005.

Macmillan, Fiona, *The World Trade Organization and Human Rights*, Oxford: Hart, forthcoming.

Man, Paul de, *Allegories of Reading: Figural Language in Rousseau, Nietzsche, Rilke, and Proust*, New Haven: Yale University Press, 1979.

Mashelkar, R. A., 'Intellectual Property Rights and the Third World' *Current Science* 81, 2001, 955.

Matsushita, Mitsuo, Schoenbaum, Thomas and Mavroidis, Petros, *The World Trade Organisation*, Oxford: Oxford University Press, 2004.

Meenakshisundaram, S. S., 'Rural Development for Panchayati Raj' in L. C. Jain (ed.), *Decentralisation and Local Governance: Essays for George Mathew*, Hyderabad: Orient Longman, 2005.

Menon, P. S. K., and Sinha, Bakshi, *Panchayati Raj in Scheduled Areas: A Critical Study*, New Delhi: Concept Publishing, 2003.

Monier-Williams, Monier, *Modern India and the Indians: Being a Series of Impressions, Notes and Essays*, 3rd ed. 1879, Delhi: Oriental Publishers, 1971.

Monsanto, 'Latest Evidence on True Causes of Indian Farmer Suicides', at: http://www.monsanto.co.uk/news/ukshowlib.php?uid=13478 (last accessed 6 December 2011).

Moran, Katy, 'Benefit Sharing Under the Convention on Biological Diversity' in Mary Riley (ed.), *Indigenous Intellectual Property Rights: Legal Obstacles & Innovative Solutions*, California: AltaMira Press, 2004.

Mueller, Janice, 'The Tiger Awakens: The Tumultuous Transformation of India's Patent System and the Rise of Indian Pharmaceutical Innovation', *University of Pittsburgh Law Review* 68, 2007, 491.

Nancy, Jean-Luc, *The Inoperative Community*, ed. and tr. Peter Connor, Minneapolis: University of Minnesota Press, 1991.

Nancy, Jean-Luc, *The Birth to Presence*, tr. Brian Holmes *et al.*, Stanford: Stanford University Press, 1993.

Nancy, Jean-Luc, *The Experience of Freedom*, tr. Bridget McDonald, Stanford: Stanford University Press, 1993.

Nancy, Jean-Luc, *Being Singular Plural*, trs Robert Richardson and Anne O'Byrne, Stanford: Stanford University Press, 2000.

Nancy, Jean-Luc, 'L'antrus', tr. Susan Janson, *New Centennial Review* 3(2), 2002, 1.

Nancy, Jean-Luc, 'Démocratie Finie et Infinie' in La Fabrique (ed.), *Démocratie dans quel état?*, Paris: La Fabrique editions, 2009.

Narayanan, P., *Patent Law*, Kolkata: Eastern House, 2006.

Nehru, Jawaharlal, *The Discovery of India*, New Delhi: Penguin, 2004.

New York Times, 'India's Choice', Editorial, 18 January 2005, at: http://www.nytimes.com/2005/01/18/opinion/18tues2.html?oref=login (last accessed 6 December 2011).

Oxford English Dictionary, 2nd ed., Oxford: Oxford University Press, 1989.

Palmeter, David and Mavroidis, Petros, *Dispute Settlement in the World Trade Organisation: Practice and Procedure*, Cambridge: Cambridge University Press, 2004.

Pant, Alok, 'Panchayats – An Institutional Myth or Viable Reality' in M. P. Dubey and Munny Padalia (eds), *Democratic Decentralisation and Panchayati Raj in India*, New Delhi: Anamika, 2002.

Parliament of India, 'Combined Discussion on the Statutory Resolution Regarding Disapproval of Patents (Amendment) Ordinance, 2004 (No.7 of 2004) and passing of the Patents (Amendment) Bill, 2005' Lok Sabha Debates, 22 March 2005, at: http://164.100.47.132/LssNew/psearch/result14.aspx?dbsl=1866 (last accessed 6 December 2011).

Parliament of India, 'Consideration of the Biological Diversity Bill, 2001' Lok Sabha Debates, 2 December 2002, at: http://164.100.47.132/LssNew/psearch/Result13.aspx?dbsl=4790 (last accessed 6 December 2011).

Parry, C., (ed.), *The Consolidated Treaty Series; Treaty of Münster* (1648) and Treaty of Osnabrück (1648), vol. 1, New York: Oceana Publications, 1969.

Pascal, Blaise, *Pensees*, tr. A. J. Krailsheimer, London: Penguin, 1995.

Permanent Mission of Brazil on behalf of the delegations of Brazil, China, Cuba, Dominican Republic, Ecuador, India, Pakistan, Thailand, Venezuela, Zambia and Zimbabwe, 'The Relationship Between the TRIPS Agreement and the Convention on Biological Diversity and the Protection of Traditional Knowledge', submission to the Council for Trade-Related Aspects of Intellectual Property Rights, World Trade Organisation (IP/C/W/356), 24 June 2002.

Philpott, Daniel, *Revolutions in Sovereignty: How Ideas Shaped Modern International Relations*, Princeton: Princeton University Press, 2001.

Plato, *Symposium*, tr. Christopher Gill, London: Penguin Books, 1999.

Poggi, Gianfranco, *The Development of the Modern State: A Sociological Introduction*, London: Hutchinson, 1987.

Prakash, Gyan, 'Writing Post-Orientalist Histories of the Third World: Perspectives from Indian Historiography', *Comparative Studies in Society and History* 32, 1990, 383.

Pufendorf, Samuel, *On the Law of Nature and Nations, Eight Books*, tr. Basil Kennet, 3rd ed., London, 1717.

Pushpangadan, P., *et al.*, '"Arogyapacha" (Trichophus Zeylanicus Gaertn.): The "Ginseng" of Kani Tribes of Agasthyar Hills (Kerala) for Ever Green Health and Vitality', *Ancient Science of Life* 8, 1988, 13.

Randeria, Shalini, 'Entangled Histories of Uneven Modernities: Civil Society, Caste Solidarities and Legal Pluralism in Post-Colonial India' in Yehuda Elkana *et al.* (eds), *Unraveling Ties: From Social Cohesion to New Practices of Connectedness*, New York: Campus Verlag, 2002.

Rangnekar, Dwijen, 'No Pills for Poor People? Understanding the Disembowelment of India's Patent Regime', *CSGR Working Paper*, 176/05, 2005.

Rangnekar, Dwijen, 'Is Plagiarism the Only Problem with the Mashelkar Report?', *Economic and Political Weekly* 42, 2007, 816.

Rao, Shiva (ed.), *The Framing of India's Constitution*, New Delhi: The Indian Institute of Public Administration, 1968.

Ray, Tinku, 'Indian GM Crops Battle Heats Up', BBC news, 18 December 2008, at: http://news.bbc.co.uk/2/hi/business/7785212.stm (last accessed 6 December 2011).

Research Foundation for Science, Technology and Ecology, 'Notices Served to Biopirates', at: http://www.ratical.org/co-globalize/BPandWTO.html (last accessed 6 December 2011).

Rousseau, Jean-Jacques, *The Social Contract*, tr. Christopher Betts, Oxford: Oxford University Press, 1994.

Rwanda, 'Notification under Paragraph 2(A) of the Decision of 30 August 2003 on the Implementation of Paragraph 6 of the Doha Declaration on the TRIPS Agreement and Public Health' (IP/N/9/RWA/1), 19 July 2007.

Saha, Rohan, 'Recent Developments in the "Arogyapacha: Kani" Case', 1 Oct 2008, Spicy IP (Blog), http://spicyipindia.blogspot.com/2008/10/guest-post-recent-developments-in.html (last accessed 6 December 2011).

Sahai, Suman, Kumar, Ujjawal and Ahmed, Waquar, *Indigenous Knowledge: Issues for Developing Countries*, New Delhi: Gene Campaign, 2005.

Sahai, Suman, Pavithran, Prasmi and Barpujari, Indrani, *Biopiracy: Imitations Not Innovations*, New Delhi: Gene Campaign, 2007.

Sarooshi, Dan, *International Organisations and their Exercise of Sovereign Powers*, Oxford: Oxford University Press, 2005.

Sassen, Saskia, *Losing Control? Sovereignty in an Age of Globalisation*, New York: Columbia University Press, 1996.

Scherer, F. M. and Watal, Jayasharee, 'Post-Trips Options for Access to Patented Medicines in Developing Nations', *Journal of International Economic Law* 5, 2002, 913.

Schmitt, Carl, *The* Nomos *of the Earth*, tr. G. Ulmen, New York: Telos Press, 2003.

Schmitt, Carl, *Political Theology: Four Chapters on the Concept of Sovereignty*, tr. George Schwab, Chicago: University of Chicago Press, 2005.

Schmitt, Carl, *Constitutional Theory*, ed. and tr. Jeffrey Seitzer, Durham: Duke University Press, 2008.

Sell, Susan K., *Power and Ideas: North-South Politics of Intellectual Property and Anti-Trust*, New York: State University of New York Press, 1998.

Sell, Susan K., *Private Power, Public Law: The Globalisation of Intellectual Property Rights*, Cambridge: Cambridge University Press, 2003.

Shah, M. C. (ed.), *Rajiv Gandhi in Parliament*, Delhi: Shipra, 1991.

Shaji, Ka, 'Herbal Wars', *Tehelka Magazine* 5(38), 27 September 2008, at: http://www.tehelka.com/story_main40.asp?filename=Ne270908herbalwars.asp (last accessed 6 December 2011).

Sharma, Devinder, 'Selling Biodiversity: Benefit Sharing is a Dead Concept', 3 May 2004, at: http://www.mindfully.org/WTO/2004/Selling-Biodiversity-Sharma3may04.htm (last accessed 6 December 2011).

Shiva, Vandana, *Biopiracy: Plunder of Nature and Knowledge*, New Delhi: Research Foundation for Science, Technology and Ecology, 1997.

Shiva, Vandana, *Patents: Myths and Reality*, New Delhi: Penguin, 2001.

Shiva, Vandana and Jalees, Kunwar, *Seeds of Suicide: The Ecological and Human Costs of Seed Monopolies and Globalisation of Agriculture*, 4th ed., New Delhi: Navdanya, 2006.

Shiva, Vandana, Jafri, Afsar, Bedi, Gitanjali and Holla-Bhar, Radha, *The Enclosure and Recovery of the Commons: Biodiversity, Indigenous Knowledge and Intellectual Property Rights*, New Delhi: Research Foundation for Science, Technology and Ecology, 1997.

Sieyès, Emmanuel, *Political Writings*, ed. and tr. Michael Sonenscher, Indianapolis: Hackett Publishing Company, 2003.

Singh, Hoshiar, 'Constitutional Base for Panchayati Raj in India: The 73rd Amendment Act', *Asian Survey* 34, 1994, 818.

Singh, Manmohan, 'PM's speech at the conference on "The State of the Panchayats"', 22 November 2006, New Delhi, at: http://pmindia.nic.in/speeches.htm (last accessed 6 December 2011).

Strathern, Marilyn, 'Introduction: Rationales of Ownership' in Lawrence Kalinoe and James Leach (eds), *Rationales of Ownership: Transactions and Claims to Ownership in Contemporary Papua New Guinea*, Wantage: Sean Kingston, 2004.

Tuck, Richard, *The Rights of War and Peace: Political Thought and the International Order from Grotius to Kant*, Oxford: Oxford University Press, 1999.

United States of America, *Pledge of Allegiance*, at: http://www.sos.wa.gov/flag/pledge.aspx (last accessed 6 December 2011).

Vattel, Emer de, *The Law of Nations*, ed. Joseph Chitty, Philadelphia: Johnson & Co, 1863.

Vitoria, Francisco de, *Political Writings*, eds Anthony Pagden and Jeremy Lawrence, Cambridge: Cambridge University Press, 1991.

Watal, Jayasharee, 'Implementing the TRIPS Agreement: Policy Options Open to India', *Economic and Political Weekly* 32(39), 1997, 2461.

Wolfrum, Rüdiger, Stoll, Peter-Tobias and Kaiser, Karen (eds), *WTO: Institutions and Dispute Settlement*, Leiden: Martinus Nijhoff, 2006.

World Intellectual Property Organisation, *Intellectual Property Needs and Expectations of Traditional Knowledge Holders: WIPO Report on Fact-Finding Missions on Intellectual Property and Traditional Knowledge (1998–1999)*, Geneva: WIPO, 2001, at: http://www.wipo.int/tk/en/tk/ffm/report/final/index.html (last accessed 6 December 2011).

World Trade Organisation, 'Amendment of the TRIPS Agreement', Decision of the General Council, 6 December 2005, WT/L/641, at: http://www.wto.org/english/tratop_e/trips_e/wtl641_e.htm, (last accessed 6 December 2011).

World Trade Organisation, 'Declaration on the TRIPS Agreement and Public Health', Ministerial Conference, 14 November 2001, WT/MIN(01)/DEC/2, at: http://www.wto.org/English/thewto_e/minist_e/min01_e/mindecl_trips_e.htm (last accessed 6 December 2011).

World Trade Organisation, 'Implementation of Paragraph 6 of the Doha Declaration on the TRIPS Agreement and Public Health', Decision of the General Council, 30 August 2003, WT/L/540 and Corr.1, at: http://www.wto.org/English/tratop_e/trips_e/implem_para6_e.htm (last accessed 6 December 2011).

World Trade Organisation, 'Members and Observers', at: http://www.wto.org/english/thewto_e/whatis_e/tif_e/org6_e.htm (last accessed 6 December 2011).

World Trade Organisation, 'Overview: The TRIPS Agreement', at: http://www.wto.org/english/tratop_e/trips_e/intel2_e.htm (last accessed 6 December 2011).

World Trade Organisation, 'TRIPS Reviews, Article 27.3(b) and Related Issues: Background and Current Situation', at: http://www.wto.org/english/tratop_e/trips_e/art27_3b_background_e.htm (last accessed 6 December 2011).

World Trade Organisation, 'What is the World Trade Organisation?', at: http://www.wto.org/english/thewto_e/whatis_e/tif_e/fact1_e.htm (last accessed 6 December 2011).

World Trade Organisation, 'Who's WTO is it anyway?' at: http://www.wto.org/english/thewto_e/whatis_e/tif_e/org1_e.htm (last accessed 6 December 2011).

World Trade Organisation, 'WTO legal texts', at: http://www.wto.org/english/docs_e/legal_e/legal_e.htm (last accessed 6 December 2011).

Index

For Product Safety Concerns and Information please contact our EU
representative GPSR@taylorandfrancis.com
Taylor & Francis Verlag GmbH, Kaufingerstraße 24, 80331 München, Germany

www.ingramcontent.com/pod-product-compliance
Ingram Content Group UK Ltd.
Pitfield, Milton Keynes, MK11 3LW, UK
UKHW022024061126
477531UK00002B/11

* 9 7 8 0 4 1 5 6 7 8 1 4 8 *